BEST RECIPES

of the

GREAT FOOD COMPANIES

BEST RECIPES
of the
GREAT FOOD COMPANIES

COMPILED & WRITTEN BY
JUDITH ANDERSON

GALAHAD BOOKS
NEW YORK

First Galahad Books edition published in 1997.

Galahad Books
A division of BBS Publishing Corporation
386 Park Avenue South
New York, NY 10016

Galahad Books is a registered trademark of BBS Publishing Corporation.

Published by arrangement with Ten Speed Press.

Library of Congress Catalog Card Number: 96-79827

ISBN: 0-88365-996-4

Printed in the United States of America.

Contents

Preface

This book celebrates the marvelous contributions made by our great American food companies to our diets, nutrition, and dining pleasures. The recipes included in it are the crowning achievements of years of testing by the most qualified home economists in the United States. Some are classics that have been enjoyed for years. A few were so innovative when they were introduced that they started new trends. Many are new, designed for today's lighter dietary interests.

These are the kinds of foods people really cook and eat. The recipes are easy to prepare and require ingredients that are readily available in supermarkets everywhere.

Stories of the origins of our important foods and recipes and of our major brand-name products included in this cookbook will make interesting dinner-time conversation. In researching the histories of these companies, products, and recipes, I discovered that Americans today regularly enjoy foods that were reserved exclusively for royalty and the privileged upper classes in other times and places. These histories tell of many of the great discoveries and innovations that have led to our incredible variety of food products from around the world, the ease with which we prepare food, and the excellent nutrition available to us in our varied diets.

The companies included in this book became great because they offered so much to our food heritage. *Best*

Recipes of the Great Food Companies extols their achievements.

Note: Microwave ovens vary in wattage and power output. Cooking times in some recipes may need to be adjusted.

Acknowledgments

BEATRICE CHEESE, INC. COUNTY LINE and TREASURE CAVE are registered trademarks of BEATRICE CHEESE, INC. Thanks for permission to use recipes go to Tom Hickey and Katherine Coupoulous.

BORDEN FOODS CORPORATION PRODUCT PUBLICITY—Eagle Brand Sweetened Condensed Milk, Wyler's and Steero bouillons, ReaLemon Lemon Juice from Concentrate, and ReaLime Lime Juice from Concentrate, Creamette Pasta, Classico Pasta Sauces, None Such Mincemeat, Cary's and Maple Orchards syrups are registered trademarks. MacDonald's is a common law trademark. Permission was granted to use the recipes featuring such trademarks. Thank you to Veronica Petta.

CAMPBELL SOUP COMPANY CAMPBELL'S, VLASIC, and FRANCO-AMERICAN are registered trademarks of CAMPBELL SOUP COMPANY. Permission was granted to use recipes. Thank you to Justine Good and Donna Skidmore.

CPC INTERNATIONAL INC. HELLMANN'S, BEST FOODS, SKIPPY, SUPER CHUNK, KARO, MAZOLA, MUELLER'S, TWIST TRIO, ARGO, KINGSFORD'S, MAZOLA, SAHARA, and THOMAS' are registered trademarks of CPC International Inc. Recipes are courtesy of Best Foods, a division of CPC International Inc. Thanks go to Elizabeth Strauss.

DOLE FOOD COMPANY Dole is a registered trademark of DOLE FOOD COMPANY. Recipes courtesy of Dole Test Kitchens.

GENERAL MILLS, INC. SUPERMOIST, BISQUICK, GOLD MEDAL, SOFTASILK, and GOLDEN GRAHAMS are registered trademarks of GENERAL MILLS, INC. Recipes are used with permission of GENERAL MILLS, INC. Thank you to Mary Bartz, Gretchen Beede, and Judy Lund.

HERSHEY FOODS CORPORATION HERSHEY'S, REESE'S, SKOR, and MINICHIPS are registered trademarks of HERSHEY FOODS CORPORATION. All recipes are used with permission. Thank to you Cheryl Reitz and Bonnie Glass.

JFC INTERNATIONAL, INC. DYNASTY is a registered trademark of JFC IN-TERNATIONAL, INC. All recipes used with permission. Thank you to Diane Plocher.

KELLOGG'S® KELLOGG'S CORN FLAKES®, RICE KRISPIES®, ALL-BRAN®, are trademarks of Kellogg Company. Recipes courtesy of Kellogg Kitchens™. Thanks to Debra Moody.

KRAFT GENERAL FOODS, INC. PHILADELPHIA BRAND, MIRACLE WHIP, SAUCEWORKS, JELL-O, CASINO, BIRDS EYE, PARKAY, VELVEETA, BREAKSTONE'S, BAKER'S, GERMAN'S, ANGEL FLAKE, CALUMET, DREAM WHIP, COOL WHIP, POST, and GRAPENUTS are registered trademarks of KRAFT GENERAL FOODS, INC. Recipes are used with permission. Thank you to Denise Henderson, Kathy Knuth, Lisa K. Van Riper, and Maryellen Clark.

LAWRY'S FOODS, INC. is a registered trademark of Lawry's Foods, Inc., Los Angeles, CA 90065. Recipes are used with permission. Thanks to Maribeth Drogosz.

LINDSAY INTERNATIONAL, INC. on behalf of Lindsay Olive Growers is appreciated for their contribution of recipes. LINDSAY is a registered trademark. Thanks to Eric M. Boyle for permission to use recipes.

LIPTON. LIPTON, WISH-BONE, and CUP-A-SOUP are registered trademarks of Lipton, Englewood Cliffs, New Jersey 07632. Recipes are used with permission. Thanks to Anna Marie Cesario.

McCORMICK & COMPANY, INC. McCORMICK/SCHILLING and BON APPÉTIT are registered trademarks of McCORMICK & COMPANY, INCOR-PORATED. Permission received to use recipes. Thank you to Diane Hamel.

NABISCO FOODS GROUP NABISCO, BLUE BONNET, KNOX, WRIGHT'S, REGINA, GREY POUPON, A.1., DAVIS, FLEISCHMANN'S, EGG BEATERS, CREAM OF WHEAT, BRER RABBIT, ROYAL, COLLEGE INN, and NILLA are registered trademarks of NABISCO BRANDS COMPANY. Recipes are used with permission. Thank you to Judith Fadden.

NESTLÉ FOOD COMPANY LIBBY'S, CONTADINA, and CARNATION are registered trademarks. Libby's is a division and Contadina Foods, Inc. a subsidiary of NESTLÉ FOOD COMPANY. Recipes are used with permission. Thank you to Vivian Manuel and Mary Ann Bydlon.

OSCAR MAYER FOODS CORPORATION d/b/a/ LOUIS RICH COMPANY and KEMP SEAFOOD COMPANY. Oscar Mayer and Louis Rich are registered trademarks of Oscar Mayer Foods Corporation. Louis Kemp is a trademark of Oscar Mayer Foods Corporation. Recipes are courtesy of Oscar Mayer Foods Corporation. Thanks to Shelagh Hackett Thomee.

PEPPERIDGE FARM, INC. PEPPERIDGE FARM is a registered trademark of PEPPERIDGE FARM, INC. Recipes are used with permission. Thank you to Elizabeth Gabriele.

RAGÚ FOODS CO. RAGÚ and ADOLPH'S are registered trademarks of RAGÚ FOODS CO. Recipes are used with permission. Thanks to Rosemary Smalberg

RECKITT & COLMAN, INC. FRENCH'S and FRANK'S REDHOT are registered trademarks of RECKITT & COLMAN, INC. Permission was granted to use recipes. Recipes provided by Janet Andreas, Test Kitchen Leader.

SARGENTO CHEESE COMPANY, INC. SARGENTO and PREFERRED LIGHT are registered trademarks of SARGENTO CHEESE COMPANY, INC. whose recipes are used with permission. Thank you to Barbara Ganon.

Party Beverages

MAI TAI PUNCH
Dole Food Company
5

SUNNY HOLIDAY PUNCH
Dole Food Company
6

SIR TEA
The Story of Sir Thomas Lipton
6

FIRESIDE PUNCH
Lipton
9

BLOODY MARY'S REDHOT® STYLE
Reckitt & Colman Inc.
9

FIRESIDE WARMER
Lipton
10

Mai Tai Punch

Dole Food Company

Makes 25 servings, 4 ounces each

3 quarts Dole® Pineapple Juice

¼ cup lemon juice

¼ cup lime juice

½ cup sugar

1 cup dark rum *or* orange juice

1 cup light rum *or* sparkling water

2 cups sparkling water

Combine fruit juices and sugar. Stir until sugar dissolves. Add rum. Chill. Just before serving, pour over block of ice in punch bowl. Add sparkling water and stir gently.

Serve in punch cups.

Sunny Holiday Punch

Dole Food Company

Makes about 4 quarts

1½ quarts Dole® Pineapple Juice, chilled

1 quart mineral water, chilled

1 can (6 ounces) frozen orange juice concentrate

1 Dole® Lemon *or* Lime, thinly sliced

2 cups fresh strawberries or drained frozen strawberries

1 bottle (750 milliliters) chilled champagne

Combine all ingredients in a punch bowl.

SIR TEA

The Story of Sir Thomas Lipton

The rags-to-riches story of Sir Thomas Lipton begins in a walk-up tenement in Glasgow, Scotland, in 1850. There Lipton was born of Irish parents. After quitting school at age ten so that he could supplement the pinched family coffers, he started working in a stationery store where he was an unusually hard worker from the start and took in every detail about the steps required to retail successfully and to achieve customer satisfaction.

Around this time, droves of immigrants were sailing to America, where the streets were paved with gold, they had heard. Some came to stay, others to make their fortunes or to learn how Americans succeeded before returning to their homeland. Lipton saw the Statue of Liberty at age fifteen, with eight dollars pushed deeply in his pocket.

He moved around the vast, young country, holding manual jobs in New York City, New Orleans, and South Carolina. He liked Americans, and they liked him. He watched the people of the thriving marketplaces and learned how shrewd businessman competed. Enthusiastically, he absorbed all the skills he would need to become a great success when he returned to Glasgow to open his grocery store at age twenty-one.

Lipton's ability to keep the customers' interests as his highest priority made him so successful that he was able to build that first grocery store into the largest company in Great Britain. What made a customer want to purchase again, he wanted to know. How could he save the consumer money, yet offer the highest-quality product available?

By the time he approached his thirtieth year, Lipton owned a chain of more than twenty stores. At forty, he was a millionaire, even before he had sold a single ounce of the tea that would make his name a household word in all tea-drinking countries.

Tea drinking had long been an expensive habit enjoyed only by the elite because the long voyage around the Cape of Good Hope had kept the price of importing the dried leaves high. The opening of the Suez Canal in 1869 shortened the distance to tea-growing countries and brought the price to a level that allowed the masses to consume the brew.

Brokers streamed through Lipton's office trying to convince him to carry the product. He was thinking. Wanting to eliminate the middlemen and keep the price down for his customers, he decided to buy his own estates in Ceylon. At this time, stores kept tea in huge chests and sold it to customers by the individual scoop, with each order individually weighed. Questions of cleanliness, accuracy of weight measurement, and freshness were always in customers' minds. Lipton's genius was to package the blended product in pound, half-pound, and quarter-pound containers. Customers were impressed with this innovation, and demand exploded. In India and Ceylon, Lipton expanded with more tea plantations, then with coffee and cocoa plantations. Later he built a meat-packing business in Chicago. Never having forgotten his respect for Americans, in 1915 he formed the Thomas J. Lipton Company of the United States. Lipton® tea boxes now depict a charming likeness of Thomas Lipton wearing a yachtsman's cap and holding a teacup.

Besides being famous in our country as "Sir Tea," Lipton was America's favorite good sport. He had tried to win the America's Cup in the international yacht race five times with five different green-hulled yachts named *Shamrock*. Each time he failed. But his good-natured and chivalrous comments with the press after each failure caused his popularity with the American public to skyrocket. After his last failure in 1930, he told reporters, "It's no use, I can't win, I can't win." Americans were so affected that they contributed thousands to buy the captivating man a gold Tiffany-designed loving cup.

Thomas Lipton had been knighted and made a baronet in recognition of his philanthropy. But his response to this outpouring of affection by the American people was most emotional. "Although I lost, you make me feel as though I had won."

Fireside Punch

Lipton

Makes about 5 (5 oz.) servings

1½ cups cranberry juice
  cocktail
1½ cups water
  4 Lipton® Soothing Moments®
  Cinnamon Apple *or* Gentle
  Orange Herbal Tea Bags

2 tablespoons brown sugar
Cinnamon sticks for
  garnish (optional)

In medium saucepan, bring cranberry juice and water to
a boil. Add herbal tea bags; cover and steep 5 minutes.
Remove tea bags; stir in sugar. Garnish with cinnamon
sticks.

Bloody Mary's REDHOT® Style

©1996 Reckitt & Colman Inc.

Makes 4 servings

1 quart tomato juice
½ cup vodka
2 tablespoons FRANK'S®
  Original REDHOT® Cayenne
  Pepper Sauce

2 tablespoons FRENCH'S®
  Worcestershire Sauce
2 tablespoons prepared
  horseradish
1 tablespoon lemon juice
1 teaspoon celery salt

Combine all ingredients in pitcher; chill. Serve over ice.

Preparation time: 5 minutes   *Chill time:* 15 minutes

Fireside Warmer

Lipton

Makes 6 servings

1⅓ cups water	2 whole cloves
3 Lipton® Flo-Thru® Regular *or* Naturally Decaffeinated Tea Bags	⅓ cup sugar
	1⅓ cups cranberry juice cocktail
1 cinnamon stick, broken	1 cup dry red wine

In medium saucepan, bring water to a boil. Add tea bags and spices; cover and brew 5 minutes.

Remove tea bags. Stir in sugar, cranberry juice, and wine; heat through. Remove spices and garnish, if desired, with orange wedges.

Snack Mixes

PEANUT BUTTER SNACK MIX
Reckitt & Colman Inc.
15

HOTSY TOTSY SNACK MIX
Reckitt & Colman Inc.
15

HOLIDAY TRAIL MIX
Dole Food Company
16

Peanut Butter Snack Mix

©1996 Reckitt & Colman Inc.

Makes about 7 cups

2 tablespoons butter *or* margarine

⅓ cup creamy peanut butter

2 cans (1½ ounces *each*) FRENCH'S® Potato Sticks

2 cups toasted oat cereal

2 cups bite-size shredded wheat

1 cup chocolate chips

Preheat oven to 350°F. Place butter and peanut butter in 9-by-13-inch baking dish. Heat in oven 4 minutes until melted. Stir in potato sticks, cereal, and shredded wheat. Toss well to coat.

Bake 20 minutes, stirring halfway. Cool mixture to room temperature. Stir in chocolate chips.

Preparation time: 15 minutes   *Cook time:* 20 minutes

Hotsy Totsy Snack Mix

©1996 Reckitt & Colman Inc.

Makes about 2 quarts

3 tablespoons butter *or* margarine, melted

¼ cup FRANK'S® Original REDHOT® Cayenne Pepper Sauce

1 tablespoon FRENCH'S® Worcestershire Sauce

¼ cup grated Parmesan cheese

2 cans (1½ ounces *each*) FRENCH'S® Potato Sticks

1 can (8 ounces) salted nuts

3 cups corn cereal squares

1 cup bite-size pretzels

Preheat oven to 250°F. In small bowl, combine butter, RedHot® Sauce, Worcestershire and cheese. Place remaining ingredients into jelly roll or roasting pan. Pour RedHot® mixture over dry ingredients; toss well to coat.

Bake for 45 minutes, stirring every 15 minutes. Cool slightly. Store in airtight container.

To microwave: Prepare mixture as above. Place into 3-quart microwave-safe bowl.

Microwave on HIGH 6 minutes, stirring every 2 minutes. Transfer to paper towels; cool.

Preparation time: 10 minutes   *Cook time:* 45 minutes

Holiday Trail Mix

Dole Food Company

Makes 11 servings, ½ cup each

1 box (8 ounces) Dole® Chopped Dates	1 cup Dole® Raisins
1 cup Dole® Whole Almonds, toasted	1 cup dried banana chips
	1 cup dried apricots
	½ cup sunflower seed nuts

Combine all ingredients. Store in closed container in refrigerator. Will keep 2 weeks.

To toast almonds: Preheat oven to 350°F. Place almonds in a shallow pan and bake for 10 minutes. Toasting time will vary depending on the size of the almonds.

Breakfast Delights

Good Morning Pumpkin Pancakes

Libby's, Nestlé Food Company

Makes about 16 pancakes

2 cups biscuit mix

1½ cups (12-ounce can) *undiluted* Carnation® Evaporated Milk

½ cup Libby's® Solid Pack Pumpkin

2 eggs

2 tablespoons firmly packed light brown sugar

2 tablespoons vegetable oil

2 teaspoons ground cinnamon

1 teaspoon ground allspice

1 teaspoon vanilla extract

Combine all ingredients in a medium bowl. Beat until smooth. Pour ¼ to ½ cup of batter onto heated and lightly greased griddle. Cook until edges are dry. Turn; cook until golden. Serve with syrup, honey, or jam.

PB&J French Toast

Best Foods, a division of CPC International Inc.

Makes 4 sandwiches

8 tablespoons Skippy® Creamy *or* Super Chunk® Peanut Butter

4 tablespoons jelly

8 slices bread

1 egg

¼ cup skim milk

Spread peanut butter and jelly on 4 bread slices; top with remaining 4 slices. In shallow bowl, beat egg with milk. Dip both sides of each sandwich into egg mixture. Cook in greased hot skillet or on griddle over medium heat until browned on both sides.

Cranberry Crumb Coffee Cake

Nabisco Foods Group

Makes 8 servings

1½ cups all-purpose flour
⅓ cup CREAM OF WHEAT Cereal (½-minute, 2½-minute *or* 10 minute stovetop cooking)
1 tablespoon DAVIS Baking Powder
1 teaspoon ground cinnamon
½ cup sugar
¼ cup FLEISCHMANN'S Margarine, softened
½ cup EGG BEATERS Healthy Real Egg Product
½ cup skim milk
½ cup apple juice
¾ cup frozen cranberries, coarsely chopped
Crumb Topping, recipe follows
Powdered Sugar Glaze, optional

Preheat oven to 375°F. In medium bowl, combine flour, cereal, baking powder, and cinnamon; set aside.

In large bowl, with electric mixer at medium speed, beat sugar and margarine until creamy. Beat in egg product. Blend in flour mixture alternately with milk and apple juice; beat 2 minutes at medium speed. Fold in cranberries. Spread batter into greased 9-inch round cake pan; top with Crumb Topping. Bake for 35 to 40 minutes or until toothpick inserted in center comes out clean. Cool in pan on wire rack for 10 minutes; remove from pan. Serve warm or cooled drizzled with Powdered Sugar Glaze if desired.

Crumb Topping

Mix ⅓ cup flour, 2 tablespoons sugar, 2 tablespoons CREAM OF WHEAT Cereal (½-minute, 2½-minute or 10-minute stovetop cooking), 1 teaspoon cinnamon. Stir in 1 tablespoon melted FLEISCHMANN'S Margarine and 1 tablespoon apple juice until crumbly.

Fruit Swirl Coffee Cake

General Mills, Inc.

Makes 30 bars or 18 squares

1½ cups sugar
½ cup margarine *or* butter, softened
½ cup shortening
1½ teaspoons baking powder
1 teaspoon vanilla
1 teaspoon almond extract

4 eggs
3 cups Gold Medal® All-Purpose Flour
1 can (21 ounces) cherry, apricot, *or* blueberry pie filling
Glaze (see below)

Preheat oven to 350°F. Generously grease jelly-roll pan, 15½-by-10½-by-1 inch, or 2 square pans, 9-by-9-by-2 inches. Beat sugar, margarine, shortening, baking powder, vanilla, almond extract, and eggs in large bowl on low speed, scraping bowl constantly. Beat 3 minutes on high speed, scraping bowl occasionally. Stir in flour. (Note: If using self-rising flour, omit baking powder.) Spread two-thirds of batter in jelly-roll pan or one-third in each square pan. Spread pie filling over batter. Drop remaining batter by tablespoonfuls onto pie filling.

Bake about 45 minutes or until light brown. While warm, drizzle with Glaze. Cut coffee cake in jelly-roll pan into 2½-by-2-inch bars; cut coffee cake in square pans into 2¾-inch squares.

Glaze

1 cup confectioners' sugar   1 to 2 tablespoons milk

Combine sugar and milk. Mix thoroughly.

Blackberry-Lemon Coffeecake

Kellogg Company

Makes 8 servings

3 cups *KELLOGG'S® RICE KRISPIES®* cereal, crushed to ¾ cup
1½ cups all-purpose flour
¾ cup sugar
½ cup margarine
½ teaspoon baking powder
½ teaspoon baking soda
¼ teaspoon salt
1 egg
¾ cup buttermilk
1 teaspoon grated lemon peel
½ cup seedless blackberry spreadable fruit
Vegetable cooking spray

Preheat oven to 350°F. In large mixing bowl, stir together *KELLOGG'S® RICE KRISPIES®* cereal, flour, and sugar. Using pastry blender cut in margarine. Remove ½ cup mixture and set aside for topping. To remaining mixture, stir in baking powder, soda, and salt.

Beat together egg, buttermilk, and lemon peel. Add to cereal mixture, stirring only until combined. Spread ⅔ batter evenly over bottom of 9-by-1½-inch round cake pan that has been coated with cooking spray. Evenly spread fruit over batter to ½-inch of pan. Dot with remaining dough and carefully spread over fruit. (All of fruit will not be covered.) Sprinkle top completely with reserved topping mixture.

Bake about 40 minutes or until toothpick inserted in center comes out clean. Cool 15 minutes. Cut into wedges to serve.

Preparation time: 30 minutes   *Baking time:* 40 minutes

Brunch Dishes

CHEESY BRUNCH CASSEROLE
Kraft General Foods, Inc.
29

DINER SKILLET POTATOES
Lipton
29

TOSTADA CASSEROLE
Beatrice Cheese, Inc.
30

MOZZARELLA SAUSAGE AND PEPPER BAKE
Beatrice Cheese Inc.
31

CRABMEAT QUICHE
Lipton
32

BREAKFAST MUFFIN QUICHES
Reckitt & Colman Inc.
32

MINI ITALIAN QUICHES
Specialty Brands

33

BRUNCH QUESADILLAS WITH FRUIT SALSA
Sargento Cheese Company, Inc.
34

Cheesy Brunch Casserole

Kraft General Foods, Inc.

Makes 8 to 10 servings

18 slices (1 regular loaf) white *or* wheat bread, cubed

1 cup broccoli florets

⅓ cup chopped red bell pepper

2 packages (8 ounces each; 4 cups total) Kraft® Natural Shredded Sharp Cheddar Cheese

8 eggs

3 cups milk

½ cup Parkay® Margarine, melted

Preheat oven to 350°F. In greased 13-by-9-inch baking dish, layer half each of the bread, broccoli, bell pepper, and cheese. Repeat layers. In large bowl, beat eggs. Add milk and margarine, beating until smooth. Pour evenly over casserole. Bake 50 minutes to 1 hour or until golden brown.

Preparation time: 20 minutes   *Cook time:* 1 hour

Diner Skillet Potatoes

Lipton

Makes 6 servings

1½ pounds all-purpose potatoes, peeled and diced

2 large red *and/or* green bell peppers, chopped

1 envelope Lipton® Recipe Secrets® Onion Soup Mix

2 tablespoons olive *or* vegetable oil

In large bowl, combine potatoes, peppers, and onion soup mix until evenly coated.

In 12-inch nonstick skillet, heat oil over medium heat and cook potato mixture, covered, stirring occasionally, 12 minutes. Remove cover and continue cooking, stirring occasionally, 10 minutes or until potatoes are tender.

Tostada Casserole

Beatrice Cheese, Inc.

Makes 6 to 8 servings

1 pound lean ground beef
1 cup salsa (mild, medium, or hot)
½ teaspoon ground cumin
Salt to taste
5 green onions, thinly sliced
3 cups (12 ounces) County Line® Shredded Taco Cheese

1 can (16 ounces) refried beans
1 can (2¼ ounces) pitted, sliced ripe olives, drained
Shredded lettuce
Chopped tomato
Sour cream
Guacamole
Tortilla chips

Preheat oven to 350°F. Lightly grease 3-quart casserole. In skillet, brown beef. Drain any fat. Add salsa, cumin, and salt. Simmer until thick and all liquid has been absorbed. Place meat mixture in casserole. Top with onions, 2 cups cheese, refried beans, olives, and remaining 1 cup cheese. Bake 30 minutes. To serve, spoon each casserole portion on a bed of shredded lettuce and top with chopped tomato, sour cream, and guacamole. Serve with tortilla chips.

For real convenience, assemble ahead and refrigerate until ready to bake.

Mozzarella Sausage and Pepper Bake

Beatrice Cheese, Inc.

Makes 8 servings

2 tablespoons olive oil
2 green peppers, seeded and thinly sliced
2 cloves garlic, minced
1¼ pounds mild *or* spicy Italian sausage, sliced into 1-inch circles
1 jar (32 ounces) meatless spaghetti sauce
1 package (16 ounces) rigatoni *or* ziti, cooked and drained
3 cups (12 ounces) County Line® Shredded Mozzarella Cheese

Preheat oven to 350°F. In large skillet, heat oil and sauté peppers and garlic until peppers are crisp-tender. Remove and set aside. Sauté sausage circles until brown. Drain any fat. Combine peppers, garlic, sausage, spaghetti sauce, pasta, and *2½ cups* cheese in 4-quart casserole. Cover and bake 40 to 45 minutes. Top casserole with remaining *½ cup* cheese. Bake, uncovered, only until cheese melts, about 5 minutes.

Crabmeat Quiche

Lipton

Makes 6 servings

1 9-inch unbaked pastry shell
4 eggs
1½ cups light cream *or* half and half
1 envelope Lipton® Recipe Secrets® Savory Herb with Garlic Soup Mix
1 cup flaked crabmeat (about 6 ounces)
1 to 2 tablespoons dry sherry (optional)
2 cups shredded Swiss cheese (about 8 ounces)

Preheat oven to 400°. Bake pastry shell 10 minutes. Remove from oven; reduce oven temperature to 375°.

In large bowl, beat eggs. Blend in cream, savory herb with garlic soup mix, crabmeat and sherry. Sprinkle cheese in pastry shell; pour in egg mixture.

Bake 40 minutes or until knife inserted in center comes out clean and pastry is golden. Garnish, if desired, with orange slices, grapes and fresh herbs. Serve hot or cold.

Variation: Also terrific with Lipton® Recipe Secrets® Onion-Mushroom or Golden Onion Soup Mix.

Breakfast Muffin Quiches

©1996 Reckitt & Colman Inc.

Makes 18 muffins

1½ cups milk
3 large eggs
3 tablespoons FRENCH'S® Classic Yellow® Mustard
1⅔ cups buttermilk baking mix
2 cups (8 ounces) shredded Cheddar cheese, divided
1 small zucchini, shredded and squeezed dry
1 tablespoon instant minced onion
1 tablespoon bacon bits

Preheat oven to 375°F. Lightly coat 18 muffin cups with vegetable cooking spray.

In medium bowl, beat together milk, eggs, and mustard.

In large bowl, combine baking mix, *1 cup* cheese, zucchini, onion, and bacon bits. Pour wet ingredients into dry; stir just until dry ingredients are moistened.

Spoon ¼ cup batter into prepared muffin cups. Evenly sprinkle tops with remaining cheese. Bake 25 minutes or until knife inserted in center comes out clean. Cool in pan 5 minutes. Loosen edges with knife and invert. Serve warm.

Preparation time: 15 minutes   *Cook time:* 25 minutes

Mini Italian Quiches

Specialty Brands

Makes 6 servings, 2 mini quiches each

1 (9-inch) folded refrigerated unbaked pie crust	1 tablespoon flour
1 cup (4 ounces) shredded mozzarella cheese	1 teaspoon Durkee® Italian Seasoning
4 large eggs	½ teaspoon Durkee® Garlic Powder
1 cup half-and-half	½ teaspoon Durkee® Onion Powder

Preheat oven to 400°F. On lightly floured board, roll dough into 15-inch circle; cut 12 circles from crust using 4-inch cookie cutter (reroll dough if necessary). Grease twelve 2-inch muffin or tart tins with vegetable cooking spray; line tins with pastry. Place on baking sheet. Divide cheese evenly among tins. In medium bowl, combine eggs, half-and-half, flour, and seasonings. Pour egg mixture over cheese, filling tins about three-fourths full. Bake 30 to 40 minutes or until crust is browned. Remove from tins and cool.

Variation: Pastry can be placed in 9-inch pie plate. Continue recipe as above. Bake, uncovered, at 400°F for 45 to 50 minutes.

Brunch Quesadillas with Fruit Salsa

Sargento Cheese Company, Inc.

Makes 4 servings

1 pint fresh strawberries, hulled and diced

1 fresh ripe Anjou pear, cored and diced

1 tablespoon chopped fresh cilantro

1 tablespoon honey

4 8-inch flour tortillas

2 teaspoons light margarine, melted

1 cup (4 ounces) Sargento® Preferred Light® Fancy Shredded Mozzarella Cheese

2 tablespoons light sour cream for garnish

Combine first 4 ingredients to make Fruit Salsa. Set aside. Brush 1 side of each tortilla with melted margarine. Place brushed side down and sprinkle *2 tablespoons* cheese on half of each tortilla. Top with *⅓ cup* salsa (drain and discard any liquid that has formed from the fruit) and remaining 2 tablespoons of cheese. Fold tortilla in half. Grill folded tortillas in a dry preheated frying pan until light golden brown and crisp, about 2 minutes. Turn and brown other side. Remove to a serving plate or platter. Cut each tortilla in half.

Serve with remaining Fruit Salsa and garnish of sour cream. Serve immediately.

Extraordinary
Sandwiches

FRUIT OF THE ANCIENTS
The Story of Olives

Growing wildly, the silvery gray olive plant of prehistory was a low, thorny shrub. First cultivated more than five thousand years ago in Egypt for its oil, the plant developed in stature to become a tree, bearing a nearly inedible, hard, yellowish-green fruit. The people of the Nile learned the secrets of extracting oil and pickling the fruit in brine or in a lime mixture to make it edible. One tree provided a family with nutritious food and essential oil for cooking, skin and hair moisturization, and lamp and stove fuel.

According to Greek legend, humans first learned that the olive could be transformed into a savory morsel when a bountiful branch dipped in a river and the salty water leached the fruit's natural bitterness. The gift from Pallas Athene, goddess of wisdom and the arts, became sacred. To destroy an olive tree was deemed a sacrilege. A crown of olive branches became the highest honor the Greek state could bestow. Unbeknownst to the Greeks, the olive tree actually does approach immortality: Two-thousand-year-old trees are still producing fruit today.

The Roman legions brought the olive tree and knowledge of oil extraction and fruit processing to the Mediterranean countries. To this day, the peoples of Greece, Italy, Portugal, and Spain extract the fruity oil to export and use in all their cooking. Even their pastries include the distinctively flavored olive oil.

Sixteenth-century Peruvians and Chileans saw the first olive trees planted in the New World. The original California olive trees are believed to have been planted at the first Franciscan mission in San Diego in 1775; eventually the trees were cultivated throughout California in all twenty-one Franciscan missions.

California's rich soil and sunny climate have proved to be ideal for olive growing and have made the state one of the world's premier growing regions. At first, California olives were grown only for their oil, but olive growers began canning the fruit in the early twentieth century.

A grower-owned cooperative, the Lindsay Ripe Olive Company, was formed in 1916. Now known as Lindsay Olive Growers, this cooperative has become the world's largest canner of ripe olives. Lindsay has developed olive making into a fine art form through its years of experience. The olives that will become green Spanish olives, the type usually stuffed with a red pimiento pepper, and those selected for curing in the distinctive California black ripe style are harvested by hand between mid-September and November. Two different curing processes transform the fruit into the two distinct products.

Olive batches vary in such qualities as size, ripeness, and sugar content of the fruit. Just as the wine maker uses specialized knowledge to develop grape harvests into fine and consistent wine, the olive maker draws on expertise to consistently bring out exactly the right color, texture, and flavor qualities in the green fruit.

Green Spanish olives are fermented in brine in a manner similar to that used for making a pickle from a cucumber. California black olives receive special treatment indeed. The olive maker determines exactly what degree of curing will purge the natural bitterness, soften the texture, and develop the tantalizing flavor in each batch. Natural air bubbles are filtered through the curing tanks to oxidize the olives, thus changing the California-style "ripe" olive from green to black, the natural color of a fully ripe olive.

The specially cured California black olive is an exquisite and unique ingredient that blends easily in recipes without overpowering other food flavors. For example, California black olives combined with delicately flavored foods such as smoked salmon will not be overwhelming. California black olives are also an excellent food for the diet-conscious individual. The low amount of fat they contain is monounsaturated, the fat that is beneficial to health, and the largest black olive contains only 12 to 13 calories. For these reasons, the fruit of the ancients remains a favorite for visual appeal, taste, and texture in today's light recipes.

New Orleans Muffuletta

Lindsay International, Inc.

Makes 6 servings

½ cup Lindsay® Pimiento-Stuffed Green Olives, drained and chopped

½ Cup Lindsay® Extra Large Pitted Ripe Olives, drained and chopped

½ cup chopped celery

½ cup chopped, mixed, pickled vegetables

⅓ cup olive *or* salad oil

¼ cup snipped parsley

3 tablespoons lemon juice

1 clove garlic, minced

1 teaspoon dried oregano, crushed

Several dashes freshly ground pepper

1 loaf (1½ pounds) Italian bread

4 ounces thinly sliced Genoa salami

4 ounces sliced provolone *or* mozzarella cheese

4 ounces sliced cappicola *or* fully cooked ham

Combine first 10 ingredients. Cover; chill, tossing several times. Drain, reserving liquid. Cut bread in half horizontally. Remove a ½-inch-thick slice from cut side of bottom.

Brush cut sides of remaining bread with reserved liquid. Layer bottom half with salami, cheese, cappicola, and olive mixture. Cover with top half of bread.

Reuben Sandwiches

Oscar Mayer Foods Corporation

Makes 4 sandwiches

1	cup well drained sauerkraut	16	slices sandwich rye bread
¼	cup Thousand Island dressing	8	slices (4 by 4 inches) Swiss cheese
2	packages (½ pound each) Louis Rich® Turkey Pastrami		Butter

Combine sauerkraut with dressing. Trim slices of meat to fit bread. To assemble each sandwich, place 1 slice meat (and trimmings) on bread slice, spread with 2 tablespoons sauerkraut mixture, top with cheese slices and another slice of turkey pastrami, and cover with bread. Butter outsides of sandwiches. Grill slowly on both sides until bread is toasted and cheese is melted.

Variations

Party Reuben: Makes about 8 sandwiches. Use snack rye bread and cut slices of meat and cheese in half. Serve hot or cold.

Oven Reuben: Make 4 at a time and serve 4 at a time by baking sandwiches open-faced in the oven. Preheat oven to 400°F. Place 4 slices of bread in 9-inch square pan and top each with 2 slices turkey pastrami. Add a layer of drained sauerkraut and top with a cheese slice. Bake 15 minutes.

Zorba's Pocket Sandwich

Oscar Mayer Foods Corporation

Makes 8 sandwiches

1 medium cucumber, thinly sliced
1 medium onion, thinly sliced
12 pitted ripe olives, sliced
¾ cup low-cal Italian dressing
1 package (8 ounces) Oscar Mayer® Cotto Salami
1 package (8 ounces) Oscar Mayer® New England Brand Sausage
8 lettuce leaves
4 pita breads (6- to 7-inch diameter) cut in half

Combine salad ingredients. Cover; refrigerate at least 1 hour. For each sandwich, place 2 meat slices and 1 lettuce leaf in pita pocket. Add salad mixture.

Turkey Waldorf Pitas

Best Foods, a division of CPC International Inc.

Makes 4 sandwiches

4 loaves (2 ounces each) regular-size Sahara® Pita Bread
1 cup diced cooked turkey
1 apple, diced
⅓ cup sliced celery
¼ cup roasted sunflower seeds (optional)
½ cup Hellmann's® *or* Best Foods® Mayonnaise
1 teaspoon lemon juice
1 teaspoon chopped crystalized ginger
Lettuce leaves

Cut one-third off each pita. Combine turkey, apple, celery, and sunflower seeds. Stir in mayonnaise, lemon juice, and ginger. Spoon into lettuce-lined pitas.

Kielbasa & Kraut Manwiches

©1996 Reckitt & Colman Inc.

Makes 6 to 8 servings

1 tablespoon vegetable oil

2 large red onions, cut in half lengthwise and thinly sliced

2 pounds kielbasa, thickly sliced

2 pounds sauerkraut, rinsed and drained well

1 can (12 ounces) beer *or* non-alcoholic malt beverage

½ cup FRENCH'S® Deli Brown Mustard

1 tablespoon caraway seeds

6 hot dog *or* hero-style buns

Heat oil in large nonstick skillet over medium heat. Add onion; cook 5 minutes or just until tender, stirring often. Remove from skillet.

Add kielbasa to skillet; cook and stir 5 minutes or until lightly browned; drain well. Stir in onion, sauerkraut, beer, mustard, and caraway seeds. Cook over low heat 10 minutes until most of liquid is absorbed, stirring occasionally. Spoon mixture into buns to serve.

Tip: This recipe may be prepared ahead. To reheat, place mixture into 12-by-9-inch disposable foil pan. Cover. Place on grid; cook over medium heat 15 minutes, stirring halfway.

Preparation time: 20 minutes   *Cook time:* 20 minutes

Sports Fan's Souper Sandwich

Lipton

Makes about 8 servings

- 1 envelope Lipton® Recipe Secrets® Onion Soup Mix
- 1 container (16 ounces) sour cream
- ½ cup chopped pitted ripe olives
- ½ cup chopped sweet pickles
- 2 loaves unsliced round bread (about 9-inch diameter)

Lettuce
- 1½ pounds thinly sliced cooked roast beef
- ½ pound thinly sliced Swiss cheese
- 2 tomatoes, sliced
- 2 green bell peppers, cut into rings

In medium bowl, combine onion soup mix, sour cream, olives, and pickles; chill. Cut thin lengthwise slice off top of each loaf of bread; reserve tops. Hollow out center of each loaf, leaving ¼-inch shell. Spread ¾ cup mixture into each shell. Place lettuce on top mixture, lining sides. Evenly layer roast beef, cheese, tomatoes, and green peppers; top with remaining mixture. To serve, replace reserved tops and cut into wedges.

Special San Francisco Pita Pocket

Lawry's Foods, Inc.

Makes 8 servings

- 1 package (10 ounces) frozen chopped spinach
- ¾ pound lean ground beef
- ½ pound fresh mushrooms, sliced
- ½ cup chopped onion
- 3 tablespoons butter *or* margarine
- ¾ teaspoon dill weed

- ½ teaspoon Lawry's® Seasoned Salt
- ½ teaspoon Lawry's® Garlic Powder with Parsley
- ½ teaspoon Lawry's® Seasoned Pepper
- 2 cups (8 ounces) grated cheese, half Cheddar and half Monterey Jack
- 4 pita breads, cut in half

To microwave: Make slit in spinach package; place package, slit side up, on paper towel. Microwave on HIGH 5 minutes. Remove spinach from package; squeeze liquid from spinach. In microwave-safe pie plate or dish, microwave ground beef on HIGH 6 to 7 minutes, stirring once or twice. Drain fat. In 13-by-9-by-2-inch microwave-safe baking dish, microwave mushrooms, onion, and butter on HIGH 8 to 10 minutes. Stir in seasonings. Microwave on HIGH 3 minutes, stirring once. Stir spinach and cooked ground beef into mushroom-onion mixture. Fold in cheese. Cover with waxed paper and microwave on HIGH 3 minutes. Wrap pita breads loosely in plastic wrap; microwave on HIGH 30 seconds to warm. Open pita breads and fill with meat mixture. Serve immediately with fresh fruit.

Variation: Substitute ground turkey for ground beef. Microwave on HIGH 4 to 5 minutes, stirring twice.

Party Pinwheel Sandwiches

Lipton

Makes 10 dozen pinwheel sandwiches

1 envelope Lipton® Recipe Secrets® Onion Soup Mix

1 container (16 ounces) sour cream

2 loaves unsliced white *or* pumpernickel bread, sliced lengthwise (8 slices each)

Festive Fillings (choose any 2 from below)

Blend onion soup mix with sour cream; chill. Trim crust from bread; flatten bread with rolling pin. Spread 1 filling mixture evenly on 8 slices of bread; roll, starting at narrow end, jelly-roll style. Repeat with remaining filling and bread. Wrap in waxed paper or plastic wrap and chill. To serve, cut into ½-inch slices.

To freeze and thaw: Tightly wrap pinwheels in waxed paper or plastic wrap, then heavy-duty aluminum foil; freeze. To serve, partially thaw frozen rolls; unwrap and cut into ½-inch slices. Continue thawing at room temperature for 1 hour.

Festive Fillings

Blue Cheese Walnut Filling: Combine 1 cup sour cream mixture, 2 ounces crumbled blue cheese, and ½ cup finely chopped walnuts.

Fruity Curry Filling: Combine 1 cup sour cream mixture, ¾ teaspoon curry powder, ½ cup raisins, ½ cup finely chopped apple, and 1 tablespoon milk.

Ham and Cheese Filling: Use 1 cup sour cream mixture. Top each prepared slice with 1 thin slice cooked ham, then Swiss or American cheese. Place quartered dill pickle across end of bread; roll starting at pickle end.

Wine, Cheese 'n Olive Filling: Combine 1 cup sour cream mixture, ¾ cup shredded Cheddar cheese, and 2 tablespoons red wine. Place 3 ripe olives across one end of each prepared slice; roll starting at olive end.

California Tuna Sandwich Spread

Lipton

Makes about 2½ cups

1 can (6½ ounces) chunk-style tuna, drained and flaked	Bread slices
	Cucumber for garnish
	Tomato wedges for garnish
2 teaspoons lemon juice	Potato chips for garnish
2 cups Lipton® California Dip (see below)	

Blend tuna with lemon juice, then combine with California Dip; chill thoroughly. Spread mixture on bread slices. Garnish sandwiches with cucumber slices, tomato wedges, and potato chips.

California Dip:

Makes about 2 cups

1 envelope Lipton® Recipe Secrets® Onion Soup Mix	1 container (16 ounces) sour cream

Blend together.

Tuna Bruschetta

Sargento Cheese Company, Inc.

Makes 4 servings

- 1 cup (4 ounces) Sargento® Preferred Light® Fancy Shredded Mozzarella Cheese
- 1 can (3½ ounces) water-packed tuna, well drained and flaked
- 4 plum tomatoes, seeded and chopped
- 2 tablespoons minced onion
- 2 teaspoons minced fresh parsley
- ½ teaspoon dried oregano
- 4 slices Italian bread (6-by-½-inch each)
- 2 tablespoons olive oil
- 2 cloves garlic, halved

Combine, cheese, tuna, tomatoes, onion, parsley, and oregano. Set aside. Brush both sides of bread with olive oil and rub surface with cut side of garlic. In a dry, pre-heated frying pan, grill bread until light golden brown. Turn and top each toasted surface with one-fourth of the cheese mixture. Continue to grill until cheese melts and bread is golden brown on bottom. Serve immediately.

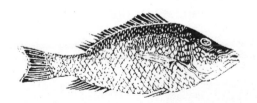

Hot Turkey Sandwiches

Kellogg Company

Makes 6 sandwiches

3 cups *KELLOGG'S®
RICE KRISPIES®* cereal,
crushed to ¾ cup
½ cup skim milk
3 egg whites
3 tablespoons brown
mustard
2 tablespoons light, reduced
calorie mayonnaise
½ teaspoon dill weed

¼ teaspoon horseradish
12 slices French bread,
diagonally cut (about
½-inch thick, 5-inches long)
12 ounces sliced, roasted
turkey breast
6 slices (¾ ounces each) fat-
free Swiss cheese
Vegetable cooking spray

Preheat oven to 400°F. Place *KELLOGG'S® RICE KRISPIES®* cereal in shallow pan or plate. Set aside. In second shallow pan or plate, combine milk and egg whites. Set aside.

In small bowl, combine mustard, mayonnaise, dill weed, and horseradish. Evenly spread on one side of bread. Place turkey on 6 slices of the bread and top each with cheese. Place remaining bread slices on cheese to form sandwiches. Carefully and quickly dip each sandwich into milk mixture, then coat with cereal. Place on baking sheet coated with cooking spray.

Bake about 10 minutes or until golden brown and hot. Serve immediately.

Preparation time: 25 minutes　　　*Baking time:* 10 minutes

A.1. Cheesesteak Sandwich

Nabisco Foods Group

Makes 12 mini sandwiches

2 cups thinly sliced red *and/or* green pepper strips
1 cup thinly sliced onions
1 tablespoon margarine
6 (2-ounce) Steak-umm Beef Sandwich Steaks, cut crosswise into 8 strips
1 cup A.1.® Steak Sauce
6 slices American cheese, halved
12 (2½-inch) dinner rolls, split

In skillet, over medium-high heat, cook peppers and onions in margarine until tender, stirring occasionally; remove from skillet. In same skillet, cook steak strips until browned, about 1 to 2 minutes, stirring occasionally. Stir in pepper mixture and A.1. Steak Sauce; heat through. Spoon into rolls and top with cheese.

Appetizers

TOASTED ALMOND PARTY SPREAD
Kraft General Foods, Inc.
59

EXTRA SPECIAL SPINACH DIP
Lipton
60

PINEAPPLE-ALMOND
CHEESE SPREAD
Dole Food Company
60

CHICKEN LIVER-PIMIENTO
SPREAD
Lindsay International, Inc.
61

WHITE PIZZA DIP
Lipton
62

HUMMUS-TOPPED PITAS
Lindsay International, Inc.
62

WARM MUSHROOM & BACON DIP
Lipton
63

NUTTY CHEESE CROCK
Nabisco Foods Group
65

REUBEN ROLL-UPS
Reckitt & Colman Inc.
65

FIESTA GUACAMOLE DIP
ReaLime® Lime Juice
from Concentrate
66

JIM BOWIE CAJUN DIP
Beatrice Cheese, Inc.
67

CLASSIC NACHO DIP
Kraft General Foods, Inc.
68

LAYERED TACO DIP
Reckitt & Colman Inc.
69

TWO-CHEESE PESTO DIP
Sargento Cheese Company, Inc.
70

TRISCUIT QUESADILLAS
Nabisco Foods Group
70

SAVORY PEPPER-HERB
CHEESECAKE
Sargento Cheese Company, Inc.
71

GUACAMOLE
Lipton
72

GUACAMOLE BITES
Pepperidge Farm, Inc.
73

ITALIAN BREAD WITH TOMATO
APPETIZERS
Lipton
73

FRENCH'S® DEVILISH EGGS
Reckitt & Colman Inc.
74

Toasted Almond Party Spread

Kraft General Foods, Inc.

Makes 2⅓ cups

1 package (8 ounces) Philadelphia® Brand Cream Cheese, softened

1½ cups (6 ounces) shredded Casino® Natural Swiss Cheese

⅓ cup Miracle Whip® Salad Dressing

⅓ cup sliced almonds, toasted

2 tablespoons chopped green onion

⅛ teaspoon ground nutmeg

⅛ teaspoon pepper

Additional sliced almonds, toasted, for garnish (optional)

Preheat oven to 350°F. Combine all ingredients; mix well. Spread mixture into 9-inch pie plate or quiche dish. Bake 15 minutes, stirring after 8 minutes. Garnish with additional toasted sliced almonds, if desired.

Serve with assorted crackers or toasted bread cut-outs.

Preparation time: 10 minutes   *Cook time:* 15 minutes

Variations

Omit: Nutmeg and pepper.

To toast almonds: Preheat oven to 350°F. Place almonds in a shallow pan and bake for 10 minutes. Toasting time will vary depending on the size of the almonds.

Extra Special Spinach Dip

Lipton

Makes 3 cups dip

1 envelope Lipton® Recipe Secrets® Vegetable Soup Mix

8 ounces regular *or* light sour cream

1 cup regular *or* light mayonnaise

1 package (10 ounces) frozen chopped spinach, thawed and squeezed dry

1 can (8 ounces) water chestnuts, drained and chopped (optional)

In medium bowl, combine all ingredients; chill at least 2 hours. Serve with your favorite dippers.

Variation: Also terrific with Lipton® Recipe Secrets® Savory Herb with Garlic Soup Mix.

Pineapple-Almond Cheese Spread

Dole Food Company

Makes 4 cups

1 package (8 ounces) cream cheese, softened

4 cups shredded sharp Cheddar cheese

½ cup mayonnaise

1 tablespoon soy sauce

2 cans (8 ounces each) Dole® Crushed Pineapple, drained

1 cup chopped toasted Dole® Almonds

½ cup finely chopped green bell pepper

¼ cup minced green onion *or* chives

Celery stalks

Assorted crackers

Beat together cream cheese, Cheddar cheese, mayonnaise, and soy sauce until smooth. Stir in pineapple, almonds, bell pepper, and green onion. Use to stuff celery stalks or heap in a bowl surrounded by crackers, with a knife for spreading. Serve at room temperature.

Chicken Liver-Pimiento Spread

Lindsay International, Inc.

Makes about 2 cups

½ pound chicken livers, finely chopped

2 tablespoons chopped onion

1 tablespoon butter *or* margarine

1 can (2.25 ounces; ½ cup) Lindsay® Sliced Ripe Olives, drained

2 hard-cooked eggs, finely chopped

¼ cup chopped pimiento

¼ cup plain yogurt

1 teaspoon Dijon mustard

¼ teaspoon garlic salt

Several dashes Worcestershire sauce

Snipped parsley

Party rye bread or crackers

Cook chicken livers and onion in butter about 5 minutes or until livers just begin to lose their pink color. Remove from heat; drain. In a mixing bowl, combine the cooked livers and onion, olives, eggs, pimiento, yogurt, mustard, garlic salt, and Worcestershire sauce. Cover the mixture and chill at least 3 hours. Sprinkle with snipped parsley just before serving. Serve spread with party rye bread or crackers.

White Pizza Dip

Lipton

Makes 2 cups dip

1 envelope Lipton® Recipe Secrets® Savory Herb with Garlic Soup Mix
8 ounces sour cream
8 ounces ricotta cheese
1 cup shredded mozzarella cheese (about 4 ounces)
¼ cup (1 ounce) chopped pepperoni (optional)
1 loaf Italian *or* French bread, sliced

Preheat oven to 350°. In shallow 1-quart casserole, combine savory herb with garlic soup mix, sour cream, ricotta cheese, ¾ cup mozzarella cheese, and pepperoni. Sprinkle with remaining ¼ cup mozzarella cheese.

Bake uncovered 30 minutes or until heated through. Serve with bread.

Hummus-Topped Pitas

Lindsay International, Inc.

Makes 8 appetizers

1 can (15 ounces) garbanzo beans
3 tablespoons lemon juice
Several dashes hot pepper sauce
¼ cup chopped onion
1 clove garlic, minced
2 teaspoons cooking oil
½ cup sesame seeds, toasted
¼ cup tahini (sesame seeds paste)
¼ cup chopped green pepper
4 small pita-bread rounds
1½ cups shredded lettuce
1½ cups (6 ounces) crumbled feta cheese
1 medium tomato, chopped
1 can (2.25 ounces; ½ cup) Lindsay® Sliced Ripe Olives, drained

Preheat oven to 350°F. Drain beans, reserving 3 tablespoons liquid. Place beans, liquid, lemon juice, and pepper sauce in a blender container or food processor; cover and blend or process until pureed. Cook onion and garlic in oil until tender. Stir together bean mixture, onion mixture, sesame seed, tahini, and green pepper. Split pita rounds horizontally; bake 5 minutes. Top with lettuce and ½ cup bean mixture. Add cheese, tomato, and olives.

Warm Mushroom & Bacon Dip

Lipton

Makes about 2 cups

6 slices bacon	⅛ teaspoon pepper
½ pound mushrooms, thinly sliced	1 package (8 ounces) cream cheese, softened
2 medium cloves garlic, finely chopped	½ pint (8 ounces) sour cream
1 envelope Lipton® Recipe Secrets® Golden Onion Soup Mix	Assorted sliced breads *or* crackers

In 10-inch skillet, cook bacon; remove and crumble. Reserve 1½ tablespoons drippings. Add mushrooms and garlic to reserved drippings and cook over medium heat, stirring occasionally, 5 minutes or until mushrooms are tender and liquid is almost evaporated. Add golden onion soup mix and pepper, then cream cheese; combine thoroughly. Simmer, stirring constantly, until cream cheese is melted. Stir in sour cream and bacon; heat through. Garnish, if desired, with parsley and additional mushrooms and bacon. Serve with breads.

To microwave: In 2-quart casserole, arrange bacon; loosely cover with paper towel. Microwave at HIGH (Full Power) 6 minutes or until done, turning casserole once; remove bacon and crumble. Reserve 2½ tablespoons drippings. Add mushrooms and garlic to reserved drippings and microwave, uncovered, 2 minutes or until mushrooms are tender, stirring once. Add golden onion soup mix and pepper, then cream cheese; combine thoroughly. Decrease heat to MEDIUM (50% Power) and microwave, uncovered, stirring frequently, 3 minutes or until cream cheese is melted. Stir in sour cream and bacon. Microwave, uncovered, at MEDIUM 3 minutes or until heated through, stirring once. Garnish and serve as above.

Variation: Also terrific with Lipton® Recipe Secrets® Onion Soup Mix.

Nutty Cheese Crock

Nabisco Foods Group

Makes 2 cups

1 cup shredded Cheddar cheese (4 ounces)

1 (8-ounce) package cream cheese, softened

½ cup grated Parmesan cheese

¼ cup GREY POUPON Dijon Mustard

¼ cup walnuts, chopped

2 cloves garlic, crushed

RITZ Crackers, TRISCUIT Wafers *or* WHEAT THINS Snack Crackers

In bowl, with electric mixer at medium speed, blend all ingredients except crackers until smooth. Serve as a spread on crackers.

Reuben Roll-Ups

©1996 Reckitt & Colman Inc.

Makes 4 servings

8 (7-inch) flour tortillas (10-ounce package)

½ cup FRENCH'S® Deli Brown Mustard

½ pound thinly sliced corned beef

8 thin slices (6 ounces) Swiss cheese

½ cup sauerkraut, well drained

Spread each tortilla with 1 tablespoon mustard. Layer corned beef, cheese, and sauerkraut on tortillas, dividing evenly. Roll up tortillas jelly-roll style. Secure with toothpicks. Cut into 2-inch pieces to serve.

Tip: To pack for picnics, wrap tortilla rolls in foil. If desired, heat roll-ups on grill over low heat until cheese melts.

Preparation time: 20 minutes

Fiesta Guacamole Dip

ReaLime® Lime Juice from Concentrate

Makes 12 to 15 servings

2 (15- *or* 16-ounce) cans refried beans

1 4-ounce can chopped green chilies, undrained

1 16-ounce container sour cream

1 package taco seasoning mix

3 ripe avocados, pitted and peeled

2 tablespoons ReaLime® Lime Juice from Concentrate *or* ReaLemon® Lemon Juice from Concentrate

½ teaspoon seasoned salt

⅛ teaspoon garlic salt

Shredded cheddar *or* Monterey Jack cheese, chopped tomatoes, sliced green onions, sliced ripe olives

In small bowl, combine refried beans and chilies; spread on large serving plate. Combine sour cream and taco seasoning; spoon over bean mixture, spreading evenly. In small bowl, mash avocados; stir in ReaLime® and salts; spoon evenly over sour cream mixture. Cover; chill several hours. Just before serving, garnish with cheese, tomatoes, green onions, and olives. Serve with tortilla chips. Refrigerate leftovers.

Jim Bowie Cajun Dip

Beatrice Cheese, Inc.

Makes 10 to 12 servings

¼ cup butter *or* margarine
1 cup chopped onion
2 cloves garlic, minced
1 can mushroom soup
1 package (12 ounces) small frozen shrimp
8 ounces (2 cups) County Line® Cheddar Cheese, shredded
1 can (4 ounces) chopped mushrooms

2 packages (10 ounces each) frozen chopped broccoli
1 tablespoon hot pepper sauce
1 teaspoon salt
1 cup cashews *or* pecans, chopped
1 can (6 ounces) water chestnuts, sliced

Melt butter in 3-quart saucepan. Sauté onion and garlic until tender; add soup, shrimp, cheese, mushrooms, broccoli, pepper sauce, salt, nuts, and water chestnuts. Cook over low heat for 15 minutes.

Serve in chafing dish or other heated server with Melba toast, toasted bread, or crackers.

Variation: Substitute horseradish for hot pepper sauce for a different taste. If famished guests eat too fast, melt another stick of butter and another package of County Line® Cheddar Cheese.

Classic Nacho Dip

Kraft General Foods, Inc.

Makes 3 cups

½ cup chopped onion
2 tablespoons Parkay®
   Margarine
1 pound Velveeta®
   Pasteurized Process
   Cheese Spread, cubed

1 jar (8 ounces) salsa
2 tablespoons chopped
   cilantro

Sauté onions in margarine, reduce heat to low. Add remaining ingredients; stir until cheese spread is melted. Serve hot with tortilla chips or vegetable dippers, if desired.

To microwave: Microwave onions and margarine in 1½-quart bowl on HIGH 1½ minutes or until tender. Add remaining ingredients; mix well. Microwave on HIGH 5 minutes or until thoroughly heated, stirring after 3 minutes. Serve hot with tortilla chips or vegetable dippers, if desired.

Variations

Substitute 1 can (14½ ounces) tomatoes, chopped and drained, for salsa.

Substitute 1 can (10 ounces) tomatoes and green chilies, chopped, drained, for salsa.

Substitute Velveeta® Mexican Pasteurized Process Cheese Spread with Jalapeño Pepper, cubed, for Velveeta® Pasteurized Process Cheese Spread.

Substitute Velveeta® Light Pasteurized Process Cheese Spread, cubed, for Velveeta® Pasteurized Process Cheese Spread.

Substitute Parkay® Soft Diet Reduced-Calorie Margarine for Parkay® Margarine.

Preparation time: 10 minutes

Layered Taco Dip

©1996 Reckitt & Colman Inc.

Makes 8 to 10 servings

1 can (16 ounces) refried beans

1 can (16 ounces) pinto beans, drained

1 package (1¼ ounces) taco seasoning mix

3 tablespoons FRANK'S® Original REDHOT® Cayenne Pepper Sauce

½ cup water

1 container (16 ounces) sour cream

1½ cups (6 ounces) shredded Cheddar cheese

1 tomato, chopped

1 small avocado; peeled, chopped and tossed in 1 tablespoon lemon juice

Tortilla chips

Combine refried beans, drained pinto beans, taco mix, RedHot® sauce, and water in medium skillet. Simmer 10 minutes, stirring often. Cool slightly.

Spread bean mixture onto large platter. Spoon sour cream evenly over beans and sprinkle with cheese. Garnish with tomatoes and avocado. Chill 1 hour. Serve with tortilla chips.

Preparation time: 20 minutes   *Cook time:* 10 minutes

Two-Cheese Pesto Dip

Sargento Cheese Company, Inc.

Makes 2 cups

1 cup light sour cream
½ cup light mayonnaise
½ cup finely chopped fresh
  parsley
¼ cup finely chopped walnuts
1 clove garlic, minced
1½ teaspoons dried basil *or*
  3 tablespoons fresh minced
  basil

½ cup (2 ounces) Sargento®
  Preferred Light® Fancy
  Shredded Mozzarella
  Cheese
2 tablespoons Sargento®
  Grated Parmesan Cheese

Combine all ingredients. Cover and refrigerate several hours or overnight. Serve with assorted fresh vegetable dippers.

Triscuit Quesadillas

Nabisco Foods Group

Makes 6 appetizers

12 TRISCUIT Wafers
2 ounces Monterey Jack
  cheese, cut into 6 pieces

6 slices jalapeño peppers
Chili powder

On each of 6 wafers, place cheese pieces and jalapeño slices; top with remaining wafers to form a sandwich. Microwave 6 sandwiches on HIGH for 15 to 20 seconds or until cheese melts. Serve warm, sprinkled with chili powder.

Savory Pepper-Herb Cheesecake

Sargento Cheese Company, Inc.

Makes 10 servings
Crust

1¼ cups fresh dark rye *or* pumpernickel breadcrumbs (about 2 slices, processed in blender *or* food processor)

3 tablespoons melted margarine

Filling

1 container (15 ounces) Sargento® Light Ricotta Cheese
½ cup half-and-half
2 tablespoons flour
2 eggs
⅓ cup chopped mixed fresh herbs (such as basil, mint, tarragon, rosemary, thyme, oregano, and parsley)

¼ cup chopped fresh chives *or* green onion tops
1½ teaspoons finely shredded lemon peel
½ teaspoon cracked black pepper
¾ teaspoon salt

Preheat oven to 350°F. Lightly grease sides of 8- or 9-inch springform pan. Combine crust ingredients; press evenly over bottom of pan. Chill while preparing filling.

In bowl of electric mixer, combine ricotta cheese, half-and-half, and flour; blend until smooth. Add eggs, 1 at a time; blend until smooth. Blend in fresh herbs, chives, lemon peel, pepper, and salt. Pour into crust; bake 30 to 35 minutes or until center is just set. Remove to wire cooling rack; cool to room temperature.

Guacamole

Lipton

Makes about 2 cups

- 1 cup Lipton® California Dip (see below)
- 1 medium avocado, mashed
- 1 medium tomato, chopped
- 1 can (4 ounces) chopped green chilies, drained
- ¼ teaspoon garlic powder
- ⅛ teaspoon hot pepper sauce
- 2 tablespoons chopped cilantro

In medium bowl, blend all ingredients; cover and chill.

California Dip

Makes about 2 cups

- 1 envelope Lipton® Recipe Secrets® Onion Soup Mix
- 1 container (16 ounces) sour cream

Blend together and chill.

Guacamole Bites

Pepperidge Farm, Inc.

Makes 24 hors d'oeuvres

1 package (9½ ounces) Pepperidge Farm® Frozen Mini Puff Pastry Shells

1 medium ripe avocado, peeled, pitted, and cubed

⅓ cup mayonnaise

1 tablespoon lime juice

1¼ teaspoons minced garlic

¾ teaspoon chili powder

½ teaspoon salt

⅓ cup canned green chilies, minced

Dash cayenne pepper *or* Tabasco sauce

Cucumber *or* tomato, finely chopped, for garnish

Prepare pastry shells according to package directions.

Coarsely mash avocado. Mix with mayonnaise, lime juice, garlic, chili powder, salt, green chilies, and cayenne pepper. Spoon avocado mixture into pastry shells, mounding high. Garnish with cucumber or tomato. Serve cold.

Italian Bread with Tomato Appetizers

Lipton

Makes 18 servings

3 medium tomatoes, seeded and finely chopped

2 tablespoons finely chopped red onion

1 tablespoon chopped fresh basil leaves

¼ teaspoon ground black pepper (optional)

8 tablespoons Wish-Bone® Italian Dressing

1 loaf Italian *or* French bread (about 18 inches long)

In small bowl, combine tomatoes, onion, basil, pepper, and 2 tablespoons Italian dressing; set aside.

Slice bread diagonally into 18 slices. Brush 1 side of each slice with remaining 6 tablespoons dressing. Grill or broil bread until golden, turning once. Evenly top grilled slices with tomato mixture.

Note: Tomato mixture can be prepared ahead.

Variation: Also terrific with Wish-Bone® Robusto Italian or Lite Italian Dressing.

French's® Devilish Eggs

© 1996 Reckitt & Colman Inc.

Makes 12 servings

12 hard-cooked eggs, halved
6 tablespoons low-fat mayonnaise
2 tablespoons FRENCH'S® Classic Yellow® Mustard (see Note)
¼ teaspoon salt
⅛ teaspoon ground red pepper

In medium bowl, press yolks through a sieve with back of spoon or mash with fork. Stir in remaining ingredients; mix well.

Spoon or pipe into egg whites. Garnish as desired. Place on platter. Cover; chill in refrigerator.

Zesty Additions—Stir in *one* of the following:

- 2 tablespoons minced red onion and 1 tablespoon horseradish.
- 2 tablespoons pickle relish and 1 tablespoon minced fresh dill.
- 2 tablespoons *each* minced onion and celery, and 1 tablespoon minced fresh dill.
- ¼ cup shredded Cheddar cheese and ½ teaspoon FRENCH'S® Worcestershire Sauce.

Note: Great also with either FRENCH'S® Deli Brown Mustard *or* FRENCH'S® Dijon Mustard.

Preparation time: 40 minutes

Deluxe Nacho Platter

Lipton

Makes about 8 servings

2 tablespoons butter *or* margarine
½ cup chopped onion
½ cup chopped green bell pepper
2 cups water
1 package Lipton® Rice & Sauce—Spanish
½ teaspoon ground cumin (optional)

2 cups (about 8 ounces) shredded Cheddar cheese
1 can (4 ounces) chopped green chilies, drained
1 bag (7 ounces) corn tortilla chips
1 cup chopped tomato
½ cup sliced pitted ripe olives

In medium saucepan, melt butter and cook onion with green pepper over medium-high heat, stirring occasionally, 3 minutes or until tender. Stir in water, Rice & Sauce, and cumin, and bring to a boil. Reduce heat and simmer, stirring occasionally, 10 minutes or until rice is tender. Stir in 1 cup cheese and chilies until cheese is melted; let cool slightly.

In large, round, shallow, broiler-proof baking dish or pie plate, layer half of the chips, rice mixture, tomato, olives, and ½ cup cheese; repeat layering, ending with remaining cheese. Broil 1 minute or until cheese is melted. Garnish, if desired, with chili peppers, sliced avocado, sour cream, fresh cilantro, and additional cheese.

Pepperoni Pizza Hors D'oeuvre

Best Foods, a division of CPC International Inc.

Makes 32 hors d'oeuvre

- 4 Thomas'® English Muffins
- 1 can (10¼ ounces) marinara sauce
- 1 package (4 ounces) shredded mozzarella cheese
- 1 package (4 ounces) sliced pepperoni

Split English muffins by scoring with tines of fork and gently pull apart. Toast. Spread sauce on 8 muffin halves. Sprinkle with cheese and arrange 4 pepperoni slices on each muffin half. Broil 4 to 5 inches from source of heat 2 to 3 minutes or until cheese bubbles and browns. Cut each muffin into 4 wedges.

Turkey Cranberry Topper

Nabisco Foods Group

Makes 24 appetizers

- 24 RITZ Crackers
- 2 ounces Swiss cheese, cut into 1-inch squares (⅛-inch thickness)
- ¼ cup whole berry cranberry sauce
- 3 ounces cooked turkey pieces
- Parsley sprigs, for garnish

Preheat oven to 350°F. Top each cracker with 1 piece cheese, ½ teaspoon cranberry sauce, and turkey piece. Place on baking sheet and bake for 2 to 3 minutes or until cheese melts. Garnish with parsley.

To microwave: Place 6 topped crackers in circular pattern on microwave-safe plate. Microwave on HIGH for 20 to 30 seconds or until cheese melts.

Savory Seafood Spread

Makes 3 cups

- 2 packages (8 ounces *each*) cream cheese, softened
- 8 ounces imitation crab meat, flaked
- 2 tablespoons minced green onion
- 2 tablespoons FRANK'S® Original REDHOT® Cayenne Pepper Sauce
- 1 tablespoon prepared horseradish
- 1 teaspoon FRENCH'S® Worcestershire Sauce
- ½ cup sliced almonds

Paprika

Preheat oven to 375°F. In mixer bowl or food processor, beat cream cheese until smooth. Beat in remaining ingredients *except* almonds and paprika.

Spread into 9-inch pie plate. Sprinkle with almonds and paprika. Bake for 20 minutes until hot and nuts are golden. Serve with crackers or vegetable dippers.

Preparation time: 10 minutes   *Cook time:* 20 minutes

Florentine Crescents

Kraft General Foods, Inc.

Makes 32 appetizers

1 package (10 ounces) Birds Eye® Chopped Spinach, thawed and well drained

1 cup (4 ounces) Casino® Shredded Natural Swiss Cheese

½ cup (2 ounces) Kraft® Grated Parmesan Cheese

½ cup Miracle Whip® Salad Dressing

¼ teaspoon ground nutmeg

2 cans (8 ounces each) refrigerated quick crescent dinner rolls

Preheat oven to 375°F. Mix spinach, cheese, salad dressing, and nutmeg until well blended. Unroll dough; separate into 16 triangles. Cut each triangle lengthwise, forming 32 triangles. Spread each triangle with 1 rounded teaspoonful of spinach mixture. Roll up, starting at wide end. Place on greased cookie sheet. Bake 11 to 13 minutes or until golden brown.

Preparation time: 15 minutes   *Cook time:* 13 minutes per batch

Golden Ham Puffs

Beatrice Cheese, Inc.

Makes 24 rounds or 48 quarters

1 cup ground cooked ham

2 teaspoons prepared mustard

1 teaspoon horseradish sauce

¼ cup mayonnaise

1 teaspoon grated onion

1 teaspoon baking powder

2½ cups grated County Line® Cheddar Cheese

1 egg, beaten

1 teaspoon grated onion

1 teaspoon baking powder

12 slices bread

In small bowl, stir together ham, mustard, horseradish sauce, mayonnaise, onion, and baking powder. In another small bowl, stir together cheese, egg, onion, and baking powder. Set aside. Toast 12 slices of bread and cut into 24 rounds with 1½-inch food cutter, or cut crusts off bread and quarter. Spread ham mixture onto bread rounds, then cheese mixture. Place on metal baking pan under broiler until mixture puffs up and turns slightly brown, about 5 minutes.

Pâté Maison

Lindsay International, Inc.

Makes 1 loaf

½ turkey breast (2 pounds), skinned and boned	½ teaspoon dried basil, crushed
3 ounces pork fat *or* salt pork, cut up	½ teaspoon dried savory, crushed
2 beaten eggs	⅛ teaspoon pepper
⅓ cup dry white wine	¾ pound ground pork
¼ cup brandy	¾ pound ground veal
4 teaspoons vinegar	4 slices bacon
¾ teaspoon salt	½ cup Lindsay® Medium Pitted Ripe Olives, drained
½ teaspoon dried thyme, crushed	3 or 4 bay leaves

Preheat oven to 350°F. Cut strips of turkey to make 1½ cups of meat; set aside. Grind remaining turkey and pork fat or salt pork through fine blade of food grinder or in a food processor. Combine eggs, wine, brandy, vinegar, salt, thyme, basil, savory, and pepper. Add ground-turkey mixture, pork, and veal; mix well. Lay bacon crosswise in bottom and up sides of 9-by-5-by-3-inch loaf pan.

Press in half of the ground-meat mixture; arrange turkey strips and olives atop. Spoon in remaining ground-meat mixture. Top with bay leaves. Cover with foil. Bake about 1¾ hours. Remove from oven. Drain off fat; replace foil. Place the bottom of another 9-by-5-by-3-inch pan atop the hot loaf. Press very firmly to compact mixture; fill the empty pan with dry beans. Chill overnight. Remove bay leaves. Turn the pâté onto a serving plate and slice.

FRUIT OF KINGS
The Story of Pineapple and James Dole

The New World gold that Columbus discovered in Guadeloupe in 1493 was a pineapple: a fragrant, golden fruit shaped like a pine cone with a beautiful, spiny crown. The fruit and plant proved impossible to ship unspoiled on the long voyage back to Spain. Little more than a century later, living plants or shoots were successfully transported to Asia. In 1640 the emperor of China sent Oliver Cromwell pineapple plants through the East India Company.

The rare pineapple became highly prized in the Old World during the seventeenth century. Grown in hothouses at great expense, they adorned the sumptuous banquet tables of the elite and were considered a status symbol. The Spanish copied the West Indies natives, who put pineapples and pineapple tops near the entrances of their huts as welcome signs, by carving pineapple motifs above their doorways and on their gateposts. Caricaturists used pineapple art to symbolize the excesses of high living during the Napoleonic wars.

In the 1880s, a sea captain brought a variety of pine-apple, the Smooth Cayenne, from Florida for cultivation in Hawaii. In 1899, James Dole, a recent Harvard gradu-ate, arrived on the islands at this fortuitous time to seek adventure and fortune. At first, he wasn't quite certain how he would do this, but he soon proposed to "extend the market for the Hawaiian Pineapple into every grocery store in the United States."

There were many detractors of Dole's pioneering ef-forts. Sugar was the crop of Hawaii. Most certainly, the pineapple fruit couldn't withstand long ocean voyages.

Determined, Dole started with several hundred plants on sixty acres north of Honolulu. At Wahiawa he built his first cannery to preserve the fruit, then convinced the American Can Company to build a manufacturing plant nearby to save the cost of shipping cans. A young Dole engineer, Henry Ginaca, cut production costs further by inventing a machine to peel, core, and cut flawless pine-apple cylinders at the rate of one hundred per minute.

By 1922 Dole had purchased the island of Lanai for $1.1 million. Lanai was barren except for the five-foot cacti Dole pushed over to make room for fields and roads. He tapped into underground water and built a dry dock for shipping pineapple to his canning facilities in Honolulu. Lanai City, with houses, stores, schools, and a hospital, was developed for the labor pool.

To familiarize Americans with canned pineapple, Dole's first ads proclaimed, "It Cuts With a Spoon—Like A Peach." Two company engineers discovered the process for extracting tangy pineapple juice in 1934, just in time for mixing with post-Prohibition gin.

Dole died in Hawaii in 1958, leaving behind his com-plete organization to place the rare and exotic fruit of Old World courts on the dining tables of every American household.

Aloha Chicken Wings

Dole Food Company

Makes 25 servings, 2 pieces each

25 chicken wings
3 tablespoons cider vinegar
2 tablespoons garlic salt
1 tablespoon onion powder
1 teaspoon ground ginger

1 teaspoon paprika
1 can (20 ounces) Dole®
  Crushed Pineapple
1 cup ketchup
¼ cup brown sugar, packed
¼ cup soy sauce

Preheat oven to 400°F. Have butcher cut wings at joints into 3 pieces. Discard bony end of wing tip or reserve for another use (such as in soup). Arrange remaining chicken parts in single layer in well-oiled baking pans. Prick skin with fork. Combine vinegar, garlic salt, onion powder, ginger, and paprika to make a baste; brush over chicken. Bake 30 minutes. Turn once. Combine pineapple and juice with ketchup, brown sugar, and soy sauce. Spoon sauce over wings. Continue roasting 15 minutes more. Turn wings; spoon on more sauce. Roast 15 minutes more, or until done. Remove wings to serving platter. Serve immediately or refrigerate until serving time. Wings may be reheated in oven or over hot coals on a grill.

Buffalo Wings

Lipton

Makes 24 wings

24 chicken wings (about 4 pounds)
1 envelope Lipton® Recipe Secrets® Golden Onion Soup Mix
½ cup margarine *or* butter, melted
2 tablespoons white vinegar
2 tablespoons water
2 cloves garlic
1½ to 2 teaspoons ground red pepper
1 teaspoon ground cumin (optional)
1 cup Wish-Bone® Chunky Blue Cheese Dressing

Cut tips off chicken wings (save tips for soup). Halve remaining chicken wings at joint.

In food processor or blender, process golden onion soup mix, margarine, vinegar, water, garlic, pepper, and cumin until blended; set aside.

Broil chicken 12 minutes or until brown, turning after 6 minutes. Brush with half of the soup mixture, then broil 2 minutes or until crisp. Turn, then brush with remaining soup mixture and broil an additional minute. Serve with Wish-Bone dressing and, if desired, celery sticks.

Variation: Also terrific with Lipton® Recipe Secrets® Onion Soup Mix.

Easy Bean Appetizer

Kellogg Company

Makes 16 servings

1 can (16 ounces) fat free refried beans

½ package (2 tablespoons + 2 teaspoons) taco seasoning mix

¼ teaspoon liquid pepper sauce

1 cup diced light pasteurized process cheese

4 cups *KELLOGG'S® RICE KRISPIES®* cereal

1 cup salsa (optional)

Vegetable cooking spray

In 3-quart saucepan, combine beans, taco seasoning, and pepper sauce. Cook over low heat, stirring constantly, until mixture starts to bubble. Add cheese. Continue cooking and stirring until cheese melts and mixture is smooth. Remove from heat.

Stir *KELLOGG'S® RICE KRISPIES®* cereal into hot bean mixture, until thoroughly combined. Spread mixture evenly in 8-by-8-by-2-inch pan coated with cooking spray. Cool completely. Cut into 1-inch squares. Serve with salsa and garnish with jalapeño slices or cherry tomato halves, if desired. Store in refrigerator.

Optional Garnishes: Jalapeño slices, Cherry tomato halves

Preparation time: 15 minutes

Garlic Herb Spread

Nabisco Foods Group

Makes ½ cup spread

½ cup (1 stick) BLUE BONNET 53% Vegetable Oil Spread, softened

2 cloves garlic, finely chopped

2 tablespoons chopped parsley

1 teaspoon each chopped chives, thyme and basil

1 teaspoon coarsely ground black pepper

1 teaspoon grated lemon peel

In small bowl, blend all ingredients until well combined. Form mixture into 5-inch log. Wrap in plastic wrap; chill until firm. Serve as a spread on crackers or toss with hot cooked pasta or steamed vegetables.

Pineapple-Sausage Appetizers

Kellogg Company

Makes about 3 dozen meatballs

1 pound spicy pork sausage

1½ cups *KELLOGG'S® RICE KRISPIES®* cereal, crushed to ¾ cup

1 can (20 ounces) pineapple chunks in juice

2 tablespoons firmly packed brown sugar

2 tablespoons cornstarch

2 tablespoons soy sauce

2 tablespoons vinegar

1 medium green pepper, cut into 1-inch pieces

Mix together sausage and *KELLOGG'S® RICE KRISPIES®* cereal. Shape into 1-inch meatballs. Brown meatballs in 12-inch frypan. Drain and set aside.

Drain pineapple, reserving juice. Add enough water to juice to measure 2 cups.

In 3-quart saucepan, mix together sugar and cornstarch. Stir in juice, soy sauce, and vinegar. Cook over medium heat, stirring constantly, until mixture boils and thickens.

Reduce heat and add meatballs. Cover and simmer for 15 minutes, stirring occasionally. Add pineapple chunks and green pepper. Simmer 3 minutes longer or until hot. Serve with cocktail picks.

Preparation time: 50 minutes

Roast Beef Spirals

Nabisco Foods Group

Makes 16 appetizers

1 (3-ounce) slice deli roast beef

3 tablespoons garlic n' herb spread

16 TRISCUIT Wafers

3 tablespoons Russian dressing

Sliced pimiento-stuffed olives, for garnish

Place roast beef slice flat on plastic wrap. Spread garlic spread evenly over slice. Roll up from end jelly-roll style. Wrap in plastic wrap and freeze for 15 to 20 minutes for easier slicing. Slice roll into 16 slices. Top each cracker with ½ teaspoon dressing and 1 roast beef sliced roll. Top each with a sliced olive. Serve immediately.

Frank's® Original Buffalo Chicken Wings

©1996 Reckitt & Colman Inc.

Makes 24 to 30 individual pieces

2½ pounds chicken wings, split and tips discarded

½ cup FRANK'S® Original REDHOT® Cayenne Pepper Sauce (or more to taste)

⅓ cup butter *or* margarine, melted

Zesty Blue Cheese Dip (recipe follows)

Celery sticks

Deep fry* wings at 400°F (HIGH) for 12 minutes or until cooked and crispy; drain.

In large bowl, combine RedHot® sauce and butter. Toss wings in sauce to coat completely. Serve with Zesty Blue Cheese Dip and celery.

*Alternate cooking directions
Prepare wings using one of the cooking methods below. Toss in sauce.

Bake: Place wings single layer on a rack in a foil-lined roasting pan. Bake at 425°F for 1 hour until fully cooked and crispy, turning halfway.

Broil: Place wings single layer on a rack in a foil-lined roasting pan. Broil 6 inches from heat for 15 to 20 minutes until cooked and crispy, turning once.

Grill: Place wings on an oiled grid; grill over medium heat for 30 to 40 minutes until fully cooked and crispy, turning often.

Preparation time: 10 minutes   *Cook time:* 15 minutes

Zesty Blue Cheese Dip

Makes ¾ cup

½ cup blue cheese salad
    dressing
¼ cup sour cream

2 teaspoons FRANK'S®
    Original REDHOT®
    Cayenne Pepper Sauce

Combine all ingredients; mix well. If desired, garnish with crumbled blue cheese.

Preparation time: 5 minutes

Breads & Muffins

BLACK BREAD
McCormick & Company, Inc.
93

PEANUT BUTTER HEALTH BREAD
Best Foods, a division of
CPC International Inc.
94

PINEAPPLE-ORANGE
WALNUT BREAD
Dole Food Company
94

PIZZA BREAD
Lindsay International, Inc.
95

SILO BREAD
Beatrice Cheese, Inc.
96

HOT PEPPER BREAD
Kellogg Company
97

ORANGE APRICOT TEA BREAD
Lipton
98

BISCUIT SOUP STICKS
Kellogg Company
99

WHEAT GERM BISCUITS
Nestlé Food Company
100

BRAN-RAISIN MUFFINS
Nestlé Food Company
100

APPLE STREUSEL MUFFINS
Libby's, Nestlé Food Company
101

APPLE MUFFINS
Nabisco Foods Group
102

APPLESAUCE CHEDDAR MUFFINS
Sargento Cheese Company, Inc.
103

CINNAMON-APPLE WALNUT
MUFFINS
Lipton
104

PINEAPPLE CARROT RAISIN
MUFFINS
Dole Food Company
105

BANANA MUFFINS
Kellogg Company
105

SPICE AND PEACH MUFFINS
Kellogg Company
106

PEANUT BUTTER CEREAL
MUFFINS
Best Foods, a division of
CPC International Inc.
107

ORANGE BRAN MUFFINS
Best Foods, a division of
CPC International Inc.
108

VEGETABLE DINNER ROLLS
Kellogg Company
108

Black Bread

McCormick & Company, Inc.

Makes 2 loaves

½ cup cornmeal
2 cups water
¼ cup butter, cut in pieces
1 ounce unsweetened
    chocolate
½ cup dark molasses
1½ teaspoons salt

2 tablespoons McCormick/
    Schilling® Caraway Seed
2 teaspoons instant coffee
¼ cup lukewarm water
1 package (¼ ounce) active
    dry yeast
5½ cups flour

Preheat oven to 350°F. In saucepan, combine cornmeal and water. Cook, stirring, over medium heat until mixture comes to a boil. Simmer 1 minute. Remove from heat. Add next 6 ingredients. Stir well. Cool to lukewarm. Combine lukewarm water and yeast. Let stand 5 minutes. Stir into cornmeal mixture. Beat in 4½ cups flour, ½ cup at a time. Place dough on well-floured surface and knead in remaining flour. Continue kneading until dough is smooth and elastic, about 5 minutes. Butter the inside of large bowl. Place dough in bowl. Turn dough until entire surface is lightly buttered. Cover with towel. Set in warm, draft-free place and let rise 1½ hours, or until double in size. Punch dough down. Knead 2 minutes on floured surface. Divide dough in half and shape each half into small loaf. Place each in a buttered 2¼-by-3½-by-7½-inch loaf pan. Cover with towel and let rise 40 minutes. Bake 1 hour or until loaves shrink away from sides of pan. Cool on wire racks.

Peanut Butter Health Bread

Best Foods, a division of CPC International Inc.

Makes 1 loaf

2 cups flour	¾ cup firmly packed brown sugar
1 cup quick oats	
1 tablespoon baking powder	1 egg
	1⅔ cups milk
1 teaspoon salt	1 cup raisins
1 cup Skippy® Creamy *or* Super Chunk® Peanut Butter	

Preheat oven to 350°F. In medium bowl, stir flour, oats, baking powder, and salt. In large bowl with mixer at medium speed, beat peanut butter and brown sugar until smooth. Beat in egg. Gradually add milk. With mixer at low speed, beat in dry ingredients until smooth. Stir in raisins. Pour into greased 9-by-5-by-3-inch loaf pan. Bake 70 to 75 minutes or until toothpick inserted in center comes out clean. Cool in pan 10 minutes. Remove and cool completely on wire rack.

Pineapple-Orange Walnut Bread

Dole Food Company

Makes 1 loaf, 28 servings

1 cup walnut pieces	1 egg
2 cups flour	Zest and juice from
1 teaspoon baking powder	1 Dole® Orange
1 teaspoon baking soda	1 can (8¼ ounces) Dole®
¼ teaspoon salt	Crushed Pineapple,
¾ cup sugar	undrained
¼ cup margarine	1 cup Dole® Raisins

Preheat oven to 350°F. Pulverize walnuts in blender. Combine nuts with flour, baking powder, baking soda, and salt. Beat sugar and margarine until light and fluffy. Beat in egg, 1 tablespoon orange zest, and ¼ cup orange juice. Stir in one-third flour mixture until blended. Stir in one-half undrained pineapple. Repeat, ending with flour. Stir in raisins. Pour batter into greased 9-by-5-inch loaf pan. Bake 65 to 70 minutes until toothpick inserted in center comes out clean. Cool in pan 10 minutes. Turn out onto wire rack to cool completely.

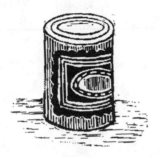

Pizza Bread

Lindsay International, Inc.

Makes 2 pizzas

1 package (16 ounces) hot roll mix

2 cans (8 ounces each) pizza sauce

2 cans (2.25 ounces each; 1 cup total) Lindsay® Wedged Ripe Olives, drained

1 cup Lindsay® Pimiento-Stuffed Green Olives, drained and sliced

2 cans (4 ounces each) mushroom stems and pieces

6 tablespoons thinly sliced green onion

Shredded mozzarella or grated Parmesan cheese

Preheat oven to 400°F. Prepare the hot roll mix according to package directions, except decrease water by ¼ cup when dissolving the yeast and stir ¼ cup of the pizza sauce into the flour mixture. Turn the dough out onto a lightly greased surface; knead in ripe olives. Cover dough; let rise until double. Punch down; divide in half. Pat each half of the dough onto a greased 12-inch round baking pan. Let rise in a warm place for 30 minutes.

Spread remaining pizza sauce over the dough. Sprinkle each pizza with half the green olives, half the mushrooms, and half the green onion. Sprinkle with desired amount of mozzarella or Parmesan cheese. Bake 20 to 25 minutes or until edges begin to pull away from sides of the pan. Cut into thin wedges and serve immediately.

Silo Bread

Beatrice Cheese, Inc.

Makes 2 loaves

1 cup finely chopped onions	1 teaspoon onion salt
1¼ cups water	¼ cup vegetable oil
1 package active dry yeast	2 eggs, slightly beaten
4 cups all-purpose flour	2 cups grated County Line®
2 tablespoons sugar	Extra Sharp Cheddar
1 teaspoon salt	Cheese

Preheat oven to 375°F. In small saucepan, cook onion in 1 cup water until tender; set aside to cool. Dissolve yeast in remaining ¼ cup warm water. Mix flour, sugar, salt, and onion salt. In large bowl, mix together 2 cups sifted flour mixture, cooked onion, yeast, vegetable oil, and eggs. Add remaining 2 cups flour mixture. Turn out onto floured board. Knead until smooth and elastic (about 10 minutes). Divide into 2 equal portions. Roll each portion of dough into a 17-by-5-inch rectangle; sprinkle with 1 cup cheese each. Roll up; place each portion end side down into a 1-pound greased coffee can. Cover cans with plastic lids or aluminum foil and set in warm place until dough rises to top of cans (about 1 hour). Remove covering. Bake 20 to 25 minutes. Let stand in can 5 minutes. Remove bread from cans. Serve warm.

Hot Pepper Bread

Kellogg Company

Makes 2 loaves, 12 slices each

5½ cups all-purpose flour
  4 cups *KELLOGG'S CORN FLAKES*® cereal, crushed to 1 cup
  1 tablespoon sugar
  1 tablespoon salt
  2 packages active dry yeast
1½ cups skim milk
  ⅓ cup vegetable oil

2 eggs
1½ cups (6 ounces) shredded low-fat, low sodium, sharp Cheddar cheese
½ cup finely chopped onion
¼ cup finely chopped hot chili peppers
2 tablespoons margarine, melted
Vegetable cooking spray

Preheat oven to 350°F. In electric mixer large bowl, combine 2 cups flour, *KELLOGG'S CORN FLAKES*® cereal, sugar, salt, and yeast. Set aside. In small saucepan, heat milk and vegetable oil over low heat, until very warm (120°F to 130°F).

Gradually add to cereal mixture and beat until well combined. Add eggs. Beat on medium speed for 2 minutes. Stir in cheese, onions, and chili peppers. By hand, stir in enough remaining flour to make a stiff dough. On well-floured surface, knead dough about 5 minutes or until smooth and elastic. Place in large bowl coated with spray, turning once to grease surface. Cover lightly. Let rise in warm place until double in volume (about 1 hour). Punch down dough. Divide in half. Place into 2 1½-quart round casseroles dishes coated with cooking spray. Cover and let rise in warm place until double in volume. Bake about 25 minutes or until golden brown. To prevent overbrowning, cover loosely with foil during last few minutes. Remove loaves from dishes and cool on wire racks. Brush with melted margarine. Serve warm or cold.

Orange Apricot Tea Bread

Lipton

Makes 1 loaf

¾ cup water
6 Lipton® Soothing Moments® Orange & Spice Flavored Tea Bags
½ cup chopped dried apricots
2½ cups all-purpose flour
1 cup sugar
1½ teaspoons baking powder
1 teaspoon salt
⅓ cup butter *or* margarine, softened
2 eggs
8 ounces vanilla yogurt

Preheat oven to 350°. Spray 9-by-5-inch loaf pan with nonstick cooking spray; set aside.

In 1-quart saucepan, bring water to a boil. Remove from heat and add orange & spice flavored tea bags and apricots; cover and steep 5 minutes. Remove tea bags and squeeze; cool.

In large bowl, mix flour, sugar, baking powder, and salt. With electric mixer, cut in butter until mixture is size of small peas. Add eggs beaten with cool tea and yogurt; stir just until flour is moistened. Turn into prepared pan.

Bake 1 hour 5 minutes or until toothpick inserted in center comes out clean. On wire rack, cool 10 minutes; remove from pan and cool completely.

Variation: Also terrific with Lipton® Soothing Moments® Gentle Orange Herbal Tea Bags.

Biscuit Soup Sticks

Kellogg Company

Makes 5 servings

1 cup *KELLOGG'S® RICE KRISPIES®* cereal, crushed to ½ cup	1 tube (7.5 ounce) refrigerated biscuits
½ teaspoon garlic salt	2 tablespoons skim milk
½ teaspoon caraway seeds	Vegetable cooking spray

Preheat oven to 400°F. In shallow pan or plate, combine *KELLOGG'S® RICE KRISPIES®* cereal, garlic salt, and caraway seeds. Set aside.

Cut biscuits in half and pull or roll into 3-inch sticks. Dip each stick in milk and coat with cereal mixture. Place on baking sheet coated with cooking spray.

Bake about 10 minutes or until golden brown. Serve hot with soup or salad.

Preparation time: 20 minutes   *Baking time:* 10 minutes

Wheat Germ Biscuits

Nestlé Food Company

Makes 8 servings

1¾ cups buttermilk baking mix

⅓ cup wheat germ

⅔ cup *undiluted* Carnation® Evaporated Milk

Preheat oven to 450°F. Combine ingredients. Knead 10 times on floured surface. Roll to ½-inch thickness. Cut into 3-inch rounds. Bake on ungreased cookie sheet 8 minutes.

Bran-Raisin Muffins

Nestlé Food Company

Makes 16 to 18 muffins

Boiling water

¾ cup raisins

⅓ cup oil

1 slightly beaten egg

1 cup liquid Carnation® Nonfat Dry Milk

1 tablespoon lemon juice

1 cup flour

½ cup sugar

¾ cup unprocessed bran

2 teaspoons baking powder

1 teaspoon baking soda

½ teaspoon salt

¼ teaspoon cinnamon

Preheat oven to 400°F. Pour boiling water over raisins; let stand 10 minutes. Drain. Combine oil and egg in small bowl. Combine liquid nonfat milk and lemon juice. Stir into egg mixture. Combine flour, sugar, bran, baking powder, baking soda, salt, and cinnamon. Make a well in center of flour mixture. Pour in milk mixture all at once, stirring just until dry ingredients are moistened. Stir in raisins. Spoon into buttered muffin-pan cups, filling two-thirds full. Bake 15 minutes.

To freeze: Allow muffins to cool completely on wire racks. Place in heavy plastic bag; seal. Freeze.

To heat in conventional oven: Wrap 1 or 2 frozen muffins in foil. Heat at 350°F for 15 minutes, or until heated through.

To heat in microwave oven: Microwave 1 frozen muffin, uncovered, 1 minute on MEDIUM (1½ minutes for 2 muffins).

Apple Streusel Muffins

Libby's, Nestlé Food Company

Makes 18 muffins

2½ cups all-purpose flour	1 cup Libby's® Solid Pack Pumpkin
2 cups granulated sugar	½ cup vegetable oil
1 tablespoon pumpkin pie spice	2 cups peeled, finely chopped apples
1 teaspoon baking soda	Streusel Topping (see below)
½ teaspoon salt	
2 eggs, lightly beaten	

Preheat oven to 350°F. In large bowl, combine flour, sugar, pumpkin pie spice, baking soda, and salt; set aside. In medium bowl, combine eggs, pumpkin, and oil. Add liquid ingredients to dry ingredients; stir just until moistened. Stir in apple. Spoon batter into greased or paper-lined muffin-pan cups, filling three-fourths full. Sprinkle Streusel Topping over batter. Bake 35 to 40 minutes, or until toothpick comes out clean.

Streusel Topping

2 tablespoons all-purpose flour	½ teaspoon ground cinnamon
¼ cup sugar	4 teaspoons butter

In small bowl, combine flour, sugar, and cinnamon. Cut in butter until mixture is crumbly.

Variation: For 6 giant muffins, follow directions above, increasing baking time to 40 to 45 minutes.

Apple Muffins

Nabisco Foods Group

Makes 12 muffins

⅓ cup sugar
1¼ cups all-purpose flour
½ cup CREAM OF WHEAT Cereal (½-minute, 2½-minute *or* 10-minute stovetop cooking)
1 tablespoon baking powder
1½ teaspoons ground cinnamon

½ cup apple juice
½ cup skim milk
¼ cup EGG BEATERS Healthy Real Egg Product
2 tablespoons margarine, melted
1 teaspoon vanilla extract
1 cup peeled, chopped apple

Preheat oven to 400°F. Reserve 1 tablespoon sugar. In medium bowl, combine remaining sugar, flour, cereal, baking powder, and cinnamon; set aside.

Reserve 2 tablespoons apple juice. In small bowl, combine remaining apple juice, milk, egg product, margarine, and vanilla; stir into dry ingredients just until moistened. Blend in apple. Spoon mixture into 12 greased 2½-inch muffin-pan cups. Bake for 18 to 20 minutes or until toothpick inserted in center comes out clean. Remove from pan; brush tops of muffins with reserved apple juice and roll in reserved sugar. Serve warm.

Applesauce Cheddar Muffins

Sargento Cheese Company, Inc.

Makes 12 muffins

2 cups baking powder biscuit mix
¼ cup sugar
1 teaspoon cinnamon
1 egg, well beaten
½ cup unsweetened applesauce
¼ cup skim milk
2 tablespoons oil
1 cup (4 ounces) Sargento® Preferred Light® Fancy Shredded Cheddar Cheese
1 tablespoon light margarine
2 tablespoons sugar

Preheat oven to 400°F. Combine biscuit mix, ¼ cup sugar, and cinnamon. In separate bowl, combine egg, applesauce, milk, oil, and cheese. Add to dry ingredients and mix lightly. Coat muffin-pan cups with a nonstick vegetable spray or paper liners. Fill each cup two-thirds full. Bake 20 minutes. Remove muffins from pan and brush tops lightly with melted margarine, roll in 2 tablespoons sugar.

Cinnamon-Apple Walnut Muffins

Lipton

Makes 12 muffins

8 ounces boiling water	½ teaspoon ground ginger (optional)
4 Lipton® Soothing Moments® Cinnamon Apple Herbal Tea Bags	½ teaspoon salt
	½ cup butter, softened
2 cups all-purpose flour	2 eggs, beaten
1 cup sugar	1 teaspoon vanilla extract
1½ teaspoons baking powder	1 cup chopped walnuts, toasted
1 teaspoon ground nutmeg (optional)	

Preheat oven to 375°. Spray muffin pan with nonstick cooking spray or line with cupcake liners; set aside.

In teapot, pour boiling water over cinnamon apple herbal tea bags; cover and steep 5 minutes. Remove tea bags and squeeze; cool.

In large bowl, combine flour, sugar, baking powder, nutmeg, ginger, and salt. With electric mixture, blend in butter until mixture is size of small peas. Make well in center of flour mixture. Add eggs beaten with cool tea and vanilla; with fork or spoon, stir just until flour is moistened. Fold in walnuts. Turn into prepared pan.

Bake 18 minutes or until toothpick inserted in center comes out clean. On wire rack, cool 10 minutes; remove from pan and cool completely.

Variation: Also terrific with Lipton® Soothing Moments® Cinnamon Flavored Tea Bags.

Pineapple Carrot Raisin Muffins

Dole Food Company

Makes 12 muffins

2 cups all-purpose flour
1 cup sugar
2 teaspoons baking powder
½ teaspoon ground cinnamon
¼ teaspoon ground ginger
½ cup shredded Dole® Carrots

½ cup Dole® Raisins
½ cup chopped walnuts
1 can (8 ounces) Dole® Crushed Pineapple
2 eggs
½ cup margarine, melted
1 teaspoon vanilla extract'

Preheat oven to 375°F. Combine flour, sugar, baking powder, cinnamon, and ginger. Stir in carrots, raisins, and nuts. Separately, combine undrained pineapple, eggs, margarine, and vanilla. Stir into dry ingredients until just blended. Spoon batter into greased muffin-pan cups. Bake 20 to 25 minutes. Turn out onto wire rack to cool.

Banana Muffins

Kellogg Company

Makes 12 muffins

1¼ cups all-purpose flour
1 tablespoon baking powder
½ teaspoon salt
½ teaspoon cinnamon
¼ teaspoon nutmeg
½ cup firmly packed brown sugar

2 cups *KELLOGG'S CORN FLAKES®* cereal, crushed to 1 cup
1 egg
⅓ cup milk
¼ cup vegetable oil
1 cup mashed ripe bananas
Vegetable cooking spray

Preheat oven to 400°F. Stir together flour, baking powder, salt, cinnamon, nutmeg, brown sugar, and *KELLOGG'S CORN FLAKES®* cereal. Set aside. In large bowl, combine egg, milk, and oil. Stir in bananas. Add flour mixture, stirring only until combined. Portion evenly into 12 2½-inch muffin-pan cups coated with cooking spray. Bake for 20 minutes or until lightly browned. Serve warm.

Spice and Peach Muffins

Kellogg Company

Makes 12 muffins

1½ cups all-purpose flour
½ cup granulated sugar
1 tablespoon baking powder
¼ teaspoon salt
1 teaspoon cinnamon
¼ teaspoon nutmeg
1 can (16 ounce) sliced peaches

4 cups *KELLOGG'S® RICE KRISPIES®* cereal
3 egg whites
1 cup powdered sugar
2 tablespoons sliced almonds
Vegetable cooking spray

Preheat oven to 400°F. In large mixing bowl, stir together flour, granulated sugar, baking powder, salt, and spices. Set aside.

Drain peaches, reserving liquid. Place peaches, *KELLOGG'S® RICE KRISPIES®* cereal, egg whites and ¾ cup of the peach liquid in food processor bowl. Using metal blade, process mixture about 45 seconds or until smooth. Add to flour mixture stirring only until combined. Portion evenly into 12 2½-inch muffin-pan cups coated with cooking spray.

Bake about 23 minutes or until golden brown. Remove from pan and drizzle with mixture of powdered sugar and 2 tablespoons peach liquid or hot water. Sprinkle with almonds. Serve warm.

Preparation time: 20 minutes   *Baking time:* 23 minutes

Peanut Butter Cereal Muffins

Best Foods, a division of CPC International Inc.

Makes 12 muffins

1¼ cups unsifted flour
 ⅓ cup sugar
 1 tablespoon baking powder
 ½ teaspoon salt
 2 cups whole bran cereal,
    corn flakes, *or*
    whole wheat flakes

1¼ cups skim milk
 ½ cup Skippy® Creamy *or*
    Super Chunk®
    Peanut Butter
 1 egg, slightly beaten
 ½ cup raisins

Preheat oven to 400°F. Grease twelve 2½-by-1¼-inch muffin-pan cups. In small bowl, stir flour, sugar, baking powder, and salt. In medium bowl, combine cereal and milk. Let stand 1 to 2 minutes or until cereal is softened. Stir in peanut butter and egg until well mixed. Add raisins. Stir in flour mixture just until mixed. Divide among prepared muffin-pan cups, nearly filling. Bake 25 to 30 minutes or until golden brown. Immediately remove muffins from pan. Cool on wire rack or serve warm.

Orange Bran Muffins

Best Foods, a division of CPC International Inc.

Makes 12 muffins

Mazola® No Stick™
  Corn Oil Cooking Spray
1¼ cups whole-bran cereal
1 cup orange juice
2 eggs, slightly beaten
⅓ cup Mazola® Corn Oil
1½ to 2 teaspoons grated
  orange peel
1 teaspoon vanilla
1¼ cups flour
½ cup quick oats
⅓ cup firmly packed
  brown sugar
¼ cup wheat germ
1 tablespoon baking powder
¼ teaspoon cinnamon

Preheat oven to 350°F. Coat twelve 2½-by-1¼-inch muffin-pan cups with cooking spray. In medium bowl, combine cereal, orange juice, eggs, corn oil, orange peel, and vanilla. Let stand 2 minutes. In large bowl, combine flour, oats, brown sugar, wheat germ, baking powder, and cinnamon. Add cereal mixture to flour mixture all at once, stirring just until moistened. Spoon into prepared muffin-pan cups. Bake 20 minutes or until lightly browned and firm to the touch. Cool in pan on wire rack about 5 minutes.

Vegetable Dinner Rolls

Kellogg Company

Makes 14 rolls

2 cups all-purpose flour
1 cup whole wheat flour
2 cups *KELLOGG'S®*
  COMPLETE® BRAN
  FLAKES cereal
1 cup water
2 tablespoons margarine
2 egg whites
1 cup shredded zucchini
½ cup shredded carrots

2 tablespoons sugar
½ teaspoon salt
1 teaspoon herb-spice
   seasoning
1 package active dry yeast

¼ cup sliced green onions
2 teaspoons sesame seeds
   (optional)
   Vegetable cooking spray

Preheat oven to 400°F. Stir together flours. Set aside.

In large mixing bowl, combine *KELLOGG'S® COMPLETE® BRAN FLAKES* cereal, 1 cup of the flour mixture, sugar, salt, seasoning, and yeast. Set aside.

Heat water and margarine until warm (115°F to 120°F). Using regular beaters, add water mixture and egg whites to cereal mixture. Beat on low speed with electric mixer 30 seconds or until thoroughly combined. Increase speed to high, beating 3 minutes longer, scraping bowl frequently. Mix in vegetables.

By hand, stir in remaining flour to make sticky dough. Cover loosely. Let rise in warm place until double in volume. Stir down batter. Divide evenly into 12 2½-inch muffin-pan cups coated with cooking spray. Sprinkle with sesame seeds, if desired.

Let rise in warm place until double in volume.

Bake about 17 minutes or until golden brown. Serve warm.

Soups & Stews

Pear-Raspberry Soup

McCormick & Company, Inc.

Makes 4 cups

6 large ripe pears
¾ cup water
½ cup sugar
¾ cup extra dry vermouth
6 McCormick/Schilling®
   Cardamom Seeds

1 2-inch piece McCormick/
   Schilling Vanilla Bean
1 2-inch piece McCormick/
   Schilling Stick Cinnamon
8 McCormick/Schilling
   Whole Allspice
1 tablespoon Red Raspberry
   Purée (see below)

Peel pears and cut into small pieces. In large saucepan, combine pears and next 7 ingredients. Bring to a boil. Reduce heat and simmer 10 minutes. Cool slightly. Remove whole spices. Purée pear mixture in food processor. Add 1 tablespoon raspberry purée. Mix well. Chill. To serve, ladle pear mixture into individual serving dishes. Dip the tip of a teaspoon into Red Raspberry Purée and draw a spiral on the surface of soup. Draw the tip of the spoon across the spiral to form a design.

Red Raspberry Purée

Makes ½ cup

1 package (10 ounces)
   frozen red raspberries
   in heavy syrup
1 tablespoon sugar

4 McCormick/Schilling®
   Whole Cloves
1 teaspoon minced
   McCormick/Schilling
   Crystallized Ginger

Combine ingredients in a saucepan. Bring to a boil. Reduce heat and simmer 10 minutes. Strain and chill.

"Show Stopper" Soup

McCormick & Company Inc.

Makes 6 servings, 1 cup each

1 package (10 ounces) frozen chopped spinach
3½ cups milk
½ cup drained oysters
¼ cup butter
¼ cup flour
¼ teaspoon McCormick/ Schilling® Ground Nutmeg
½ teaspoon McCormick/ Schilling Ground White Pepper

2 teaspoons McCormick/ Schilling Instant Minced Onion
1 teaspoon McCormick/ Schilling Chicken Flavor Base
¾ teaspoon McCormick/ Schilling Bon Appétit®
1 cup whipping cream
Whipping cream for garnish
Crushed McCormick/ Schilling Red Pepper for garnish

Thaw spinach; drain excess liquid. Pour 1½ cups milk into blender jar. Gradually add spinach, blending until smooth after each addition. Pour into a bowl. Puree oysters in blender. Add to spinach mixture. Set aside. Melt butter in large saucepan. Stir in next 6 ingredients. Cook over medium heat until bubbly. Stir in spinach mixture. Add remaining 2 cups milk and 1 cup whipping cream. Cook, stirring constantly, over medium heat, until mixture begins to boil. Reduce heat and simmer 2 minutes. Garnish with dollops of unsweetened whipped cream topped with crushed red pepper.

Sweet Potato Soup with Scallops

McCormick & Company, Inc.

Makes 5 servings, 1 cup each

- 4 teaspoons McCormick/ Schilling® Chicken Flavor Base
- 1 quart water
- 1 cup mashed cooked sweet potatoes
- 1 teaspoon McCormick/ Schilling Instant Minced Onion
- ¾ teaspoon McCormick/ Schilling Bon Appétit®
- ⅛ teaspoon McCormick/ Schilling Ground Black Pepper
- 1 cup diced (½-inch) cooked sweet potatoes
- 1 cup finely chopped scallops

In 4-quart saucepan, combine first 6 ingredients. Heat to a boil. Reduce heat. Add diced sweet potatoes and scallops. Simmer 15 minutes.

Thai Chicken and Rice Soup

JFC International, Inc.

Makes about 6 cups

- 1 tablespoon Dynasty® Chinese Stir-Fry Oil
- 1 whole chicken breast, skinned, boned, and cut into small bite-size pieces
- 1 small onion, chopped
- 1 can (14½ ounces) Dynasty® Chicken Stock
- 1 can (14 ounces) coconut milk*
- 1 cup fresh *or* frozen (thawed) whole kernel corn
- 1 cup cooked rice
- 2 tablespoons Dynasty® Oyster-Flavored Sauce
- 2 tablespoons rice vinegar
- 1 tablespoon minced fresh coriander (cilantro) *or* parsley
- 1 to 2 teaspoons Dynasty® Hot Chili Oil

Heat medium saucepan over high heat. Add oil; coat pan. Add chicken and onion; sauté 4 to 5 minutes, or until chicken is lightly browned and onion is translucent. Add chicken stock, coconut milk, corn, rice, oyster sauce, and rice vinegar. Cook and stir until mixture boils. Remove from heat; stir in coriander and chili oil. Serve while hot.

Note: If coconut milk is unavailable, combine 1¼ cups shredded unsweetened coconut and 2 cups hot water in electric blender container. Whir on high speed 1 minute; strain milk and use as directed above.

To microwave: Combine oil, chicken, and onion in 3-quart microwave-safe dish. Cover with lid or plastic wrap, venting corner. Microwave on HIGH 3 to 4 minutes, or until chicken is cooked and onion is translucent, stirring halfway through cooking. Stir in remaining ingredients. Cover and microwave on HIGH 6 to 8 minutes, or until heated through, stirring halfway through cooking.

Chicken Vegetable Soup, Hong Kong Style

JFC International, Inc.

Makes 4 to 5 servings, about 10 cups total

1 package (5.29 ounces) Dynasty® Saifun

4 Dynasty® Shiitake

1 package (10.5 ounces) tofu, drained well

3 to 4 cups vegetable oil

¼ pound lean, ground chicken, turkey, *or* pork

4 cans (14½ ounces each) Dynasty® Chicken Stock

1 medium zucchini, halved lengthwise and cut crosswise into ½-inch lengths

1 carrot, halved lengthwise and cut crosswise into ¼-inch lengths

3 green onions and tops, halved lengthwise and cut crosswise into ½-inch lengths

1 teaspoon Dynasty® Sesame Oil (optional)

Soak 1 bundle saifun in hot water 20 minutes. Save remaining saifun for use some other time. Drain saifun; coarsely chop. Set aside. Cover shiitake with hot water; let stand 20 minutes. Drain shiitake. Remove and discard shiitake stems; thinly slice shiitake. Blot tofu with paper towel to dry; cut into ¾- to 1-inch cubes. Heat oil in medium saucepan to 350°F. Add tofu cubes to hot oil, a few at a time; cook 2 to 3 minutes, or until lightly browned. Remove with slotted spoon; drain on paper towel. Heat large saucepan over high heat. Add chicken; stir-fry 2 to 3 minutes, or until browned. Stir in chicken stock, zucchini, carrot, and shiitake. Bring to a boil. Reduce heat; cover and simmer 5 minutes, or until vegetables are tender. Stir in tofu, saifun, and green onions; heat through. Remove from heat; stir in sesame oil. Salt to taste and serve.

Variation: Substitute with ½ package (3½ ounce size) Dynasty® Saifun/Harusame. Soak 25 minutes; continue as directed.

Brunswick Stew

Campbell Soup Company

Makes 12 servings, 1 cup each

5 pound stewing chicken, cut up
6 cups water
2 bay leaves
2 teaspoons salt
½ teaspoon pepper
4 slices bacon, cut into ½-inch pieces
2 medium onions, sliced and separated into rings
2 medium potatoes, peeled and cubed
1 can (16 ounces) whole tomatoes, undrained, cut up
1 can (8 ounces) whole-kernel golden corn, drained
1 cup frozen lima beans
1 tablespoon Worcestershire sauce
1 can (20¾ ounces) Campbell's® Pork & Beans in Tomato Sauce
2 tablespoons chopped fresh parsley (optional)

In 6-quart Dutch oven, combine chicken, water, bay leaves, salt and pepper. Heat to boil. Reduce heat; simmer, covered, 2½ hours or until tender. Strain broth; skim fat. Reserve 4 cups broth (add water to equal 4 cups). Discard bay leaves. When cool, remove chicken from bones; cut up. In same Dutch oven, cook bacon until crisp. Drain on paper towels. Spoon off all but 2 tablespoons drippings. Add onions; cook until tender, stirring often. Stir in potatoes, tomatoes, corn, lima beans, Worcestershire sauce, reserved broth, and chicken. Heat to boiling. Reduce heat; simmer, uncovered, 30 minutes. Stir in pork and beans. Simmer, uncovered, 30 minutes longer. Stir in bacon. Add parsley, if desired.

Caribbean Pork Stew

Specialty Brands

Makes 6 servings

2 tablespoons vegetable oil
1½ pounds boneless pork loin (rib end), cubed
1 can (13¾ ounces) chicken broth
1 can (8 ounces) tomato sauce
1 pound sweet potatoes, peeled and cut in 1-inch cubes
2 teaspoons Durkee® Onion Powder
2 teaspoons Durkee® Garlic Powder
½ teaspoon Durkee® Ground Cinnamon
½ teaspoon Durkee® Ground Cumin
⅛ teaspoon Durkee® Crushed Red Pepper
1 red pepper, cut in strips
1 green pepper, cut in strips
⅓ cup orange juice
1 cup sliced green onion

Heat oil in Dutch oven over high; cook pork until evenly browned, about 5 minutes; drain. Add broth, tomato sauce, potatoes, and seasonings. Bring to a boil; simmer, covered, 25 minutes. Add peppers, orange juice and green onions. Simmer, covered, 5 minutes. Serve with cooked rice.

Mexican Vegetable Beef Soup

Lawry's Foods, Inc.

Makes 6 servings

1 pound lean ground beef
½ cup chopped onions
1 package (1.25 ounces) Lawry's® Taco Spices and Seasonings
1 can (28 ounces) whole tomatoes, cut up
1 package (16 ounces) frozen mixed vegetables, thawed
1 can (15¼ ounces) kidney beans, undrained
1 can (14½ ounces) beef broth
Cilantro, chopped (optional)

In Dutch oven, brown ground beef and onions, stirring, until beef is cooked through; drain fat. Add taco spices and seasonings, tomatoes, vegetables, beans, and broth. Bring to a boil; reduce heat and simmer, uncovered, 5 minutes, stirring occasionally. For extra flavor, add chopped cilantro.

Top each serving with corn chips and grated Cheddar cheese.

Savory Herb Tomato Soup

©1996 Reckitt & Colman Inc.

Makes 4 (1 cup) servings
- 1 can (11⅛ ounces) condensed Italian tomato *or* regular tomato soup
- 1½ cups skim milk
- 1 can (14.5 ounces) diced tomatoes, undrained
- 2 tablespoons FRENCH'S® Worcestershire Sauce
- 2 tablespoons minced fresh basil *or* Italian parsley (optional)

In medium nonreactive saucepan, combine soup, milk, tomatoes, and Worcestershire. Cook and stir over low heat until hot. Do Not Boil. Stir in basil or parsley.

If desired, serve with bread sticks or Italian bread.

Preparation time: 5 minutes   *Cook time:* 5 minutes

Cuban Black Bean Soup

©1996 Reckitt & Colman Inc.

Makes 10 servings

2 tablespoons vegetable oil
1 large onion, chopped
3 large cloves garlic, minced
4 cans (15 to 19 ounces *each*) black beans, undrained
2 cans (14.5 ounces *each*) reduced-sodium chicken broth
⅓ cup FRANK'S® Original REDHOT® Cayenne Pepper Sauce
¼ cup minced fresh cilantro leaves
2 teaspoons ground cumin
Sour cream

Heat oil in 4- to 5-quart saucepot; cook onion and garlic until tender. Add beans with their liquid, broth, RedHot® sauce, cilantro, and cumin.

Bring to a boil, stirring. Reduce heat; simmer, partially covered, 30 minutes. Stir occasionally.

Remove 1 cup soup mixture. Place in blender; cover and process until smooth. Stir into soup.

Spoon soup into bowls. Serve with a dollop of sour cream, if desired.

Note: This soup freezes well. For small families, freeze leftovers in individual portions. Thaw and reheat in the microwave.

Preparation time: 10 minutes   *Cook time:* 35 minutes

Tortilla Soup

McCormick & Company, Inc.

Makes 7 cups broth

1   cup tomato juice
2   tablespoons McCormick/ Schilling® Beef Flavor Base
7   cups hot water
2   McCormick/Schilling Whole Black Peppercorns
1   McCormick/Schilling Bay Leaf
2   tablespoons McCormick/ Schilling Instant Minced Onion
¼   teaspoon McCormick/ Schilling Garlic Powder
½   cup coarsely chopped celery
½   cup thinly sliced carrots
1   can (4 ounces) mild green chilies, drained and cut in strips
2   whole hot chilies
Meatballs (see below)
Tortilla chips
Monterey jack cheese, shredded

Place first 11 ingredients in large saucepan. Bring to a boil. Reduce heat and simmer 25 minutes. Remove bay leaf and hot chilies. To serve, place a few meatballs in soup plate. Ladle broth over meatballs. Add a few tortilla chips and sprinkle with shredded cheese.

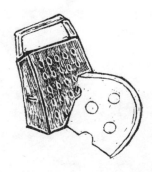

Meatballs

Makes 22 to 23 meatballs

1 tablespoon McCormick/ Schilling® Instant Minced Onion
¼ cup dry breadcrumbs
¼ cup milk
1 egg, beaten
½ pound ground beef
½ pound ground pork
½ cup chopped blanched almonds
⅛ teaspoon McCormick/ Schilling Ground Black Pepper
⅛ teaspoon McCormick/ Schilling Ground Oregano
⅛ teaspoon McCormick/ Schilling Ground Cumin
1 teaspoon McCormick/ Schilling Chervil Leaves
½ teaspoon McCormick/ Schilling Shredded Green Onion
¾ teaspoon McCormick/ Schilling Bon Appétit®
1 tablespoon peanut oil

In large bowl, mix onion, breadcrumbs, milk, and egg. Add all other ingredients except peanut oil and mix well. Shape into 1¼-inch meatballs. Heat peanut oil in skillet. Cook meatballs 4 minutes, turning to brown on all sides. Add small amount of oil if necessary.

Cream of Jalapeño Soup

Sargento Cheese Company, Inc

Makes 6 cups

4 tablespoons butter *or* margarine
1 large onion, chopped
1 large carrot, peeled and finely chopped
1 large green pepper, seeded and finely chopped
3 jalapeño peppers, seeded and finely chopped
3 tablespoons flour
3 cups chicken broth
2 cups whipping cream
1 cup (4 ounces) Sargento® Fancy Shredded Swiss Cheese
1 cup (4 ounces) Sargento® Shredded *or* Fancy Shredded Cheddar Cheese

In large saucepan, melt *2 tablespoons* butter and cook onion, carrot, and green pepper over low heat, stirring occasionally until tender, about 8 minutes. Stir in jalapeño peppers. Remove from saucepan. Melt remaining 2 table-spoons butter in separate saucepan. Stir in flour and cook, stirring constantly, 2 minutes. Gradually stir in broth and cream. Increase heat and bring to a boil, stirring constantly. Reduce heat and simmer until thickened, about 10 minutes. Stir in both cheeses; stir in vegetables.

Creamy Broccoli Soup

Kraft General Foods, Inc.

Makes 5 servings, 1 cup each

¼ cup chopped onion
1 tablespoon Parkay® Margarine
2 cups milk
1 package (8 ounces) Philadelphia® Brand Cream Cheese, cubed

¾ pound Velveeta® Pasteurized Process Cheese Spread, cubed
1 package (10 ounces) Birds Eye® Chopped Broccoli, cooked and drained
¼ teaspoon ground nutmeg Dash of pepper

In 2-quart saucepan, cook onion in margarine until tender. Reduce heat to medium. Add milk and cream cheese, stir until cream cheese is melted. Add remaining ingredients; heat thoroughly, stirring occasionally.

To microwave: Microwave onion and margarine in micro-wave-safe 2-quart bowl on HIGH 30 seconds or until on-ions are tender. Add milk; microwave on HIGH 3 to 4 minutes, stirring every 2 minutes. Stir in cream cheese;

microwave on HIGH 4 to 6 minutes or until cream cheese is melted, stirring every 2 minutes. Stir in remaining ingredients; microwave on HIGH 30 seconds or until thoroughly heated.

Variations: Substitute Birds Eye® Chopped Spinach for broccoli. Substitute Birds Eye® Cauliflower, chopped, for broccoli. Substitute Birds Eye® Asparagus Spears, chopped, for broccoli.

Preparation time: 15 minutes   *Cook time:* 15 minutes

Hearty Noodle & Spinach Soup

Lipton

Makes about 6 servings

2 tablespoons olive *or* vegetable oil
1 teaspoon finely chopped garlic
Generous dash crushed red pepper

1½ pounds spinach leaves, stems removed and torn into bite-size pieces*
5 cups water
1 package Lipton® Noodles & Sauce—Chicken Flavor
Salt and pepper to taste

In 3-quart saucepan, heat oil over medium-high heat and cook garlic with red pepper 1 minute. Stir in spinach and cook, stirring occasionally, until wilted. Add water and bring to a boil. Stir in Noodles & Sauce—Chicken Flavor and continue boiling over medium heat, stirring occasionally, 7 minutes or until noodles are tender. Add salt and pepper.

*Variation: Substitute 2 packages (10 ounces each) frozen chopped spinach, thawed and undrained.

Pizza Soup

Lipton

Makes about 3½ cups

1 medium onion, chopped
2 ounces pepperoni *or* salami, cut into small pieces
½ teaspoon garlic powder
½ teaspoon dried oregano leaves

1 envelope Lipton® Soup Secrets® Noodle Soup Mix with Real Chicken Broth
3 cups water
2 tablespoons tomato paste
½ cup (about 1½ ounces) shredded mozzarella cheese

In medium saucepan, cook onion, pepperoni, garlic powder, and oregano over medium-high heat, stirring frequently, 3 minutes or until onion is tender. Stir in remaining ingredients except cheese. Bring to a boil; then simmer, stirring occasionally, 5 minutes. To serve, sprinkle with cheese.

To microwave: In 2-quart microwave-safe casserole, microwave onion, pepperoni, garlic powder, and oregano at HIGH (Full Power) 2 minutes. Stir in remaining ingredients except cheese. Microwave, uncovered, 10 minutes, stirring once. To serve, sprinkle with cheese.

Variation: Omit pepperoni *or* salami. Add 1 tablespoon oil.

Grandma's Turkey Stew

Oscar Mayer Foods Corporation

Makes 4 servings

1 package Louis Rich®
  Fresh Turkey Wings *or*
  Drumsticks
3 tablespoons cornstarch
2 teaspoons instant chicken
  bouillon

½ teaspoon poultry seasoning
1 package (16 ounces)
  frozen mixed
  vegetables
1 cup buttermilk baking mix
⅓ cup milk

Rinse turkey. Place in skillet with 1 cup water. Bring to a boil; turn down heat. Cover. Simmer 2 hours. Remove turkey. Measure liquid; add water to make 2 cups. Return liquid to skillet; stir in cornstarch, bouillon, and poultry seasoning. Add vegetables. Bring to a boil; turn down heat. Cover. Simmer 5 minutes. Remove turkey from bones. Add turkey to skillet. Separately, combine baking mix and milk to make dumplings; drop in 4 spoonfuls onto simmering stew. Cook, uncovered, 5 minutes. Cover. Cook 5 minutes more.

Hoppin' John Soup

©1996 Reckitt & Colman Inc.

Makes 6 (1 cup) servings

4 strips bacon, chopped
1 cup chopped onion
2 teaspoons minced garlic
2 cans (15 ounces *each*)
  black-eyed peas, undrained
1 can (14.5 ounces)
  chicken broth

½ cup water
3 to 4 tablespoons FRANK'S®
  Original REDHOT®
  Cayenne Pepper Sauce
1 teaspoon dried thyme
  leaves

In large saucepan, cook and stir bacon, onion, and garlic 5 minutes until vegetables are tender.

Stir in remaining ingredients. Bring to a boil. Simmer, stirring, 15 minutes. Serve with hot cooked rice tossed with minced parsley.

Preparation time: 15 minutes *Cook time:* 20 minutes

Italian Sausage Stew

Nabisco Foods Group

Makes 6 to 8 servings

1 pound sweet Italian pork *or* turkey sausage, removed from casing	3 (13¾-fluid ounce) cans COLLEGE INN Beef Broth
1 green bell pepper, diced	1 (15-ounce) can stewed tomatoes
1 teaspoon minced garlic	½ pound small shaped pasta
	Grated Parmesan cheese

In 6-quart heavy pot, over medium heat, brown sausage, stirring to break up meat; pour off fat. Stir in green pepper and garlic; cook and stir for 2 minutes. Add broth and crushed tomatoes. Heat to a boil. Reduce heat; simmer 15 minutes. Add pasta and cook 10 minutes or until done. Serve warm sprinkled with cheese.

Salads & Salad Dressings

FRUIT SALAD DELIGHTS

Catalina Salad

McCormick & Company, Inc.

Makes 6 individual salads; 1½ cups salad dressing

2 pink grapefruit
2 ripe avocados
2 Granny Smith apples
Salad greens
1 cup mayonnaise
½ cup orange juice
¼ teaspoon McCormick/ Schilling® Ground Mustard

½ teaspoon McCormick/ Schilling Dill Weed
½ teaspoon McCormick/ Schilling Instant Minced Onion
⅛ teaspoon McCormick/ Schilling Ground White Pepper
¼ teaspoon McCormick/ Schilling Bon Appétit®

Peel and section grapefruit. Peel and slice avocados. Core and slice apples or cut apples into thin spirals as follows: Cut a thin slice from the blossom end, then use a potato peeler to cut the apple in continuous spirals. Wash and dry salad greens. Combine mayonnaise with remaining ingredients. Mix well. Chill. Arrange a bed of salad greens on each of 6 salad plates. Arrange grapefruit, avocado, and apple slices or spirals on greens. Spoon dressing over each salad.

Citrus Toss

Sargento Cheese Company, Inc.

Makes 4 servings

2 tablespoons lemon juice
2 teaspoons sugar
¼ cup hazelnut *or* vegetable oil
3 cups torn salad greens
1¼ cups (5 ounces) Sargento® Fancy Shredded Cheddar Cheese
½ cup (1½ ounces) Sargento® Fancy Shredded Parmesan Cheese

1½ cups orange sections
1 cup grapefruit sections
1 cup seedless green grapes
1 can (8 ounces) sliced water chestnuts, well drained
⅓ cup coarsely chopped hazelnuts, toasted

To make dressing, combine lemon juice and sugar in small bowl. Gradually add oil, whisking until smooth and thickened; reserve.

Place salad greens, cheeses, orange and grapefruit sections, grapes and water chestnuts in large bowl. Add dressing; toss gently. Sprinkle with hazelnuts. Serve immediately.

Poppy Fruit Salad

Sargento Cheese Company, Inc

Makes 4 servings

2 tablespoons cider vinegar
2 tablespoons honey
½ teaspoon dry mustard
⅓ cup vegetable oil
1½ teaspoons poppy seeds
2 medium pears, sliced
⅔ cup seedless red grapes, cut in half
⅔ cup seedless green grapes, cut in half
1½ cups (6 ounces) Sargento® Fancy Shredded Sharp Cheddar Cheese
½ cup coarsely chopped walnuts *or* pecans, toasted
Lettuce leaves (optional)

Combine vinegar, honey, and mustard in small bowl. Gradually add oil, whisking until smooth and thickened. Stir in poppy seeds; set aside.

Combine pears, grapes, and cheese in large bowl. Add dressing. Toss gently to coat thoroughly. Sprinkle with walnuts. Serve on lettuce-lined plates, if desired.

Lanai Fruit Salad

Dole Food Company

Makes 12 servings

1 can (20 ounces) Dole® Pineapple Chunks
4 Dole® Oranges, peeled and chunked
4 apples, seeded and chunked
3 Dole® Bananas, peeled and sliced
2 baskets strawberries
2 cups assorted seedless grapes
1 carton (8 ounces) vanilla yogurt
1 tablespoon lime juice
½ teaspoon grated lime peel
1 teaspoon honey

Drain pineapple; reserve juice for beverage. Toss together all fruit. To make dressing, stir together yogurt, lime juice and peel, and honey. Serve dressing with salad.

Festive Cranberry Mold

Dole Food Company

Makes 8 servings

1 can (8¼ ounces) Dole®
  Crushed Pineapple
1 envelope unflavored
gelatin
1 tablespoon sugar
¾ cup port wine
1 medium red apple, cored
  and diced

1 can (8 ounces) whole-
  berry cranberry sauce
⅓ cup chopped pecans *or*
  walnuts
Zest from ½ Dole® Orange
¼ teaspoon ground
  cardamom
Dole® salad greens

Drain pineapple well; reserve syrup. In medium saucepan, combine gelatin and sugar. Stir in reserved syrup and port. Heat mixture until gelatin dissolves. Chill until slightly thickened. Fold in pineapple, apple, cranberry sauce, nuts, 1 teaspoon orange zest, and cardamom. Pour into 1-quart mold. Refrigerate until set. Unmold on serving plate lined with salad greens.

Sparkling Berry Salad

Nabisco Foods Group

Makes about 12 servings, ½ cup each

2 envelopes Knox® Unflavored Gelatine

2 cups cranberry-raspberry juice

⅓ cup sugar

1 cup club soda

¼ cup creme de cassis (black-currant-flavored liqueur; optional)

1 teaspoon lemon juice

1 teaspoon fresh grated orange peel (optional)

3 cups assorted blueberries, raspberries, *or* strawberries

Sour cream (optional)

In medium saucepan, sprinkle unflavored gelatine over *1 cup* cranberry-raspberry juice; let stand 1 minute. Stir over low heat until gelatine is completely dissolved, about 5 minutes. Stir in sugar until dissolved.

In large bowl, blend remaining *1 cup* cranberry-raspberry juice, soda, gelatine mixture, liqueur, lemon juice, and, if desired, orange peel. Chill, stirring occasionally, until mixture is consistency of unbeaten egg whites, about 60 minutes. Fold in berries. Pour into 6-cup mold or bowl; chill until firm, about 3 hours. Unmold and serve, with sour cream, if desired.

Variation: Use 2 cups cranberry juice cocktail instead of cranberry-raspberry juice and increase sugar to ½ cup.

THE JELL-O WAY

The Story of Jell-O

In 1845 Peter Cooper, designer of the first American steam locomotive, popularly known as the Tom Thumb, created an entirely new dessert made of gelatin. He obtained a patent and described his creation as "a transparent, concentrated substance containing all the ingredients fitting it for table use in a portable form, and requiring only the addition of hot water to dissolve it, so that it may be poured into molds and when cold will be fit for use." Like most great thinkers, however, Cooper had many exciting and profitable inventions, plans, and ideas to keep him busy. He put his gelatin on the shelf, and there it sat for the next fifty years.

Then along came Pearl B. Wait, a carpenter by trade who had been dabbling in the business of manufacturing cough medicine and laxative tea in his home in the 1890s. Wait was interested in making his mark in the new packaged-foods industry. He and his wife, May, experimented in their kitchen and he enhanced Cooper's invention by adding fruit flavors to it. His wife excitedly proclaimed the product name should be Jell-O and told Wait to sell the creation door-to-door to housewives by demonstrating the simplicity of using it to create delicious desserts. But Wait lacked the sales skills and marketing know-how to get his fledgling company off the ground, and he grew discouraged. He was happy to get $450 for the Jell-O rights from his next-door neighbor, Orator Frank Woodward.

Overwhelming with magnetism and boundless energy in traditional Horatio Alger fashion, Woodward had quit school at age twelve and started his first company eight years later. In 1899, after great success selling

Raccoon Corn Plasters, Sherman's Headache Remedy, and other curatives of the day, he was enthusiastically promoting Grain-O, a roasted-cereal beverage for people who couldn't drink coffee or tea. Woodward decided Jell-O would be a good addition to his already-successful company.

When Woodward's salesmen showed up at church socials, picnics, fairs, and dances to demonstrate the easy creation of spectacular Jell-O desserts, they usually became the highlight of the event. Woodward gave away samples and fancy tin molds. He offered Jell-O discounts to his employees so they could advertise the product personally by selling it to family and friends.

But converting the housewife to this light and fruity dessert wasn't easy in an era of rich cakes and pies. One day when Woodward was touring his factory plant with his plant superintendent, the two stood silently before countless cases of piled-up Jell-O. Glumly, Woodward asked his companion, "Will you buy all this Jell-O and the whole Jell-O business for $35?" His manager quickly refused. Then, suddenly, the advertising campaign started producing results. People were becoming captivated by the shimmering desserts. By 1902, sales hit $250,000. Fashionable women with wavy curls and bun hairdos, wearing white aprons, smiled triumphantly from the Ladies Home Journal to proclaim Jell-O as "America's Most Famous Dessert." It could be topped with whipped cream or thin custard, and for "something very fancy, there are hundreds of delightful combinations that can be quickly prepared." Four years later sales zoomed to $1 million annually.

In 1925, with an exchange of stocks, the Postum Cereal Company of Battle Creek, Michigan, purchased and merged with the Jell-O Company. These products formed the core of the great General Foods Corporation. The $450 formula was now worth $67 million as a business. Whenever Woodward thought of the prompt rejection of his rash offer, he exhaled a sigh of relief.

Ethel Barrymore, Jack Benny, and other celebrities of the day were interviewed for their favorite Jell-O recipes. The brilliant artist Rose O'Neill, who, along with Norman Rockwell and other notable artists, illustrated Jell-O recipe booklets, was asked her opinion of the dessert. "When I tell you I haven't time to be a housewife and have never in my life made up anything edible except Jell-O, you will know I must appreciate the advantages offered by the 'easy Jell-O way.'"

The advertising agency assigned to the Jell-O account decided a child model would make a perfect trademark for Jell-O, showing how appealing the dessert is for children and how easy it is to prepare. Franklin King, the artist assigned to design the trademark, interviewed hundreds of models without finding the right image. Finally, as he watched his four-year-old daughter, Elizabeth, playing in the nursery, inspiration struck. He took some pictures and showed them to the agency. Elizabeth King became the Jell-O Girl. Every month for the next four years, new pictures were taken of Elizabeth to be used in all print ads and store displays. Since 1973, Bill Cosby has contributed to the ad campaign with his charismatic and successful Jell-O pudding television commercials geared toward children. The dessert has become one of the most popular and successful specialty grocery items of the twentieth century.

Under-the-Sea Salad

Kraft General Foods, Inc.

Makes 0 servings, about 3½ cups total

- 1 can (16 ounces) pear halves in syrup
- 1 package (4-serving size) Jell-O® Brand Lime-Flavor Gelatine
- ¼ teaspoon salt (optional)
- 1 cup boiling water
- 1 tablespoon lemon juice
- 2 packages (3 ounces each) Philadelphia® Brand Cream Cheese, softened
- ⅛ teaspoon ground cinnamon (optional)
- Salad greens (optional)
- Mayonnaise (optional)
- Pear halves, drained and diced (optional)

Drain pears, reserving ¾ cup of the syrup. Dice pears and set aside. Dissolve gelatine and salt in boiling water. Add reserved syrup and lemon juice to gelatin. Pour 1¼ cups into an 8-by-4-inch loaf pan or 4-cup mold. Chill until set but not firm, about 1 hour. Very slowly blend remaining gelatin into cream cheese, beating until smooth. Add cinnamon and pears and spoon over clear gelatin in pan. Chill until firm, about 4 hours. Unmold. Garnish with crisp salad greens, mayonnaise, and additional pears, if desired.

Note: Recipe may be doubled, using a 9-by-5-inch loaf pan.

Five-Cup Salad

Kraft General Foods, Inc.

Makes 4 to 6 servings

1 cup Kraft® Miniature Marshmallows
1 cup Breakstone's® Sour Cream
1 cup orange sections
1 cup grapes
1 cup Bakers® Angel Flake® Coconut

In large bowl, mix together ingredients. Chill.

Variations

Substitute 1 cup peach slices for orange sections.

Substitute 1 can (11 ounces) mandarin orange segments, drained, for orange sections.

Add 1 can (8 ounces) pineapple chunks, drained.

Preparation time: 10 minutes, plus chilling

ROBUST VEGETABLE SALADS

Greek Salad

Lindsay International, Inc.

Makes 8 servings

⅓ cup olive *or* salad oil
¼ cup lemon juice
¾ teaspoon dried oregano, crushed
½ teaspoon salt
¼ teaspoon pepper
8 cups torn mixed greens
2 cups cherry tomatoes, halved

1 can (6 ounces, 1½ cups) Lindsay® Large Pitted Ripe Olives, drained
1 medium cucumber, sliced
1 cup sliced radishes
½ cup sliced green onions
¼ cup snipped parsley
2 cups (8 ounces) crumbled feta cheese

For dressing, in a screw-top jar shake together oil, lemon juice, oregano, salt, and pepper. Cover and chill. In a salad bowl, combine torn greens, tomatoes, olives, cucumber, radishes, onions, and parsley over greens; top with feta cheese. Shake chilled dressing and drizzle over salad; toss gently.

Swiss Salad Medley

Beatrice Cheese, Inc.

Makes 8 servings

1 can (16 ounces) peas, drained

1 can (16 ounces) kidney beans, drained

1 can (6 ounces) black olives, drained and sliced

⅓ cup chopped green onions

½ large green pepper, chopped

3 stalks celery, chopped

10 ounces (2½ cups) County Line® Swiss Cheese, grated

4 eggs, hard cooked and chopped

¾ cup bread and butter pickles, chopped

1 cup mayonnaise

2 tablespoons horseradish sauce

½ teaspoon salt

¼ cup slivered almonds, toasted

In large mixing bowl, combine peas, kidney beans, olives, green onions, green pepper, celery, cheese, eggs, and pickles. In small bowl, mix mayonnaise, horseradish sauce, and salt; add to other ingredients along with toasted almonds. Chill and serve.

To toast almonds: Preheat oven to 350°F. Place almonds in a shallow pan and bake for 10 minutes. Toasting time will vary depending on the size of the almonds.

Seven-Layer Salad

Kraft General Foods, Inc.

Makes 8 servings

1½ quarts shredded lettuce
 2 cups chopped tomatoes
 2 cups mushroom slices
 1 package (10 ounces) Birds
   Eye® Green Peas, thawed
   and drained
 4 ounces Kraft® Natural
   Mild Cheddar Cheese,
   cubed

 1 cup red onion rings
 2 cups Miracle Whip® Light
   Reduced Calorie Salad
   Dressing
Oscar Mayer® Bacon
   slices (optional)
Kraft® Natural Mild
   Cheddar Cheese,
   shredded (optional)

In 2-quart serving bowl, layer lettuce, tomatoes, mushrooms, peas, cubed cheese, and onions. Spread salad dressing over onions, sealing to edge of bowl; cover. Chill several hours or overnight. Garnish with crisply cooked bacon slices, crumbled, and shredded Cheddar cheese, if desired.

Preparation time: 15 minutes, plus chilling

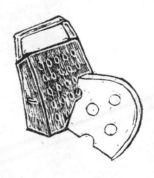

Naturally Cheesy Layered Lettuce Bowl

Beatrice Cheese, Inc.

Makes 4 servings

1 cup shredded County Line® Sharp Cheddar Cheese

1 cup plain yogurt *or* sour cream

1 large head iceberg lettuce

1½ cups shredded County Line® Old World Swiss Cheese

¾ cup fresh spinach, torn into bite-size pieces

¾ cup cooked brown *or* white rice, chilled

1 can (11 ounces) Mandarin orange segments

¾ cup chopped pecans

Dollop of plain yogurt *or* sour cream for garnish

Stir together Cheddar cheese and 1 cup yogurt; set aside. Remove inside portion of lettuce head. Spread *½ cup* of Cheddar cheese mixture inside shell. Layer with *¾ cup Swiss* cheese, spinach, rice, *½ cup* cheese mixture, orange segments, *¾ cup* Swiss cheese, remaining cheese mixture, and pecans. Refrigerate 3 hours or until ready to serve. Cut into wedges. Garnish with dollop of yogurt or sour cream.

Baked German Potato Salad

Kraft General Foods, Inc.

Makes 6 to 8 servings

6 slices Oscar Mayer® Bacon, chopped	½ cup Miracle Whip® Salad Dressing
3½ cups cooked new potatoes, quartered	1 tablespoon Kraft® Pure Prepared Mustard
¾ cup chopped celery	1 teaspoon celery seed
¾ cup chopped green bell pepper	Salt
¾ cup chopped onion	Pepper

Preheat oven to 400°F. Cook bacon until crisp; remove bacon, reserving *2 tablespoons* fat. Combine reserved fat, bacon, potatoes, celery, green bell peppers, and onions. Add combined salad dressing, mustard, and seasonings; mix lightly. Spoon into 2-quart casserole. Bake 20 minutes.

Variations

Substitute *2 tablespoons* Dijon mustard for prepared mustard.

Substitute cooked red potatoes, cut into 1-inch cubes, for quartered new potatoes.

Preparation time: 20 minutes   *Cook time:* 20 minutes

Great American Potato Salad

Kraft General Foods, Inc.

Makes 6 servings

1 cup Miracle Whip® Salad Dressing	4 cups cubed cooked potatoes
1 teaspoon Kraft® Pure Prepared Mustard	2 hard-cooked eggs, chopped
½ teaspoon celery seed	½ cup chopped onion
½ teaspoon salt	½ cup celery slices
⅛ teaspoon pepper	½ cup chopped sweet pickle

Stir together salad dressing, mustard, celery seed, salt, and pepper. Add remaining ingredients; mix lightly. Chill.

Variations
Substitute Miracle Whip® Light Reduced Calorie Salad Dressing for regular salad dressing.

Omit celery and pickle. Add 1½ cups chopped ham and ½ cup chopped green bell pepper.

Omit celery seed, celery, and pickle. Add 1 cup chopped cucumber and ½ teaspoon dill weed.

Omit mustard, celery seed and pickle. Add 3 tablespoons Sauceworks® Horseradish Sauce and 1½ cups cubed roast beef.

Preparation time: 30 minutes, plus chilling

Mozzarella, Tomato, and Basil Salad

Beatrice Cheese, Inc.

Makes 6 servings

4 cups halved cherry tomatoes, sliced plum tomatoes, *or* diced and seeded garden tomatoes

¼ cup chopped red *or* white onion

¼ cup minced fresh parsley

3 tablespoons vegetable *or* olive oil

1 tablespoon red wine vinegar

½ teaspoon dried basil *or* 2 tablespoons chopped fresh basil leaves

Freshly ground black pepper to taste

2 cups (8 ounces) County Line® Shredded Reduced Fat/Sodium Mozzarella Cheese

Salad greens

In a salad bowl, combine all ingredients except cheese and greens. Let tomatoes marinate 30 to 60 minutes. Stir in cheese and serve on a bed of salad greens.

Market Salad

Sargento Cheese Company, Inc.

Makes 8 servings

2 cups small cauliflower florets

2 cups small broccoli florets

2 medium carrots, cut into short, thin strips

1 can (16 ounces) garbanzo beans, well drained

¾ cup chopped red bell pepper *or* pimiento

2 cups (8 ounces) Sargento® Fancy Shredded Low-Moisture Part-Skim Mozzarella Cheese

⅓ cup white wine vinegar

1 teaspoon dried oregano leaves, crushed

2 cloves garlic, minced

¼ teaspoon salt

½ cup vegetable oil

2 teaspoons capers (optional)

Combine cauliflower, broccoli, carrots, beans, bell pepper, and cheese in large bowl; set aside. Combine vinegar, oregano, garlic, and salt in small bowl. Gradually add oil, whisking until smooth and thickened. Stir in capers. Add to vegetable and cheese mixture. Toss gently. Cover; chill thoroughly. Stir several times during chilling.

Garden Gazpacho Salad

Lipton

Makes about 8 side-dish servings

1 cup (8 ounces) Wish-Bone® Robusto Italian Dressing
¼ cup tomato juice
6 dashes hot pepper sauce (optional)
2 medium cucumbers, chopped

2 medium tomatoes, chopped
2 medium green bell peppers, chopped
1 medium onion, chopped
1 loaf unsliced round bread (about 9-inch diameter)
Lettuce leaves

In large bowl, blend robusto Italian dressing, tomato juice, and pepper sauce. Stir in vegetables. Cover and marinate in refrigerator, stirring occasionally, at least 2 hours. Cut lengthwise slice off top of bread. Hollow out center, leaving ½-inch shell. Just before serving, line bread shell with lettuce and fill with vegetable mixture. To serve, spoon out vegetable mixture, then cut bread shell into wedges.

Variations: Also terrific with Wish-Bone® Italian, Lite Italian, *or* Fat Free Italian Dressing.

Four-Bean Salad

Campbell Soup Company

Makes 16 servings, ½ cup each

¾ cup wine vinegar
¼ cup vegetable oil
1 tablespoon sugar
¼ teaspoon pepper
1 can (20¾ ounces) Campbell's® Pork and Beans in Tomato Sauce
1 can (16 ounces) black beans, drained

1 can (16 ounces) red kidney beans, drained
1½ cups cut green beans, cooked
1 medium red onion, halved lengthwise and sliced
Cucumber slices for garnish

In large bowl, combine vinegar, oil, sugar, and pepper. Add beans and onion; toss gently to coat. Cover; refrigerate until serving time, at least 4 hours. Serve in cucumber-lined salad bowl.

Marinated Pepper Salad

Campbell Soup Company

Makes 6 servings, 4½ cups total

⅓ cup olive oil

¼ cup lime juice

2 tablespoons chopped fresh cilantro

2 tablespoons Vlasic® Sweet Banana Pepper Juice

½ teaspoon dried oregano leaves, crushed

½ teaspoon garlic powder

¼ teaspoon salt

¼ teaspoon ground red pepper

2 cups sliced Campbell's® Fresh Mushrooms

1 cup Vlasic® Sweet Banana Pepper Rings, drained

1 medium avocado, seeded, peeled, and sliced crosswise

1 Campbell's® Fresh Tomato, chopped

1 Campbell's® Fresh Tomato, sliced, for garnish

Curly endive for garnish

Vlasic® Mild Banana Peppers for garnish

To make dressing, in a small bowl combine oil, lime juice, cilantro, pepper juice, oregano, garlic, salt, and red pepper. In medium bowl, combine mushrooms, pepper rings, avocado, and chopped tomato. Add dressing; toss gently to coat. Cover; refrigerate until serving time, at least 2 hours. To serve, line plate with tomato slices and endive. With slotted spoon, place salad on plate. Top with whole peppers.

Garden Salad with Warm Bacon Vinaigrette Dressing

Oscar Mayer Foods Corporation

Makes 4 servings

10 slices Oscar Mayer® Thick Sliced Bacon, cut into quarters

1 medium onion, coarsely chopped

¼ cup water

¼ cup vinegar

2 tablespoons sugar

⅛ teaspoon black pepper

8 cups (about 10 ounces) fresh spinach leaves *or* leaf lettuce, cleaned and torn into bite-size pieces

1 medium tomato, cut into ½-inch chunks

Place salad greens and chopped tomato in large serving bowl; set aside. Cook bacon and onion in large skillet over medium heat until bacon is crisp. Drain. Add remaining dressing ingredients to bacon and onions and cook over medium heat 3 minutes. Pour hot dressing over salad greens and toss. Serve immediately.

Layered Taco Salad

Kraft General Foods, Inc.

Makes 8 servings

1 tablespoon oil

4 boneless skinless chicken breast halves (approximately 1¼ pounds), cubed

¾ cup salsa

1 quart torn lettuce

3 cups coarsely broken tortilla chips

1 can (15 ounces) kidney beans, rinsed and drained

¼ cup green onion slices

Guacamole (see below)

1 cup (4 ounces) Kraft® Natural Shredded Sharp Cheddar Cheese

2 slices Oscar Mayer® Bacon, crisply cooked, crumbled

Heat oil in wok or 10-inch skillet over medium-high; add chicken. Stir-fry 4 to 5 minutes or until tender. Reduce heat to medium. Stir in salsa; cover. Simmer 5 minutes. In 3- to 4-quart serving bowl, layer lettuce, chips, beans, onions, and chicken mixture. Cover with Guacamole, spreading to edges of bowl to seal. Sprinkle with cheese. Cover; chill. Add bacon; toss lightly just before serving.

To microwave: Omit oil. To cook chicken, place in 1½-quart casserole; cover. Microwave on HIGH 4 to 5 minutes or until tender, stirring every 2 minutes. Drain; stir in salsa. Microwave on HIGH 1 minute. Continue as directed.

Guacamole

1 ripe avocado, peeled and mashed	½ cup salsa
½ cup Miracle Whip® Salad Dressing	¼ cup milk

Mix all ingredients until well blended.

Preparation time: 20 minutes, plus chilling

PASTA SALADS

Southwest Pasta Salad

Best Foods, a division of CPC International Inc.

Makes 6 servings

½ cup Mazola® Corn Oil
⅓ cup lime juice
⅓ cup chopped cilantro
2 tablespoons pickled jalapeño peppers, seeded and chopped
2 cloves garlic, minced
¾ teaspoon ground cumin
¾ teaspoon salt

6 ounces Mueller's® Pasta Ruffles, cooked, rinsed with cold water, and drained
1 can (16 ounces) black beans, rinsed and drained
¾ cup diced red onion
¾ cup diced red pepper
¾ cup diced yellow pepper

In small bowl, stir corn oil, lime juice, cilantro, jalapeño peppers, garlic, cumin, and salt until blended. In large bowl, combine pasta, beans, red onion, and peppers. Add dressing; toss to coat. Cover; chill 1 hour.

Curried Pineapple Pasta Salad

Dole Food Company

Makes 8 servings

1 can (20 ounces) Dole® Pineapple Chunks
3 chicken breast halves (2 cups), cooked and shredded
8 ounces macaroni (or small pasta), cooked
2 cups sliced Dole® Celery
½ cup sliced Dole® Green Onions

½ cup Dole® Red Bell Pepper, seeded and slivered
½ cup sliced ripe olives
¾ cup mayonnaise
⅓ cup chopped chutney
¼ cup dairy sour cream
2 teaspoons curry powder
1 teaspoon salt

Drain pineapple. In salad bowl, combine pineapple, chicken, pasta, celery, onion, red pepper, and olives. For dressing, blend remaining ingredients. Toss salad with dressing. Cover and refrigerate until chilled.

Bow Tie Salad

Dole Food Company

Makes 10 servings

1 package (10 ounces) bow tie pasta
1 Dole® Red Bell Pepper, seeded and slivered
2 cups Dole® Broccoli florets
1 cup Dole® Cauliflower florets
1 clove garlic, pressed
½ cup rice vinegar
¼ cup vegetable oil
2 tablespoons teriyaki sauce
1 tablespoon sesame seeds, toasted
2 teaspoons sesame oil
¼ teaspoon red pepper flakes

Cook pasta according to package directions. Combine with remaining ingredients. Refrigerate overnight.

Party Pasta Salad

Dole Food Company

Makes 12 to 15 servings

1 package (12 ounces) twistee egg noodles
1 clove garlic, pressed
1 cup vegetable oil
½ cup distilled white vinegar
¼ cup lemon juice
1 tablespoon Dijon mustard
1 tablespoon Worcestershire sauce
Salt to taste
Pepper to taste
1 red bell pepper, seeded and chunked
3 cups Dole® Broccoli florets
3 cups Dole® Cauliflower florets
1½ cups Dole® Pitted Dates, halved
1 cup Dole® Whole Natural Almonds, toasted

Cook noodles according to package directions. For dressing, combine next 8 ingredients. In large bowl, toss hot noodles and dressing. Add remaining ingredients except almonds. Refrigerate 2 hours or overnight. Toss in almonds just before serving.

To toast almonds: Preheat oven to 350°F. Place almonds in a shallow pan and bake for 10 minutes. Toasting time will vary depending on the size of the almonds.

Picnic-Perfect Pasta Salad

Dole Food Company

Makes 4 servings

- 1 can (8 ounces) Dole® Pineapple Chunks in Juice
- 2 tablespoons sesame oil
- 1 tablespoon honey
- 1 tablespoon soy sauce
- 1 tablespoon minced crystalized ginger
- 1 large clove garlic, pressed
- 2 cups cooked spiral pasta
- 1 cup cooked chunked chicken *or* deli chicken
- 2 tablespoons sliced Dole® Green Onion
- 2 cups cooked Dole® Broccoli florets
- ⅓ cup Dole® Red Bell Pepper strips
- 1 tablespoon sesame seed, toasted

Drain pineapple; reserve ⅓ *cup* juice. For salad dressing, in screw-top jar combine reserved juice, sesame oil, honey, soy sauce, ginger, and garlic. In large bowl, combine pineapple, pasta, chicken, and onion. Toss with dressing. Cover; refrigerate 2 hours or longer. Add broccoli and bell pepper. Toss well, sprinkle with sesame seeds.

Pasta Del Sol

Dole Food Company

Makes 6 to 8 servings

1 can (20 ounces) Dole® Pineapple Chunks
8 ounces spiral pasta
1 tablespoon sugar
1 small Dole® Red Bell Pepper, chunked
1½ cups slivered ham *or* Cheddar cheese
1 cup sliced Dole® Carrots
1 cup frozen peas, thawed
Zest and juice from 1 Dole® Orange
½ cup vegetable oil
1 tablespoon sweet basil, crumbled
¼ teaspoon black pepper
Dash nutmeg

Drain pineapple; reserve ½ *cup* juice. Cook pasta according to package directions. Combine pineapple, pasta, bell pepper, ham, carrots, and peas in large bowl. For dressing, combine reserved ½ *cup* pineapple juice with *1 tablespoon* orange zest, ½ *cup* orange juice, and remaining ingredients. Pour over salad. Toss well. Cover; refrigerate at least 1 hour or overnight.

Pasta Salad Niçoise

Lindsay International, Inc.

Makes 8 servings

¼ cup salad oil
3 tablespoons lemon juice
2 tablespoons vinegar
½ teaspoon dry mustard
½ teaspoon paprika
½ teaspoon dried basil, crushed
8 ounces linguine, broken in half
1 cup cherry tomatoes, halved

1 package (9 ounces) frozen French-style green beans, cooked, drained, and chilled
1 can (12 ounces) tuna, drained and flaked
4 eggs (hard cooked and sliced)
½ cup Lindsay® Small Pitted Ripe Olives, drained

For salad dressing, in a screw-top jar shake together salad oil, lemon juice, vinegar, dry mustard, paprika, and basil.

Cook linguine in boiling salted water until tender. Immediately drain in colander. Rinse with cold water; drain. In salad bowl, combine linguine, cherry-tomato halves, and green beans. Pour dressing over mixture. Toss gently to mix.

Break the tuna into bite-size chunks; mound tuna atop linguine mixture. Arrange sliced eggs and olives around tuna. Cover and chill several hours. Toss gently before serving.

Savory Shell Salad

Sargento Cheese Company, Inc.

Makes 8 servings

2 cups uncooked salad *or* medium pasta shells

2 medium tomatoes, seeded and diced

2 green onions, thinly sliced

¼ cup white wine vinegar

½ teaspoon oregano

2 cloves garlic, minced

¼ teaspoon sugar

⅓ cup olive oil

1¼ cups (5 ounces) Sargento® Fancy Shredded Cheddar Cheese

Cook pasta according to package directions; cool. In large bowl, toss together pasta, tomatoes, and onions. In small bowl, stir together vinegar, oregano, garlic, and sugar. Gradually add oil, whisking until smooth and thickened. Add to pasta. Toss to coat thoroughly. Stir in cheese. Cover and refrigerate until chilled. Toss before serving.

Tortellini Asparagus Salad

Lawry's Foods, Inc.

Makes 4 servings

1 pound fresh asparagus, cut into ½-inch pieces

2 cups tightly packed fresh spinach leaves, torn into bite-size pieces

1 cup diced red bell pepper

2 packages (9 ounces each) small cheese-filled tortellini, cooked and drained

¼ cup red wine vinegar

2 tablespoons olive *or* vegetable oil

1½ teaspoons lemon juice

1 teaspoon sugar

1 teaspoon Lawry's® Garlic Salt

Place asparagus on steamer rack; place in deep pot with 1 inch of boiling water. Cover and steam 10 minutes. Remove and set aside. Steam spinach in same pot about 45 seconds or until just wilted. In large bowl, combine asparagus, spinach, bell pepper, and tortellini; blend well. In small bowl, combine vinegar, oil, lemon juice, sugar, and garlic salt; blend well. Pour over tortellini mixture; toss well.

Serve with fresh bread.

Variations

Substitute 1½ cups broccoli florets for asparagus.
Substitute chopped pimientos for red bell pepper.

To microwave: Place asparagus and spinach in microwave-safe bowl; sprinkle with water. Cover with plastic wrap, venting 1 corner, and microwave on HIGH 2 minutes to steam. In large bowl, combine asparagus, spinach, bell pepper, and tortellini; blend well. In small bowl, combine vinegar, oil, lemon juice, sugar, and garlic salt; blend well. Pour over tortellini mixture; toss well.

Thai Salad

Best Foods, a division of CPC International Inc.

Makes 4 servings

⅓ cup Mazola® Corn Oil
⅓ cup lime juice
2 tablespoons chopped fresh mint leaves
2 tablespoons chopped cilantro
2 tablespoons pickled jalapeño peppers, chopped and seeded
½ teaspoon salt
½ teaspoon sugar
6 ounces Mueller's® Twist Trio®, cooked, rinsed with cold water, and drained
½ cup chopped red onion
1 large cucumber, sliced
12 ounces medium shrimp, shelled and cooked
Lettuce leaves

In small bowl, stir corn oil, lime juice, mint, cilantro, jalapeño peppers, salt, and sugar until blended, to make dressing. In medium bowl, combine pasta and red onion. Toss with half the dressing. Arrange on lettuce-lined platter with cucumber and shrimp; drizzle with remaining dressing.

Garden Pasta Toss

Kraft General Foods, Inc.

Makes 6 to 8 servings

- 2 cups (5½ ounces) rotini, cooked and drained
- 2 cups zucchini slices, halved
- ½ cup chopped red bell pepper
- 8 slices Oscar Mayer® Bacon, crisply cooked, crumbled
- 2 eggs, hard cooked and coarsely chopped
- 1 teaspoon dried oregano leaves, crushed
- ½ teaspoon onion powder
- ½ teaspoon pepper
- ¾ pound Velveeta® Pasteurized Process Cheese Spread, cubed
- ¾ cup Kraft® Real Mayonnaise
- 3 tablespoons milk
- 2 teaspoons Kraft® Pure Prepared Mustard
- Lettuce (optional)

Mix rotini, zucchini, red bell pepper, bacon, eggs, and seasonings in large bowl. Heat pasteurized process cheese spread, mayonnaise, milk, and mustard in saucepan over low heat, stirring until pasteurized process cheese spread is melted. Pour over rotini mixture; mix lightly. Chill. Mix lightly just before serving. Serve on lettuce-covered platter, if desired.

Preparation time: 20 minutes, plus chilling

Italian Pasta & Vegetable Salad

Lipton

Makes 8 side-dish servings

8 ounces uncooked rotelle or spiral pasta

2½ cups assorted cut-up fresh vegetables (broccoli, carrots, tomatoes, bell peppers, cauliflower, onions, and mushrooms)

½ cup cubed cheddar *or* mozzarella cheese

⅓ cup sliced pitted ripe olives (optional)

1 cup Wish-Bone® Italian Dressing

Cook pasta according to package directions; drain and rinse with cold water until completely cool.

In large bowl, combine all ingredients except Italian dressing. Add dressing; toss well. Serve chilled or at room temperature.

Note: If preparing a day ahead, refrigerate, then stir in ¼ cup additional Wish-Bone® Dressing before serving.

Variation: Also terrific with Wish Bone® Robusto Italian, Fat Free Italian, Classic House Italian, Creamy Roasted Garlic, Fat Free Creamy Roasted Garlic, Ranch, or Fat Free Ranch Dressing.

Pasta, Chicken and Broccoli Pesto Toss

Sargento Cheese Company, Inc.

Makes 8 servings

4 ounces (about 2 cups) vegetable spiral pasta

2 cups cubed, cooked chicken *or* turkey breast

2 cups small broccoli florets, cooked crisp-tender and cooled

1½ cups (6 ounces) Sargento® Fancy Shredded Low-Moisture Part-Skim Mozzarella Cheese

⅔ cup lightly packed fresh basil leaves

2 cloves garlic

1 cup mayonnaise

1 tablespoon lemon juice

½ teaspoon salt

½ cup (1½ ounces) Sargento® Fancy Shredded Parmesan Cheese

½ cup pine nuts *or* coarsely chopped walnuts, toasted

Cook pasta according to package directions until tender; drain and cool. Combine pasta, chicken, broccoli, and mozzarella cheese in large bowl. Process basil and garlic in food processor or blender until finely chopped. Add mayonnaise, lemon juice, and salt. Process to combine thoroughly. Stir in Parmesan cheese. Add to pasta mixture and toss to coat all ingredients. Stir in pine nuts. Serve immediately or cover and refrigerate. For maximum flavor, remove from refrigerator and toss gently 30 minutes before serving.

MEAT AND POULTRY SALADS

Hot and Cold Veal Salad

McCormick & Company, Inc.

Makes 4 individual salads; 1 cup sauce

- ½ pound thin veal cutlets
- ½ pound veal sweetbreads
- ½ cup butter
- 1 tablespoon flour
- ½ cup malt vinegar
- ⅔ cup water
- ¼ teaspoon McCormick/ Schilling® Ground Mustard
- ¼ teaspoon McCormick/ Schilling Paprika
- ⅛ teaspoon McCormick/ Schilling Thyme Leaves
- ⅛ teaspoon McCormick/ Schilling Tarragon Leaves
- ¼ teaspoon McCormick/ Schilling Ground Black Pepper
- ¼ teaspoon McCormick/ Schilling Instant Minced Onion
- Salad greens

Cut veal in small pieces, about 2-by-2-by-¼ inches. Parboil sweetbreads. Cool. Remove membrane and cut meat in small pieces, about 2-by-2-by-½ inches. Sauté veal and sweetbreads in butter until lightly browned. Remove meat and keep warm. Sprinkle flour over butter in skillet. Stir and cook over low heat 1 minute. Add vinegar, water, and next 6 ingredients. Cook, stirring and scraping pan 1 minute. Pour into heatproof bowl and keep warm. Arrange 4 plates of salad greens. Place meat, alternating slices of veal and sweetbreads, over center of greens. Pour ¼ *cup* of sauce over meat. Serve immediately.

Caesar Steak Salad

Nabisco Foods Group

Makes 5 servings

½　cup A.1.® ORIGINAL *or*
　　A.1.® BOLD Steak Sauce
½　cup prepared Italian salad
　　dressing
1　tablespoon chopped fresh
　　basil
1　teaspoon anchovy paste

1　(1 to 1¼-pound) beef
　　sirloin steak, trimmed
5　cups torn Romaine leaves
1　cup cherry tomato halves
1　cup shredded carrots
1　cup garlic-flavored
　　multi-grain croutons
¼　cup Parmesan cheese

In small bowl, combine steak sauce, dressing, basil, and anchovy paste. Place steak in nonmetal dish. Coat with ¼ *cup* steak sauce mixture; reserve remaining steak sauce mixture. Cover; chill 1 hour, turning occasionally.

On large platter, arrange salad greens, tomato, and carrots; set aside.

Remove steak from marinade. Grill over medium high heat for 8 minutes on each side or until desired doneness, turning once.

To serve, thinly slice steak across grain; arrange over salad greens. Top with croutons and remaining dressing mixture. Sprinkle with Parmesan cheese.

Turkey Waldorf Salad

Best Foods, a division of CPC International Inc.

Makes about 5 cups

- ⅔ cup Hellmann's® *or* Best Foods® Mayonnaise
- 2 tablespoons lemon juice
- ½ teaspoon salt
- ¼ teaspoon pepper
- 2 cups diced cooked turkey *or* chicken
- 2 apples, cored and chopped
- ⅔ cup sliced celery
- ½ cup chopped walnuts

In large bowl, stir mayonnaise, lemon juice, salt, and pepper until smooth. Add turkey, apples, celery, and walnuts; toss to coat well. Cover and refrigerate.

Smoked Turkey and Pepper Pasta Salad

Kraft General Foods, Inc.

Makes 5 to 6 servings

- ¾ cup Miracle Whip® Salad Dressing
- 1 tablespoon Dijon mustard
- ½ teaspoon dried thyme leaves
- 8 ounces fettuccine, cooked and drained
- 1 cup (8 ounces) diced Louis Rich® Smoked Boneless Turkey Breast
- ¾ cup zucchini slices, halved
- ½ cup red bell pepper strips
- ½ cup yellow bell pepper strips

Salt and Pepper to taste

Mix salad dressing, mustard, and thyme until well blended. Add pasta, turkey, and vegetables; mix lightly. Season with salt and pepper to taste. Chill. Add additional dressing before serving, if desired.

Variations

Substitute Miracle Whip® Light Reduced Calorie Salad Dressing for regular salad dressing.

Substitute rotini, shell, or elbow macaroni for fettucine.

Substitute ⅓ *cup* red bell pepper, ⅓ *cup* yellow bell pepper, and ⅓ *cup* green bell pepper for red and yellow peppers.

Preparation time: 15 minutes, plus chilling

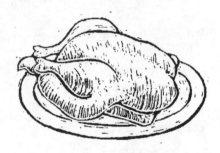

HUMANKIND'S EARLIEST PROCESSED FOOD

The Story of Hot Dogs

Sausages, the earliest known processed food, are first mentioned in history in Homer's *Odyssey.* The Gauls and ancient Romans enjoyed spiced ground meat held together with outer casings as one of their dietary mainstays.

In 1987 the Germans of Frankfurt celebrated the five hundredth anniversary of the invention of the modern frankfurter which, they claim, predates the discovery of the New World by five years. The origin of the modern frankfurter, has been disputed, however. Also called the wiener, the sausage, some say, was actually first processed in Vienna (Wien), Austria. To further complicate things, Frankfurters tend to call the sausage a wiener, and Viennese like to call it a frankfurter. Still others believe that today's frankfurter—or wiener—may have originated in neither city but rather may be a blend of sausages brought to the United States by butchers of several nationalities. A German immigrant selling hot dogs with milk rolls and sauerkraut from his pushcart in New York City's Bowery in the 1860s may have been the first to put the hot dog on a roll. Around the turn of the century, a German butcher, Charles Feltman, brought the frankfurter from his homeland and sold 3,684 "dachshund sausages" from his Coney Island stand during his first year in business. Throngs of visitors to the Chicago Columbian Exposition consumed an enormous quantity of the easy-to-eat dachshund sausages in 1893, the same year that St. Louis bar owner Chris Von de Ahe, also owner of the St. Louis Browns major league baseball team, began the great U.S. tradition of hot dogs at ball games.

The first hot dog bun was probably created for the visitors of the St. Louis Louisiana Purchase Exposition in 1904. A hot dog concessionaire, Anton Feuchtwanger, had run low on the white cotton gloves he loaned to customers to protect their fingers from the hot sausages. He sought help from his brother-in-law, a baker, who solved the problem by creating the first hot dog-size buns.

The frankfurter received its current nickname one cold April day in 1906. Concessionaire Harry Stevens, whose company is still the major concessionaire in New York and Florida ballparks and other sports stadiums, was losing money trying to sell ice cream and ice-cold sodas at the New York Polo Grounds. He sent his salesmen out to round up all the sausages and buns they could locate. Within an hour, they were promoting hot sausages, freshly retrieved from portable tanks of hot water, by hawking, "Red hots! Get your dachshund sausages while they're hot!" A sports cartoonist, Tad Dorgan, desperate for an idea before his press deadline, heard the vendors' cries and quickly drew a caricature of barking dachshund sausages snuggled in cozy buns. He couldn't spell dachshund, so he simply wrote "hot dog!"

Hot dogs have been fare fitting for royalty on occasion: In 1939, Franklin D. Roosevelt entertained King George VI of England with a hot dog and beer feast; in 1957, Queen Elizabeth II served the American Bar Association a royal hot dog banquet.

But hot dogs are truly a food for every day. Chicago's O'Hare International Airport sells more of them than any-place else in the world, ringing up more than 2 million annually at its restaurants and snack bars. Throughout the United States, 95 percent of all homes serve the country's favorite sausage. During peak outdoor cookery months— Memorial Day to Labor Day—the country consumes more than 5 billion hot dogs, according to the Oscar Mayer Company. Laid end to end, that's enough hot dogs to circle the globe more than fifteen times.

Wiener Sauerkraut Salad

Oscar Mayer Foods Corporation

Makes 6 servings

1 package (16 ounces) Oscar Mayer® Wieners	¼ cup chopped green pepper
2 cups sauerkraut, drained	½ cup sour cream
1 cup thinly sliced radishes	½ cup mayonnaise
	Lettuce leaves

Cut unheated wieners into ½-inch pieces. Combine with sauerkraut, radishes, and green pepper in large bowl. Cover; let sit 1 hour. Mix sour cream and mayonnaise in small bowl. Toss with sauerkraut; refrigerate before serving. Serve on lettuce leaves.

Scarborough Fair Salad

Oscar Mayer Foods Corporation

Makes 4 servings

1 pound Louis Rich® Breast of Turkey	1 tablespoon chopped fresh parsley
1 package (2 ounces) slivered almonds	½ cup mayonnaise
1 tart green apple	¼ teaspoon ground thyme
1 tablespoon lemon juice	⅛ teaspoon garlic powder
2 stalks celery, chopped	⅛ teaspoon oregano leaves
2 green onions with tops, chopped	⅛ teaspoon pepper
	⅛ teaspoon rosemary leaves
	⅛ teaspoon sage

Preheat oven to 350°F. Cut turkey into ½-inch cubes, set aside. Toast almonds on shallow baking sheet for 8 minutes or until lightly browned; cool. Cut apple into chunks and toss with lemon juice in large bowl. Add turkey, almonds, celery, onion, and parsley. In small bowl, combine mayonnaise, thyme, garlic powder, oregano leaves, pepper, rosemary leaves, and sage to make dressing. Add to turkey mixture and toss. Cover and chill thoroughly before serving.

Turkey in Avocados

Lindsay International, Inc.

Makes 6 servings

⅓ cup plain yogurt
¼ cup mayonnaise *or* salad dressing
1 teaspoon lemon juice
¼ teaspoon dill weed
⅛ teaspoon salt
Dash pepper
1½ cups cubed cooked turkey *or* chicken

1 small tomato, seeded and chopped
½ cup Lindsay® Colossal Pitted Ripe Olives, drained and halved
3 tablespoons sliced green onion
3 avocados
Lemon juice

Stir together yogurt, mayonnaise, 1 teaspoon lemon juice, dill weed, ⅛ teaspoon salt, and dash pepper. Stir in turkey or chicken, tomato, olives, and green onion. Cover and chill thoroughly. To serve, halve and seed avocados; brush lightly with lemon juice. Spoon about ½ cup mixture into each half.

Chunky Chicken Salad or Sandwich Spread

Lipton

Makes about 6 servings

1 cup Lipton® California Dip (see below)
2 cups cut-up cooked chicken

1 cup sliced celery
¼ cup sliced sweet gherkins
¼ cup sliced pitted ripe olives

In large bowl, toss California Dip with chicken, celery, gherkins, and olives.

California Dip

Makes about 2 cups

1 envelope Lipton® Recipe Secrets® Onion Soup Mix

1 container (16 ounces) sour cream

Blend together and chill.

Lunch Box Sandwich

Slices of bread *or* rolls

Thin slices of boiled *or* baked ham

Lightly butter slices of bread or rolls. Arrange 1 or 2 slices of ham on bread. Top with 2 to 3 tablespoons Chunky Chicken Salad. Cover with second slice of bread.

Cheddar Chicken and Apple Salad

Beatrice Cheese, Inc.

Makes 6 servings

¼ cup no-cholesterol mayonnaise

2 tablespoons skim milk

2 to 3 teaspoons snipped fresh dill *or* ½ teaspoon dill

2 cups cooked cubed chicken *or* turkey breast

1 cup diced celery

1 Granny Smith apple, cored and diced

1 Red Delicious apple, cored and diced

4 green onions with tops, thinly sliced

2 cups (8 ounces) County Line® Shredded Reduced-Fat/Sodium Cheddar Cheese

Freshly ground pepper to taste

In small bowl, combine mayonnaise, milk, and dill to make dressing. In salad bowl, combine all remaining ingredients. Toss with dressing to coat.

Serve on lettuce or stuff into pita-bread halves.

Grilled Chicken Salad Vinaigrette

Ragú Foods Co.

Makes 6 to 8 servings

- 1 package Adolph's® Marinade in Minutes— Garlic Dijon Flavor
- ½ cup wine vinegar
- ¼ cup water
- 2 pounds boneless chicken breasts
- 1 cup thinly sliced celery
- 1 medium onion, sliced
- 1 jar (7 ounces) roasted peppers, drained and sliced
- 1 jar (6 ounces) marinated artichoke hearts, drained and sliced
- 1 can (2¼ ounces) sliced ripe olives, drained
- ⅓ cup olive oil
- 3 tablespoons wine vinegar
- 1 teaspoon Dijon mustard

Salt to taste
Pepper to taste
Leaf lettuce

Preheat grill or broiler. In medium bowl, thoroughly combine contents of marinade package with ½ cup vinegar and ¼ cup water. Place chicken in marinade; pierce deeply with a fork. Marinate 15 minutes, turning chicken occasionally. Remove chicken from marinade. Grill or broil chicken 5 to 6 inches from heat, 5 to 7 minutes per side or until thoroughly cooked. Thinly slice chicken; let cool. Combine sliced chicken with celery, onion, roasted peppers, artichoke hearts, olives, olive oil, vinegar, mustard, salt, and pepper. Stir to combine thoroughly. Serve chilled over leaf lettuce.

Southwest Chicken Salad

Lindsay International, Inc.

Makes 4 servings

¼ cup salad oil
2 tablespoons white wine
   vinegar
2 tablespoon lime juice
½ teaspoon chili powder
¼ teaspoon dry mustard
Several drops bottled hot
   pepper sauce
¼ teaspoon salt
4 ounces medium shell
   macaroni, cooked,
   drained, and rinsed
   with cold water
1 can (6 ounces; 1⅔ cup)
   Lindsay® Medium Pitted
   Ripe Olives, drained

1 can (8¾ ounces) whole-
   kernel corn, drained
1 cup chopped cooked
   chicken
4 ounces Monterey jack
   cheese, cubed
½ medium avocado, seeded,
   peeled, and cut into
   bite-size chunks
2 canned jalapeño peppers,
   rinsed, seeded, and
   chopped
2 tablespoons sliced green
   onion
1 jar (2 ounces) diced
   pimiento, drained

In a screw-top jar, shake together oil, vinegar, lime juice,
chili powder, dry mustard, pepper sauce, and salt. Pour
over macaroni; stir to coat. Stir in remaining ingredients;
cover and chill.

SALAD DRESSINGS

Poppy-Seed Dijon Dressing

Nabisco Foods Group

Makes 1¾ cups

1 cup vegetable oil
¼ cup Regina® Red Wine
   Vinegar
¼ cup honey

2 tablespoons GREY
   POUPON Dijon *or*
   COUNTRY DIJON Mustard
1 tablespoon minced onion
1 tablespoon poppy seeds

In bowl, whisk oil, vinegar, honey, and mustard; blend in onion and poppy seed. Serve with tossed salad.

Store, covered, in refrigerator up to 1 week. Bring to room temperature and mix thoroughly before serving.

Last-Minute Dressing

Lawry's Foods, Inc.

Makes 1 cup

⅔ cup vegetable oil
¼ cup white wine vinegar
1½ tablespoons Dijon
   mustard
1 tablespoon water

2 teaspoons sugar
1 teaspoon Lawry's®
   Seasoned Salt
½ teaspoon Lawry's® Lemon
   Pepper Seasoning

In medium bowl or food processor, combine all ingredients. Blend well with wire whisk or process 15 seconds.

Use on any green salad or pour over grilled chicken or beef entree.

Dressed-Up Salad Dressing

Lawry's Foods, Inc.

Makes about 2 cups

1 bottle (8 ounces) Wish-Bone® Italian Salad Dressing

1 tablespoon Dijon mustard

1 tablespoon Parmesan cheese

½ teaspoon Lawry's® Garlic Powder with Parsley

1 egg white, hard cooked and finely chopped

¼ cup finely chopped green bell pepper

¼ cup finely chopped red bell pepper

¼ cup finely chopped yellow bell pepper

1 tablespoon chopped almonds

Tossed greens

Tomato wedges

In food processor or blender, combine dressing, mustard, cheese, and garlic powder with parsley; process 15 seconds to blend well. In medium bowl, combine remaining ingredients; pour dressing mixture over pepper mixture. Serve over tossed greens and tomato wedges. Add any remaining bell pepper to salad for extra color.

Note: To save time, chop egg white, peppers, and almonds in the food processor; add dressing, mustard, cheese, and garlic powder. Process to desired texture.

SAY CHEESE

The Story of Cheese

Legend has it that somewhere in an Asian desert more than four thousand years ago an Arab trader tried to take a gulp of milk stored in a pouch he had made from a calf's stomach. Attached to his camel's hump during the undulating ride through the desert, the pouch had absorbed the full blast of the sun. The milk had curdled. The Arab was too hungry to care. He poured out the clear liquid and ate the precipitate. Not a bad taste, thought the nomad. He had discovered a new way of storing milk and from that moment on cheese became a delicious and important part of the diets of most primitive and many civilized people of the world. The nomad didn't know that the acid that transformed his milk was rennet, found in the gastric juices of the fourth stomach of young milk-drinking animals. For today's cheese making, rennin, the milk-coagulating enzyme, is extracted from the lining of calves' stomachs and commercially processed. Plant-juice agents such as thistle juice and safflower juice are also used to curdle milk into cheese. These different fermenting agents produce different kinds of cheeses.

Bacteria, present in all milk, will act to sour milk and cause the solid, protein part of the milk to separate from the liquids, or the curds to separate from the whey. Hence, what Miss Muffet ate was an early stage of cottage cheese. This manner of making cheese was probably discovered independently in different parts of the world when milk accidently soured. The ancient method is still used to make cottage cheese, now usually with the addition of rennin.

The amount of water left in cheese and the ripening method used to make the product determine its hardness or softness. Hard cheeses are used for grating; best known of these, the hardest of all, is Parmesan, named for the Italian town of Parma. According to sales in the United States, our favorite hard cheese is Cheddar, originally made in Cheddar, England. Made from whole milk it contains a small amount of fat. Our most popular soft cheese is cottage cheese, manufactured from skim milk and with very little fat content.

Cheese, like wine, develops its unique flavor from the characteristics of its region of origin. The breed of cattle or goat, the kinds of grasses or flowers the animals ate, the happenstance of any of millions of microorganisms settling out of the air all act to produce the distinctive cheese flavors associated with different regions. New York Cheddar cheese, for example, tastes very different from Wisconsin Cheddar.

The final step of making cheese, the process of aging with natural enzymes and molds, defines the singular flavor and makes the cheese a gastronomic delicacy. Blue-mold cheese, among the most robust, include the famous Roquefort, from the French town of the same name, a semi-soft cheese made from rich sheep's milk and aged in ancient caves.

The best-selling blue cheese in the United States is Beatrice Cheese, Inc.'s Treasure Cave® brand, made from whole milk. Ripened in the traditional manner, Treasure Cave® is cured for one hundred days and nights in a massive labyrinth of whitewashed sandstone caves along the Straight River in Faribault, Minnesota. The temperature of the caves is a constant 54° F, the same as well water, perfect for aging a rich, full-flavored blue.

Super Dressing

Beatrice Cheese, Inc

Makes 2 cups

Salad greens

Cucumbers

Tomatoes

1 package (4 ounces) Treasure Cave® Blue Cheese, crumbled

1 cup mayonnaise

⅓ cup milk

¼ teaspoon celery salt

⅛ teaspoon garlic salt

⅛ teaspoon onion salt

Dash pepper

Prepare greens, cucumbers, and tomatoes for salad. Combine all remaining ingredients in medium-size bowl. Serve with salad. If dressing thickens on standing, add more milk.

Creamy Dressing

Beatrice Cheese, Inc.

Makes 2 cups

1 package (4 ounces) Treasure Cave® Blue Cheese

3 ounces cream cheese

½ cup milk

½ cup sour cream

2 tablespoons lemon juice

Mixed salad greens *or* cabbage

Blend two-thirds of the package of blue cheese with all of the cream cheese. Gradually add milk. Blend in sour cream and lemon juice. Spoon onto mixed salad greens or mix with shredded cabbage for salad. Crumble remaining cheese over salad.

Sweet-Sour Dressing

Beatrice Cheese, Inc.

Makes 2½ cups

2 package (4 ounces)
Treasure Cave® Blue
Cheese, crumbled

¼ cup sugar
1 teaspoon salt
⅓ cup vinegar
1 cup sour cream

Combine all ingredients. Cover and refrigerate for at least 30 minutes before serving.

Scene-Stealing
Side Dishes

CHEESY BROCCOLI POTATOES
Reckitt & Colman Inc.
207

SLOPPY JOE TOPPED POTATOES
Reckitt & Colman Inc.
208

ROASTED POTATOES POUPON
Nabisco Foods Group
208

GERMAN POTATO BAKE
Kraft General Foods, Inc.
209

SOUTHWEST BAKED BEANS
Reckitt & Colman Inc.
210

WESTERN BEAN BAKE
Campbell Soup Company
210

CAJUN-STYLE BEANS
Campbell Soup Company
211

CREAMY SPINACH BAKE
Kellogg Company
212

POLENTA WITH FRESH
TOMATO SALSA
Nabisco Foods Group
213

SESAME GREEN BEANS AND
RED PEPPER
Reckitt & Colman Inc.
214

RITZ CRACKER STUFFING
Nabisco Foods Group
215

Rice Dishes

ARTICHOKE RICE BAKE
Lawry's Foods, Inc.
216

SPANISH MILLET (OR RICE)
Beatrice Cheese, Inc.
217

ALMOND WILD RICE BAKE
Dole Food Company
217

PARMESAN RICE
Lindsay International, Inc.
218

CHEESY RICE CASSEROLE
Reckitt & Colman Inc.
219

CORN AND RICE CASSEROLE
Nabisco Foods Group
219

CHEESY BROCCOLI & RICE
Reckitt & Colman Inc.
220

HEARTY VEGETABLE DISHES

Cucumber Sauté

McCormick & Company, Inc.

Makes 4 individual salads, 3 cups total

4 slices bacon
2 cucumbers
1 medium red bell pepper
1 small yellow onion
⅛ teaspoon McCormick/ Schilling® Ground White Pepper
¼ teaspoon McCormick/ Schilling Celery Seed
¼ teaspoon McCormick/ Schilling Seasoning Salt
¼ teaspoon McCormick/ Schilling Parsley Flakes
¼ teaspoon sugar
3 tablespoons water
2 tablespoons red wine vinegar
½ teaspoon cornstarch
Additional bacon for garnish (optional)
Fresh parsley for garnish (optional)

Fry bacon. Drain. Reserve *2 tablespoons* bacon fat. Set aside. Peel, quarter, and seed cucumbers. Cut into julienne strips. Seed red pepper. Cut into thin bite-size strips.

Peel onion and cut into ⅛-inch slices. Separate onion into rings. Heat bacon fat in skillet over medium-high heat. Add cucumbers, red peppers, and onion. Stir-fry 3 minutes.

Remove vegetables from skillet. Combine remaining 8 ingredients. Mix well. Add to skillet, stirring constantly, until mixture thickens. Add vegetables and heat through. Arrange cucumbers, peppers, and onions on 4 salad plates. Crumble bacon. Garnish each serving with bacon and fresh parsley, if desired.

Cauliflower Escallop

Kellogg Company

Makes 8 servings

2 tablespoons margarine melted	¾ cup hot water
	¼ cup margarine
1½ cups *KELLOGG'S* CORN *FLAKES*® cereal, crushed to ¾ cup	¼ cup all-purpose flour
	¼ teaspoon white pepper
	1 cup skim milk
¼ teaspoon garlic powder	2 tablespoons chopped pimiento
4 cups sliced cauliflower	
1 chicken bouillon cube	1 cup sliced green onions

Preheat oven to 350°F. Combine the 2 tablespoons margarine with *KELLOGG'S CORN FLAKES*® cereal and garlic powder. Set aside for topping. Cook cauliflower in small amount of water until almost tender, about 10 minutes. Drain well. Set aside. Dissolve bouillon cube in ¾ cup hot water. Set aside. In large saucepan melt ¼ cup margarine over low heat. Stir in flour and pepper. Add bouillon and milk gradually, stirring until smooth. Increase heat to medium and cook until bubbly and thickened, stirring constantly. Remove from heat. Stir in pimiento, green onions, and cauliflower. Spoon mixture into 10-by-6-by-2-inch (1½ quart) glass baking dish. Sprinkle cereal mixture evenly over top. Bake about 20 minutes or until thoroughly heated.

DREAMS COMING TRUE

The Story of Lawry's®

In the twenties, thirties, and forties, Los Angeles was a land of dreams and Hollywood fantasies. Even the restaurants and bakeries were designed to look like something more than just buildings where food was sold. People talked business deals at lunch inside a massive brown derby, bought tasty hot dogs in a building that looked like a giant hot dog, and selected baked goods in the whimsical blue-and-white windmills of the Van de Kamp bakeries dotting the dreamscape. The Dutch were known for cleanliness, Frank Lawrence had reasoned: It made sense to dramatize that theme in the bakeries he owned with his brother-in-law, Theodore Van de Kamp.

Lawrence next used his charm and showmanship at the Tam O'Shanter, a restaurant-turned-inn that transported guests right to Normandy, France, inside and out. People were enchanted. The famous restaurant, the oldest in Los Angeles, still exists in its original location.

Then Lawrence decided to create a restaurant where prime rib would be carved and served right at the table, as it was in a place he had heard about in London, the acclaimed Simpson's-in-the-Strand. Other restaurateurs considered this a foolhardy scheme. But Lawrence chose a site in the former swampland between Santa Monica and Los Angeles, where two other restaurants sat placidly amid wild mustard on the otherwise vacant land. Today, Lawry's® The Prime Rib is the premier restaurant in its original location, now the world-famous La Cienaga Restaurant Row with thirty-five restaurants.

In his restaurant, Lawrence blended art deco and stylized Old English decor. He wanted to call the place Larry's but decided on Lawry's because it sounded more English. From the day in 1938 when the first prime ribs were wheeled on a cart to tableside, the place was a success.

Lawry's brought many firsts to the United States' restaurant scene. Valets first parked cars there. At a time when the usual restaurant salad presentation was cottage cheese, fruit, or gelatin, Lawry's began tossing salad greens tableside to serve before the main course, thus opening a whole new market for salad dressings and toppings. As far as can be determined, Lawry's was the first restaurant to feature a baked potato topped with butter and chives as an elegant side dish. The unforgettable Lawry's creamed spinach (recipe to follow) was presented with every beef dinner.

One morning, Frank Lawrence's son tasted a salt blend that he particularly liked on his eggs at his aunt's house. "If you like it so much, take it home with you," Aunt Tessie said. The blend, created by the chef of the El Paseo restaurant, intrigued Frank Lawrence. With some improvement, it might taste good on roast beef, he decided. He proceeded to turn his home kitchen into a lab for nearly a year. The final blend of 17 herbs and spices sat on every table in his restaurant. Customers were so taken with the seasoning that they kept pilfering the bottles. Even so, it didn't occur to Lawrence that the salt seasoning might be an important product idea.

The food broker wasn't certain when a visionary family member, Walter Van de Kamp, presented the seasoning to him for possible sale through Ralph's grocery chain. "I like your restaurant, Walter, and I like the product, but I doubt if it will sell," the broker said. But he agreed to show the product to Ralph's buyer. The buyer was also doubtful about its salability but agreed to try ten cases anyway.

From this tiny beginning in the land of fantasies, Lawry's® Seasoned Salt has become the world's largest-selling spice blend. In 1979 Lawry's® became a member of the Thomas J. Lipton family of companies, and it now manufactures and markets 250 products for international consumer and food service use.

Creamed Spinach à la Lawry's

Lawry's Foods, Inc.

Makes 8 servings

4 bacon slices, finely chopped	1½ to 2 cups milk
1 cup finely chopped onion	2 packages (10 ounces each) frozen spinach, cooked and drained
¼ cup all-purpose flour	Fresh basil for garnish
2 teaspoons Lawry's® Seasoned Salt	Additional cooked bacon for garnish
½ teaspoon Lawry's® Seasoned Pepper	
½ teaspoon Lawry's® Garlic Powder with Parsley	

In medium skillet, cook bacon until almost crisp. Add onion to bacon and cook until onion is tender, about 10 minutes. Remove from heat. Add flour, seasoned salt, seasoned pepper, and garlic powder with parsley; blend well. Gradually stir in milk, starting with 1½ cups; cook and stir over low heat until thickened. Add spinach and mix thoroughly. If too thick, add additional milk. Garnish with fresh basil and additional cooked bacon.

Excellent with prime ribs of beef.

Snappy Pods Amandine

Lawry's Foods, Inc

Makes 4 servings

½ cup cold water
1 tablespoon soy sauce
2 teaspoons cornstarch
1 teaspoon instant chicken bouillon granules
½ teaspoon Lawry's® Seasoned Pepper
½ teaspoon Lawry's® Garlic Salt

1 tablespoon vegetable oil
1 package (6 ounces) frozen Chinese pea pods, thawed
½ cup sliced fresh mushrooms *or* 1 can (4 ounces) sliced mushrooms, drained
2 tablespoons toasted, slivered almonds

In small bowl, combine water, soy sauce, cornstarch, bouillon granules, seasoned pepper, and garlic salt; blend well and set aside. In large skillet, heat oil and stir-fry pea pods 2 minutes. Stir in mushrooms. Add cornstarch mixture; cook and stir until thickened and glazed. Sprinkle with almonds.

Serve with other Chinese dishes or grilled steak or fish.

To toast almonds: Preheat oven to 350°F. Place almonds in a shallow pan and bake for 10 minutes. Toasting time will vary depending on size of the almonds.

Gourmet Veg-Kabobs

Lawry's Foods, Inc.

Makes 4 to 6 servings

½ cup salad oil
⅓ cup lemon juice
3 tablespoons red wine
1 tablespoon Lawry's®
Lemon Pepper Seasoning
2 teaspoons crushed red
  pepper flakes
1 teaspoon Lawry's®
  Seasoned Salt

2 yellow *or* green medium
  zucchini, cut into chunks
2 small onion, cut into
  wedges
16 medium mushroom caps
Cherry tomatoes
6 to 8 (6-inch) skewers
3 tablespoons grated
  Parmesan cheese

In medium bowl, mix together first 6 ingredients; blend well. Add vegetables; cover and refrigerate 30 minutes or overnight. Thread zucchini, onion, mushrooms, and tomatoes on skewers. Broil skewers 6 inches from heat 12 to 15 minutes; brush often with reserved marinade. Sprinkle on cheese and broil until lightly browned.

Goes well with steamed rice and oven-baked chicken.

Variation: Add chunked chicken *or* cubed beef onto skewers before broiling.

Light Batter-Fried Vegetables

Best Foods, a division of CPC International Inc.

Makes 4 cups

¾ cup Argo® *or* Kingsford's®
  Corn Starch
¼ cup unsifted flour
1 teaspoon baking powder
½ teaspoon salt
¼ teaspoon pepper
½ cup water

1 egg, slightly beaten
1 quart (about) Mazola®
  Corn Oil
4 cups cut-up vegetables,
  such as zucchini, carrots,
  onion, and mushrooms

In medium bowl, stir together corn starch, flour, baking powder, salt, and pepper. Add water and egg; stir until mixture is smooth. Pour corn oil into large skillet, filling not more than one-third full. Heat corn oil over medium heat to 375°F. Dip vegetables into batter, stirring batter occasionally. Fry a few vegetables at a time, turning once, 2 to 3 minutes or until golden brown and crisp. Drain on paper towels.

Variations

Herb Batter: Add 1 teaspoon dried basil leaves and 1 clove garlic, minced or pressed.

Beer Batter: Omit water. Add ⅓ cup cold beer.

Homestyle Zucchini and Tomatoes

Lipton

Makes about 4 servings

2 tablespoons oil
1 medium clove garlic, finely chopped
3 medium zucchini, thinly sliced (about 4½ cups)
½ teaspoon basil leaves
1 can (14½ ounces) whole peeled tomatoes, drained and chopped, with liquid reserved
1 envelope Lipton® Recipe Secrets® Golden Onion Soup Mix

In large skillet, heat oil and cook garlic with zucchini over medium-high heat, 3 minutes. Stir in tomatoes, then golden onion soup mix thoroughly blended with reserved liquid and basil. Bring to a boil; simmer, stirring occasionally, 10 minutes or until zucchini is tender and sauce is slightly thickened.

To microwave: In 2-quart casserole, combine zucchini with tomatoes. Stir in golden onion soup mix thoroughly blended with reserved liquid, garlic, and basil. Microwave, covered, at HIGH (Full Power) 5 minutes, stirring once. Remove cover and microwave 4 minutes or until zucchini is tender, stirring once. Let stand, covered, 2 minutes.

Variation: Also terrific with Lipton® Recipe Secrets® Onion Soup Mix.

Zucchini Waffles

Beatrice Cheese, Inc.

Makes three 9-inch waffles

3 cups grated zucchini	1 small onion, diced
2 eggs	Salt to taste
1½ cups buttermilk baking mix	Pepper to taste
1 cup shredded County Line® Cheddar Cheese	

Mix all ingredients well and let set overnight. Bake on preheated greased waffle baker. Serve with meat, in place of potatoes, with beef-mushroom gravy.

Provolone-Stuffed Zucchini

Lindsay International, Inc.

Makes 4 servings

2 large zucchini, halved lengthwise	½ cup Lindsay® Small Pitted Ripe Olives, drained and sliced
2 tablespoons chopped onion	
1 tablespoon butter *or* margarine	½ cup shredded carrot
½ teaspoon cornstarch	2 tablespoons grated Parmesan cheese
1 tablespoon dairy sour cream	½ teaspoon dried basil, crushed
¾ cup (3 ounces) shredded provolone cheese	

Preheat oven to 350°F. Cut off ends of zucchini. Cook zucchini, covered, in boiling water about 7 minutes or until crisp-tender; drain. Scoop out and reserve the pulp, leaving a ¼-inch shell.

Cook onion in butter until tender. Combine cornstarch and sour cream; stir in provolone cheese, olives, carrot, Parmesan cheese, basil, reserved pulp, and cooked onion.

Spoon into zucchini shells; arrange in a 12-by-7½-by-2-inch baking dish. Bake, uncovered, 20 to 25 minutes or until heated through.

Cheesy Stuffed Mushrooms

Sargento Cheese Company, Inc.

Makes 6 servings

12 large mushrooms	1 cup (4 ounces) Sargento®
½ cup finely chopped onion	Shredded *or* Fancy
1 tablespoon olive oil	Shredded Mozzarella
1 tablespoon minced parsley	Cheese
½ teaspoon basil	¼ cup (1 ounce) Sargento®
⅓ cup dry white wine	Grated Parmesan Cheese

Preheat oven to 350°F. Remove stems from mushrooms; reserve caps. Coarsely chop stems and sauté with onions in oil over medium-low heat until tender, about 5 minutes. Stir in parsley, basil, and wine. Simmer 10 minutes or until wine is absorbed; remove from heat. Cool about 5 minutes. Stir in cheeses. Fill mushroom caps with cheese mixture. Place in 9-by-9-inch baking dish. Bake, uncovered, 12 to 15 minutes.

Texas Spaghetti Squash

Beatrice Cheese, Inc.

Makes 8 to 10 servings

2 cups pinto beans, cooked
1 teaspoon ground coriander
1 teaspoon cumin
⅛ teaspoon cayenne pepper
½ cup water
1 spaghetti squash (1½ to 2 pounds)
1 cup brown rice
1½ cups chopped green onions

1 clove garlic, minced
1 egg, beaten
1½ cups County Line® Monterey jack Cheese
1 cup plain yogurt
1½ cups grated County Line® Cheddar Cheese
Tomatoes, chopped, for garnish

Preheat oven to 350°F. In small saucepan, combine pinto beans, coriander, cumin, pepper, and water. Simmer. Cut squash in half lengthwise. Remove seed and membrane. In large Dutch oven, cook squash until tender, about 35 minutes. Cool. Using a fork, scrape out squash to form spaghetti. In small saucepan, cook rice (according to package directions). Cool. Add ½ *cup* onions, garlic, egg, and yogurt. Stir.

In a 13-by-9 baking dish, layer as follows: squash, beans, Monterey jack cheese, rice mixture, 1 cup green onions, and Cheddar cheese. Bake 30 minutes. Garnish with chopped tomatoes.

Carrots au Gratin

Kellogg Company

Makes 6 servings

- 3 tablespoons margarine
- 1¾ cups *KELLOGG'S CORN FLAKES®* cereal, crushed to ¾ cup
- ⅓ cup chopped onion
- 3 tablespoons all-purpose flour
- ¼ teaspoon salt
- ¼ teaspoon pepper
- 1½ cups skim milk
- ⅔ cup (4 ounces) low fat shredded American cheese
- 4½ cups sliced carrots, cooked and drained (about 1½ pounds)
- 1 tablespoon dried parsley flakes
- Vegetable cooking spray

Preheat oven to 350°F. In large saucepan, melt margarine over low heat. Remove 1 tablespoon and mix with *KELLOGG'S CORN FLAKES®* cereal. Set aside for topping. Add onion to remaining margarine in pan. Cook, stirring frequently, until onion is softened but not browned.

Stir in flour, salt, and pepper. Add milk gradually, stir until smooth. Increase heat to medium and cook until bubbly and thickened, stirring constantly. Add cheese, stirring until melted. Remove from heat. Stir in carrots and parsley flakes. Spread mixture into a 10-by-6-by-2-inch (1½ quart) glass baking dish coated with cooking spray. Sprinkle cereal mixture evenly over top.

Bake about 20 minutes or until thoroughly heated. Remove from oven. Let stand about 5 minutes before serving.

Oven-Fried Green Tomatoes

Kellogg Company

Makes 6 servings

4 cups *KELLOGG'S CORN FLAKES®* cereal, crushed to 1 cup
1 teaspoon garlic salt
½ teaspoon oregano
¼ cup all-purpose flour
2 egg whites
2 tablespoons water
2 large green tomatoes
Vegetable cooking spray

Preheat oven to 400°F. Combine *KELLOGG'S CORN FLAKES®* cereal, garlic salt, and oregano in pie plate or shallow bowl. Place flour in second pie plate or bowl. Beat egg whites and water with fork until thoroughly combined.

Cut tomatoes in ½-inch slices. Dip tomatoes in flour, then in egg mixture, then cereal mixture. Carefully repeat dipping in egg mixture and cereal mixture to double coat completely. Place on foil-lined shallow baking pan coated with cooking spray. Lightly spray coated tomatoes with cooking spray.

Bake about 8 minutes or until lightly browned.

Green Bean and Onion Medley

Lawry's Foods, Inc.

Makes 6 servings

1 pound fresh green beans, stems and strings removed
½ pound pearl onions, peeled
1 tablespoon olive *or* vegetable oil
2 teaspoons white wine vinegar
½ teaspoon Lawry's® Seasoned Salt
½ teaspoon Lawry's® Seasoned Pepper
Romano cheese, grated (optional)

In large pot, bring 2 quarts water to a boil. Add green beans and onions. Reduce heat and simmer, partially covered, 20 minutes or until beans and onions are crisptender; drain and remove to medium bowl. Stir in remaining ingredients; toss well. Sprinkle with freshly grated Romano cheese, if desired. Serve immediately.

To microwave: In 2-quart microwave-safe casserole, combine green beans, onions, and ⅓ cup water. Cover with plastic wrap, venting corner, and microwave on HIGH 8 to 10 minutes; drain liquid. Stir in remaining ingredients. Cover and microwave 2 minutes. Serve immediately.

French's® Original Green Bean Casserole

©1996 Reckitt & Colman Inc.

Makes 6 servings

1 can (10¾ ounces) CAMPBELL'S®Condensed Cream of Mushroom Soup	2 packages (9 ounces *each*) frozen cut green beans, thawed*
¾ cup milk	1⅓ cups (2.8 ounce can) FRENCH'S® French Fried Onions
⅛ teaspoon pepper	

Preheat oven to 350°F. In 1½-quart casserole, combine soup, milk, and pepper, stir until well blended. Stir in beans and ⅔ cup French Fried Onions.

Bake, uncovered, 30 minutes or until hot. Stir. Sprinkle with remaining ⅔ cup onions. Bake 5 minutes or until onions are golden brown.

Or 2 cans (14.5 ounces *each*) cut green beans, drained.

To microwave: Prepare green bean mixture as above; pour into 1½-quart microwave-safe casserole. Cover with vented plastic wrap. Microwave on HIGH 8 to 10 minutes or until heated through, stirring halfway. Uncover. Top with remaining onions. Cook 1 minute until onions are golden. Let stand 5 minutes.

Note: You may substitute 4 cups cooked, cut fresh green beans for the frozen or canned.

Preparation time: 5 minutes   *Cook time:* 35 minutes

Cheddar Broccoli Corn Bake

Kellogg Company

Makes 6 servings

¼ cup margarine, divided
2 tablespoons all-purpose flour
¼ teaspoon salt
1½ cups skim milk
1½ cups (6 ounces) shredded low-fat, low-sodium Cheddar cheese

2 cups *KELLOGG'S CORN FLAKES®* cereal, crushed to 1 cup
1 can (16 ounces) whole-kernel corn, drained
2 packages (10 ounces each) frozen broccoli spears, thawed and drained

Preheat oven to 350°F. Melt 2 tablespoons margarine in large saucepan over low heat. Stir in flour and salt. Add milk gradually, stirring until smooth, increase heat to medium and cook until bubbly and thickened, stirring constantly. Add cheese, stirring until melted. Stir in ¼ cup *KELLOGG'S CORN FLAKES®* cereal and corn and remove from heat. Arrange broccoli in 12-by-7½-by-2–inch (2 quart) glass baking dish. Pour cheese sauce over broccoli. Melt remaining margarine in small saucepan. Stir in remaining cereal. Sprinkle over casserole. Bake about 30 minutes or until thoroughly heated.

Sweet Potatoes Anna

Specialty Brands

Makes 6 servings

  2 pounds sweet potatoes, peeled and thinly sliced
  ¼ cup melted butter
  1 tablespoon sugar
1½ teaspoons Durkee® Ground Cinnamon
  ¾ teaspoon Durkee® Ground Ginger
  ¾ teaspoon salt
  ¼ teaspoon Durkee® Ground Nutmeg
  ¼ teaspoon Durkee® Ground Black Pepper
  1 cup (4 ounces) shredded Swiss cheese

Preheat oven to 425°F. Toss potatoes with butter, sugar, and seasonings; mix well. In foil-lined 9-inch cake pan, arrange a layer of potatoes, closely overlapping slices. Sprinkle with cheese; layer remaining potatoes on top. Loosely cover pan. Bake 60 minutes or until fork-tender. Remove foil; invert onto serving plate.

Butterscotch Yams

Best Foods, a division of CPC International Inc.

Makes 6 servings

  6 medium yams
  ½ cup Karo® Light *or* Dark Corn Syrup
  ½ cup firmly packed brown sugar
  ¼ cup heavy *or* light cream *or* half-and-half
  2 tablespoons Mazola® Margarine
  ½ teaspoon ground cinnamon
  ½ teaspoon salt

Pierce yams with fork several times. Microwave on HIGH (100% Power) 12 to 14 minutes or until tender. Let stand 10 minutes. Peel yams and cut into quarters. In 3-quart microwavable baking dish, combine corn syrup, brown sugar, cream, margarine, cinnamon, and salt. Microwave on HIGH (100% Power) 3 to 4 minutes, stirring once. Add yams; toss to coat well. Microwave on HIGH (100% Power) 6 minutes or until glazed, spooning sauce over yams after 3 minutes.

Cheesy Broccoli Potatoes

©1996 Reckitt & Colman Inc.

Makes 6 servings
  6 hot baked potatoes, split
1½ cups chopped, cooked broccoli
1⅓ cups (2.8 ounce can) FRENCH'S® French Fried Onions
  ¾ cup pasteurized process cheese sauce, heated

Place potatoes on microwave dish, fluff up potatoes with fork. Top with broccoli and French Fried Onions.
    Microwave 2 minutes. Drizzle cheese sauce on top.

Quick Cook Potato Tip: Scrub and prick potatoes. Microwave on HIGH 20 minutes.

Conventional Directions: Scrub and prick potatoes. Bake 1 hour at 400°F until done. Top with broccoli and onions. Bake 3 minutes. Drizzle with cheese sauce.

Preparation time: 20 minutes   *Cook time:* 2 minutes

Sloppy Joe Topped Potatoes

©1996 Reckitt & Colman Inc.

Makes 4 servings

1 pound ground beef *or* turkey	4 medium hot baked potatoes, split
1 can (10¾ ounces) condensed tomato soup	Garnish: Shredded Cheddar cheese, sliced green
2 tablespoons FRENCH'S® Worcestershire Sauce	onions, chopped tomatoes

Cook meat in large skillet until browned; drain. Add soup, ¼ cup water, and Worcestershire. Bring to a boil. Simmer over low heat 5 minutes, stirring often.

Serve over potatoes. Top with cheese, onion, and tomatoes.

Quick Cook Potato Tip: Scrub and prick potatoes. Microwave on HIGH for 20 minutes.

Preparation time: 10 minutes   *Cook time:* 20 minutes

Roasted Potatoes Poupon

Nabisco Foods Group

Makes 6 servings

½ cup GREY POUPON COUNTRY DIJON Mustard *or* GREY POUPON Dijon Mustard	3 pounds red skinned potatoes, cut into 1½-inch cubes
½ cup olive oil	2 medium onions, sliced (about 1½ cups)
	Chopped parsley, for garnish

In small bowl, combine mustard and oil. In large bowl, combine potatoes, onions, and mustard mixture, tossing to coat well. Spread evenly on baking sheet. Bake at 400°F for 45 to 50 minutes or until potatoes are tender and crispy. Garnish with chopped parsley.

German Potato Bake

Kraft General Foods, Inc.

Makes 6 servings

- 4 cups cubed hot cooked potatoes
- ½ pound Velveeta® Pasteurized Process Cheese Spread, cubed
- 2 tablespoons Parkay® Margarine
- ¾ cup Miracle Whip® Salad Dressing

- ¼ cup sour cream
- 5 slices Oscar Mayer® Bacon, crisply cooked, crumbled
- ¼ cup green onion slices
- 1 jar (2 ounces) chopped pimiento, drained
- ¼ teaspoon pepper
- ¼ teaspoon paprika

Preheat oven to 350°F. Combine potatoes, *¼ pound* pasteurized process cheese spread, and margarine; stir over low heat until pasteurized process cheese spread is melted. Add salad dressing, sour cream, *2 tablespoons* bacon, *2 tablespoons* onion, pimiento, and pepper; mix well. Spoon into 1½-quart casserole. Top with remaining pasteurized process cheese spread, bacon, and onion. Sprinkle with paprika. Bake 20 to 25 minutes or until thoroughly heated.

Variation: Substitute ¼ cup chopped red bell pepper for pimiento.

Preparation time: 30 minutes   *Cook time:* 25 minutes

Southwest Baked Beans

©1996 Reckitt & Colman Inc.

Makes 8 to 10 servings

3 strips bacon, chopped
1 large green *or* red pepper, chopped
1 medium onion, chopped
2 cans (16 ounces *each*) pork and beans
1 can (15 ounces) red kidney beans, drained
⅓ cup FRENCH'S® Worcestershire Sauce
⅓ cup FRENCH'S® Deli Brown Mustard
¼ cup brown sugar
1 tablespoon chili powder

Preheat oven to 400°F. In medium skillet, cook and stir bacon, pepper, and onion until bacon is cooked and vegetables are tender. Transfer to 2-quart casserole. Stir in remaining ingredients.

Bake, uncovered, for 40 minutes until hot and bubbly, stirring once.

Preparation time: 15 minutes   *Cook time:* 45 minutes

Western Bean Bake

Campbell Soup Company

Makes 15 servings, ½ cup each

2 cans (16 ounces each) Campbell's® Pork & Beans in Tomato Sauce *or* 2 cans (15½ ounces each) Campbell's® Ranchero Beans
1 can (16 ounces) pinto beans, drained
1 can (16 ounces) black beans, drained
1 can (4 ounces) chopped green chilies, drained
½ cup thinly sliced onion, separated into rings
1 tablespoon chopped fresh cilantro
1 tablespoon lime juice
Lime twist for garnish
Fresh cilantro for garnish
Sour cream (optional)

Preheat oven to 350°F. In 2-quart casserole, combine beans, chilies, onions, chopped cilantro, and juice. Bake, uncovered 1 hour or until hot and bubbly. Stir before serving. Garnish with lime twist and cilantro. Serve with sour cream if desired.

Cajun-Style Beans

Campbell Soup Company

Makes 6 servings, ½ cup each

1 tablespoon butter *or* margarine
½ cup diced cooked ham
½ cup chopped onion
1 stalk celery, chopped
1 medium green pepper, chopped
1 large clove garlic, minced

1 can (16 ounces) Campbell's® Pork & Beans in Tomato Sauce
2 tablespoons chopped pimiento
¼ teaspoon black pepper
⅛ teaspoon ground red pepper

In 10-inch skillet over medium heat, in hot butter, cook ham, onion, celery, green pepper, and garlic until vegetables are tender, stirring often. Stir in beans, pimiento, black pepper, and red pepper. Heat to boiling. Reduce heat; simmer, uncovered, 5 minutes, stirring occasionally.

Creamy Spinach Bake

Kellogg Company

Makes 6 servings

- 5 tablespoons margarine
- 3 cups *KELLOGG'S CORN FLAKES®* cereal, crushed to 1½ cups, divided
- 2 tablespoons all-purpose flour
- ¼ teaspoon salt
- 3 tablespoons chopped onion
- 1¼ cups skim milk
- 1 cup (4 ounces) shredded low fat Swiss cheese
- 1 package (10 ounces) frozen chopped spinach, thawed and drained
- 2 eggs, well beaten

Preheat oven to 350°F. In large saucepan, melt margarine over low heat. Remove 2 tablespoons and mix with ¾ cup of the *KELLOGG'S CORN FLAKES®* cereal. Set aside for topping. To remaining margarine in pan, stir in flour, salt, and onion. Cook and stir about 1 minute. Add milk gradually, stirring until smooth. Increase heat to medium and cook until mixture boils, stirring constantly. Remove from heat.

Add cheese, stirring until slightly melted. Stir in spinach, eggs, and ¾ cup *KELLOGG'S CORN FLAKES®* cereal. Spread mixture in 1-quart casserole dish. Sprinkle cereal topping over spinach mixture.

Bake about 25 minutes or until thoroughly heated.

Polenta with Fresh Tomato Salsa

Nabisco Foods Group

Makes 8 servings

3 cups water	1½ cups chopped tomato
¾ cup CREAM OF WHEAT Cereal (½-minute, 2½-minute *or* 10-minute stovetop cooking)	⅓ cup chopped green pepper
	¼ cup chopped green onions
	2 tablespoons lime juice
1 clove garlic, minced	1 tablespoon diced jalapeño
4 teaspoons margarine	1 tablespoon chopped cilantro *or* parsley
½ cup shredded reduced fat Cheddar cheese	

In large saucepan, over high heat, heat water to a boil; slowly sprinkle in cereal and garlic. Cook and stir cereal until thickened, about 1 to 3 minutes, remove from heat. Spread mixture in greased 9-by-9-by-2-inch baking pan. Cover; chill until firm, about 30 minutes. Cut evenly into 4 squares; then cut each square diagonally into quarters to form 4 triangles.

In large nonstick skillet, over medium-high heat, cook half the triangles in 2 teaspoons margarine until crisp and golden on each side, about 5 minutes; remove from skillet and keep warm. Repeat with remaining triangles and margarine. Sprinkle cheese over warm polenta to melt. Meanwhile, combine tomato, green pepper, green onions, lime juice, jalapeño, and cilantro or parsley; serve with polenta.

Sesame Green Beans and Red Pepper

©1996 Reckitt & Colman Inc.

Makes 6 servings

- 3 tablespoons FRANK'S® Original REDHOT® Cayenne Pepper Sauce
- 1 tablespoon sesame seeds, toasted
- 1 tablespoon olive oil
- 1 tablespoon soy sauce
- 2 teaspoons grated gingerroot
- 1 teaspoon minced garlic
- ¼ teaspoon Oriental sesame oil
- 1 pound green beans, washed and cut in half
- ½ cup thinly sliced red bell pepper

In large bowl, whisk together all ingredients *except* vegetables.

In large skillet, cook green beans in boiling water and cover 5 minutes until crisp-tender. Rinse with cold water; drain.

Add beans and red pepper to dressing in bowl. Toss to coat. Cover; refrigerate 1 hour.

Preparation time: 20 minutes   *Cook time:* 10 minutes

Ritz Cracker Stuffing

Nabisco Foods Group

Makes about 6 cups

- 1 cup coarsely chopped mushrooms *or* broccoli
- ½ cup chopped onion
- ½ cup chopped celery
- ¼ cup FLEISCHMANN'S Margarine
- 4 Stay Fresh Packs RITZ Crackers, coarsely crushed (about 7 cups crumbs)
- 2 cups PLANTERS GOLD MEASURE Walnuts, Pecans *or* Almonds, coarsely chopped

- ¼ cup snipped parsley
- 1 tablespoon poultry seasoning
- ½ teaspoon ground black pepper
- 1 (13¾-fluid ounce) can COLLEGE INN Chicken Broth
- 2 eggs, beaten

In skillet, over medium heat, cook mushrooms or broccoli, onion, and celery in margarine until tender.

In large bowl, combine cracker crumbs, nuts, parsley, poultry seasoning, pepper, and vegetable mixture. Add broth and eggs, tossing until well combined. Spoon into 2-quart baking dish or pan; cover. Bake at 325°F for 30 to 40 minutes or until heated through. Or use as a stuffing for turkey, chicken, or pork.

To Microwave: In 2½-quart microwave-proof bowl, combine mushrooms or broccoli, onion, celery, and spread or better blend; cover. Microwave on HIGH (100% power) for 3 to 4 minutes or until tender. Stir in remaining ingredients as above; cover. Microwave on HIGH for 10 to 12 minutes or until hot, stirring after 6 minutes.

Note: For fewer servings, recipe can be halved. Spoon into 1-quart baking dish. Cover; bake at 325°F for 25 to 30 minutes, or microwave on HIGH for 6 to 8 minutes.

RICE DISHES

Artichoke Rice Bake

Lawry's Foods, Inc.

Makes 4 servings

2 tablespoons Imperial® Margarine

8 ounces fresh mushrooms, sliced

1 small onion, chopped

1½ teaspoons Lawry's® Garlic Salt

½ teaspoon Lawry's® Seasoned Pepper

2 cups chicken broth

1 cup long-grain rice

2 medium tomatoes, chopped

2 cans (7 ounces each) artichoke hearts, drained and quartered

Chopped parsley for garnish

In large skillet, melt margarine and sauté mushrooms, onion, garlic salt, and seasoned pepper until tender. Add broth and rice. Bring to a boil; reduce heat, cover, and simmer 25 minutes or until liquid is absorbed. Stir in tomatoes and artichoke hearts; let stand 2 minutes. Garnish with chopped parsley.

Variation: For a Cajun-style main dish, stir in 1 cup of cooked shrimp, chicken, or pork and ½ teaspoon hot pepper sauce.

Spanish Millet (or Rice)

Beatrice Cheese, Inc.

Makes 6 servings

2 cups cooked millet *or* brown rice

1 cup cooked lentils

1 cup tomatoes, chopped and drained

½ can tomato paste

¼ cup chopped green pepper

½ cup minced onion

½ teaspoon black pepper

1½ teaspoons garlic powder

1 teaspoon sugar

1¾ cup County Line® Sharp Colby Cheese, shredded

Preheat oven to 375°F. Mix together all ingredients except cheese. Place half of mixture in greased 2-quart baking dish. Sprinkle *1¼ cups* shredded cheese over top. Add remaining mixture. Bake 30 minutes. Remove from oven and sprinkle remaining shredded cheese on top; return to oven until cheese is melted, about 10 minutes.

Almond Wild Rice Bake

Dole Food Company

Makes 6 to 8 servings

1 cup raw wild rice

2¼ cups water, divided

½ teaspoon salt

4 cups sliced fresh mushrooms

1 small onion, chopped

½ cup sliced Dole® Celery

¼ cup margarine

1 pound lean ground beef

1 cup light sour cream

1 cup Dole® Whole Natural Almonds, toasted

¼ cup teriyaki sauce

¼ teaspoon cracked black pepper

1 cup Dole® Raisins Chopped parsley for garnish (optional)

Preheat oven to 350°F. Simmer rice, covered, in *2 cups* water with salt for 45 minutes. In large ovenproof skillet, sauté mushrooms, onion, and celery in margarine until onion is soft. Push to sides of skillet. Add beef. Cook until redness disappears. Stir and combine with sautéed vegetables in skillet. Add rice, remaining ¼ *cup* water, sour cream, almonds, teriyaki sauce, and black pepper to skillet. Bake, uncovered, 40 minutes. Stir several times. Stir in raisins. Garnish with chopped parsley, if desired.

Parmesan Rice

Lindsay International, Inc.

Makes 8 servings

½ cup chopped onion
2 tablespoons butter *or* margarine
1 can (28 ounces) tomatoes, cut up undrained
1 cup water
¾ cup long-grain rice
½ cup dry white wine

2 teaspoons instant chicken bouillon granules
Several dashes bottle hot pepper sauce
Dash pepper
⅓ cup grated Parmesan cheese
½ cup Lindsay® Small Pitted Ripe Olives, drained

In a 3-quart saucepan cook onion in butter or margarine until tender but not brown. Stir in undrained tomatoes, water, rice, wine, bouillon granules, pepper sauce, and pepper. Cover; simmer about 30 minutes or until rice is done and most of liquid is absorbed. Reserve *2 tablespoons* Parmesan cheese. Stir olives and remaining Parmesan cheese into rice mixture; heat through. Sprinkle with reserved Parmesan before serving.

Cheesy Rice Casserole

©1996 Reckitt & Colman Inc.

Makes 6 servings

2 cups hot cooked rice
1⅓ cups (2.8 ounce can) FRENCH'S® French Fried Onions

1 cup sour cream
1 jar (16 ounces) medium salsa
1 cup shredded Cheddar cheese

Mix rice and ⅔ *cup* French Fried Onions; spoon half the rice in 2-quart microwave dish. Top with sour cream.

Spoon half the salsa and cheese on top. Cover with remaining rice, salsa, and cheese.

Cover; microwave 8 minutes or until hot. Top with ⅔ *cup* onions. Microwave 1 minute.

Conventional Directions: Prepare as above. Bake, uncovered, at 350°F for 30 to 35 minutes or until hot. Top with remaining onions; bake 5 minutes until onions are golden.

Preparation time: 15 minutes   *Cook time:* 9 minutes

Corn and Rice Casserole

Nabisco Foods Group

Makes 8 servings

3 (13¾-fluid ounce) cans COLLEGE INN Garden Vegetable Broth, divided
1 cup long-grain rice
1 (15-ounce) can corn, drained

1 cup chopped onion
¾ cup chopped red *or* green bell pepper
2 cups shredded sharp Cheddar cheese (8 ounces)
Salt and pepper to taste

Preheat oven to 350°F. In 2-quart covered saucepan, over high heat, heat 2 cans broth to a boil. Stir in rice; cook according to package directions until rice is tender. In greased 2-quart oblong baking dish, combine cooked rice, corn, onion, red pepper, cheese, remaining 1 can broth, and salt and pepper to taste. Bake uncovered, for 40 to 45 minutes or until hot. Serve warm.

Cheesy Broccoli & Rice

©1996 Reckitt & Colman Inc.

Makes 6 servings

1 package (4.4 ounces) chicken flavor rice & sauce mix

1⅓ cups (2.8 ounce can) FRENCH'S® French Fried Onions

1 cup *each* chopped broccoli and red pepper

1 cup cubed pasteurized process cheese

Bring rice mix and *2 cups water* to a boil in saucepan.

Stir in ⅔ *cup* French Fried Onions, vegetables, and cheese. Simmer 10 minutes until rice is tender, stirring. Sprinkle with ⅔ *cup* onions.

Preparation time: 5 minutes   *Cook time:* 10 minutes

Pasta Main Dishes

Spicy Shrimp with Fusille

Ragú Foods Co.

Makes 4 servings

- 1 pound medium shrimp, peeled and deveined
- 2 tablespoons butter
- 1 jar (28 ounces) Ragú® Fino Italian Brand Pasta Sauce
- Tabasco sauce to taste
- Salt to taste
- Pepper to taste
- ¾ package (16-ounce size) fusille, cooked and drained
- 1 tablespoon chopped fresh parsley

In large skillet, lightly sauté shrimp in butter. Add pasta sauce, Tabasco sauce, salt, and pepper. Simmer, covered, until shrimp are cooked. Spoon sauce over hot cooked pasta; toss to coat well. Top pasta with shrimp; sprinkle with parsley.

Penńe with Mushroom Clam Sauce and Cheeses

Beatrice Cheese, Inc.

Makes 4 to 6 servings

- 2 tablespoons butter *or* margarine
- 2 tablespoons olive oil
- 1 small white onion, chopped
- ½ pound mushrooms, cleaned and sliced
- 1 teaspoon garlic powder
- ½ cup Marsala wine
- 1 can (8 ounces) clams, chopped, with juice
- 1 pound penńe (or other tubular pasta)
- ¾ cup whipping cream
- ½ cup shredded County Line® Mozzarella Cheese
- ½ cup shredded County Line® Swiss Cheese
- ½ cup crumbled blue cheese
- 6 sprigs parsley, chopped
- Fresh ground pepper

Melt butter in 12-inch skillet. Add olive oil, onion, and mushrooms; sauté until tender. Add ½ *teaspoon* garlic powder and wine. Bring to a boil; reduce heat, add clams, and cook until thickened. Cook pasta according to package instructions; drain. Meanwhile, in double boiler, mix together cream, ½ *teaspoon* garlic powder, and cheeses. Stir until melted. Keep warm.

In a large bowl, mix together pasta, cheese mixture, clam/mushroom mixture, and parsley. Serve immediately with fresh ground pepper.

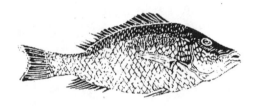

Pasta with Fish Sauce

Lindsay International, Inc.

Makes 6 servings

1 large onion, chopped
1 clove garlic, minced
2 tablespoons butter *or* margarine
1 can (28 ounces) tomatoes, cut up, undrained
½ teaspoon dried oregano, crushed
¼ teaspoon dried basil, crushed

⅛ teaspoon pepper
1 can (7½ ounces) minced clams
1 package (16 ounces) frozen fish fillets, partially thawed and cut into 1-inch cubes
½ cup Lindsay® Small Pitted drained
Hot cooked linguine *or* spaghetti

In Dutch oven, cook onion and garlic in butter until tender. Stir in *undrained* tomatoes, oregano, basil, and pepper. Drain clams, adding liquid to tomato mixture. Simmer, uncovered, about 30 minutes, stirring occasionally. Add fish, olives, and clams to sauce. Simmer, covered, 5 minutes, stirring once. Serve over pasta.

Pasta Primavera

Dole Food Company

Makes 8 servings

1 package (8 ounces) pasta	¼ cup chopped parsley
1 clove garlic, pressed	2 tablespoons olive oil
1 Dole® Red Bell Pepper, slivered	1 tablespoon sweet basil, crumbled
½ pound snow peas	Black pepper (optional)
3 cups Dole® Broccoli florets	¼ cup grated Parmesan cheese
1 cup diced Dole® Green Onions	

Cook pasta according to package directions. Meanwhile, in 12-inch skillet, sauté garlic with all remaining vegetables in oil 1 minute. Cover and steam 5 minutes. Shake skillet occasionally. Add basil and cooked pasta. Toss well until pasta is heated through. Turn onto serving platter. Sprinkle generously with black pepper, if desired, and Parmesan cheese.

Springtime Noodles Alfredo

Lipton

Makes about 4 servings

2 tablespoons butter *or* margarine	1 package Lipton® Noodles & Sauce—Alfredo
2 medium carrots, sliced	1 cup milk

1 medium zucchini *or* yellow squash, thinly sliced
1 medium clove garlic, finely chopped
1⅓ cups-water

1 tablespoon snipped fresh dill *or* ½ teaspoon dried dill weed (optional)
½ cup frozen peas, thawed (optional)
Pepper to taste

In 12-inch skillet, melt butter over medium-high heat and cook carrots, zucchini, and garlic, stirring occasionally, 3 minutes or until vegetables are tender; remove and set aside. In same skillet, add water and milk and bring to the boiling point. Stir in Noodles & Sauce—Alfredo and dill and continue boiling over medium heat, stirring occasionally, 7 minutes or until noodles are tender. Stir in vegetables, peas, and pepper; heat through. Sprinkle, if desired, with grated Parmesan cheese. Garnish with carrot and dill.

To microwave: In 1½-quart microwave-safe casserole, microwave butter, carrots, zucchini, and garlic, uncovered, at HIGH (Full Power) 6 minutes or until vegetables are tender, stirring once; remove and set aside. In same casserole, stir in water, milk, and Noodles & Sauce—Alfredo. Microwave 11 minutes or until noodles are tender. Stir in vegetables, dill, peas, and pepper; cover and let stand 2 minutes. Serve as above.

Pepperoni Pasta Ruffles

Ragú Foods Co.

Makes 4 to 6 servings

1 small green pepper, diced
1 small red pepper, diced

8 ounces mozzarella cheese, diced

1 tablespoon olive oil
1 jar (30¾ ounces) Ragú®
   Thick and Hearty Spaghetti
   Sauce
1 package (3½ ounces)
   sliced pepperoni, halved

1 package (14 ounces) pasta
   ruffles, cooked and
   drained
Salt to taste
Pepper to taste

In large skillet, sauté green and red peppers in hot olive oil until tender. Add spaghetti sauce and simmer over low heat, stirring occasionally, about 10 minutes or until heated through. Spoon sauce, pepperoni, and cheese over hot pasta; toss to coat well. Season to taste with salt and pepper.

Stuffed Shells Primavera

Ragú Foods Co.

Makes 6 servings

2 cups chopped fresh
   broccoli
2 medium zucchini,
   shredded
1 cup chopped fresh
   mushrooms
1 small onion, chopped
½ cup finely chopped carrots
2 tablespoons butter
Pinch nutmeg
Salt to taste
Pepper to taste
1 pound ricotta cheese

2 cups (8 ounces) shredded
   mozzarella cheese
1 egg, lightly beaten
¼ cup grated Parmesan
   cheese
3 tablespoons chopped fresh
   basil
1 package (12 ounces)
   jumbo pasta shells for
   stuffing, cooked and
   drained
1 jar (30 ounces) Ragú®
   Chunky Gardenstyle
   Spaghetti Sauce

Preheat oven to 350°F. In large skillet, sauté broccoli, zucchini, mushrooms, onion, and carrots in butter until vegetables are tender. Season with nutmeg, salt, and pepper. In large bowl, thoroughly combine ricotta cheese, mozzarella cheese, egg, Parmesan cheese, and basil. Add sautéed vegetables; stir to mix well. Spoon *1 cup* spaghetti sauce evenly in a 13-by-9-inch baking dish. Fill shells with vegetable/cheese mixture. Arrange in baking dish. Spoon remaining sauce over shells. Bake, covered, 45 minutes. Uncover and bake 10 minutes or until bubbly.

Vegetable Market Capellini

Classico® di Napoli Pasta Sauce

Makes 6 to 8 servings

1 cup sliced fresh mushrooms

¾ cup chopped onion

2 cloves garlic, chopped

2 tablespoons olive oil

2 (26-ounce) jars Classico® di Napoli Tomato-Basil Pasta Sauce

1½ teaspoons dried Italian seasoning

1 (6-ounce) jar artichoke hearts marinated in olive oil, drained and chopped

1½ cups fresh small broccoli florets

1½ cups fresh small cauliflowerets

½ cup coarsely chopped yellow bell pepper

1 (1-pound) package capellini, cooked as package directs and drained

Freshly grated Parmesan cheese

In large saucepan, over medium heat, cook and stir mushrooms, onion, and garlic in oil until vegetables are tender. Add pasta sauce and Italian seasoning. Cover; simmer 15 minutes. Add remaining vegetables. Cover; simmer 20 minutes longer or until vegetables are tender. Serve over hot cooked capellini with grated Parmesan cheese if desired. Refrigerate leftovers.

Florentine Stuffed Shells

Sargento Cheese Company, Inc.

Makes 8 servings

24 uncooked jumbo pasta shells for filling

1 package (10 ounces) frozen chopped spinach, thawed

1 egg, beaten

2 cups (15 ounces) Sargento® Ricotta Cheese

1½ cups (6 ounces) Sargento® Shredded *or* Fancy Shredded Mozzarella Cheese

⅓ cup finely chopped onion

2 cloves garlic, minced

¼ teaspoon salt

⅛ teaspoon ground nutmeg

2 cups meatless spaghetti sauce

½ cup (2 ounces) Sargento® Grated Parmesan Cheese

Preheat oven to 350°F. Cook pasta shells according to package directions. Squeeze spinach to remove as much moisture as possible. Combine spinach, egg, ricotta and mozzarella cheeses, onion, garlic, salt, and nutmeg; stir to blend well. Stuff shells with ricotta mixture, using about *3 tablespoons* for each shell. Arrange in lightly greased 13-by-9-inch baking dish. Pour spaghetti sauce over shells. Sprinkle with grated cheese. Bake, covered, 30 to 40 minutes.

Singapore Spicy Noodles

Lawry's Foods, Inc.

Makes 4 servings

1¼ cups water
2 tablespoons ketchup
2½ teaspoons packed brown sugar
1½ teaspoons chopped cilantro
1 teaspoon cornstarch
¾ teaspoon Lawry's® Seasoned Salt
¾ teaspoon Lawry's® Garlic Powder with Parsley

¼ teaspoon crushed red pepper
2½ tablespoons chunky peanut butter
¼ cup sliced green onions
8 ounces linguine, cooked and drained
1 cup shredded red cabbage
Green onion curls for garnish

In medium saucepan, combine water, ketchup, sugar, cilantro, cornstarch, and seasonings. Bring to a boil. Reduce heat; simmer, uncovered, 5 minutes. Cool 10 minutes; blend in peanut butter and green onions. Toss sauce with hot linguine and red cabbage. Garnish with green onion curls. Serve with a marinated cucumber salad.

Variation: For a heartier entrée, add cooked shredded chicken or pork.

Pasta Cintoro

Lawry's Foods, Inc.

Makes 4 servings

- 2 tablespoons Imperial® Margarine
- 2 tablespoons olive *or* vegetable oil
- 1 teaspoon dried basil, crushed
- ¾ teaspoon Lawry's® Garlic Powder with Parsley
- ½ teaspoon Lawry's® Lemon Pepper Seasoning
- ½ cup chopped red bell pepper
- 1 medium zucchini, cut into 1-inch julienne strips
- 1 cup thinly sliced mushrooms
- 2 medium tomatoes, chopped
- ¼ to ½ cup chicken broth
- 8 ounces angel hair pasta, cooked
- Parmesan cheese

In large skillet, melt margarine. Add olive oil, basil, garlic powder with parsley, and lemon pepper seasoning; blend well. Add vegetables and lightly sauté. Add chicken broth and heat 1 minute. Add pasta and toss to coat with vegetable mixture.

Serve with a light sprinkling of Parmesan cheese.

Veal Sauce Lucia

Lawry's Foods, Inc.

Makes 4 servings

2 tablespoons vegetable oil
1½ pounds veal stew meat, cut into bite-size cubes
1 medium onion, chopped
1 medium carrot, grated
¾ teaspoon dried basil, crushed
¾ teaspoon Lawry's® Garlic Powder with Parsley
1 package (1.5 ounces) Lawry's® Extra Rich and Thick Spaghetti Sauce Spices and Seasonings
1¾ cups water
1 can (6 ounces) tomato paste
½ cup frozen peas
8 ounces linguine *or* other pasta of your choice, cooked and drained

In Dutch oven, heat oil and brown veal; drain fat. Add onion, carrot, basil, and garlic powder with parsley; sauté 5 minutes. Add spaghetti sauce spices and seasonings, water, and tomato paste; blend well. Bring to a boil; reduce heat and simmer, covered, 30 minutes. Add peas and heat 5 minutes. Ladle sauce over hot pasta.

Serve with Caesar salad and garlic bread.

Wine-Cheese Sauced Pasta

Lindsay International, Inc.

Makes 8 servings

¼ cup chopped onion
3 tablespoons butter *or* margarine
¼ cup all-purpose flour
2½ cups (10 ounces) shredded Monterey jack cheese
1½ cups (6 ounces) shredded Gruyère cheese

1 teaspoon instant chicken
bouillon granules
¼ teaspoon white pepper
2⅓ cups milk
½ cup dry white wine

1 cup Lindsey® Extra Large
Pitted Ripe Olives, drained
2 tablespoons chopped
pimiento
Hot cooked spinach fettuccine
or other pasta

In saucepan, cook onion in butter until tender. Stir in flour, bouillon granules, and white pepper. Add milk all at once. Cook and stir until thickened and bubbly. Add wine. Gradually stir in cheeses just until melted. Stir in olives and pimiento. Serve atop fettuccine.

Fettuccine with Herbed Cheese Sauce

Sargento Cheese Company, Inc.

Makes 6 servings

3 tablespoons butter *or*
margarine
⅓ cup sliced green onion
1 clove garlic, minced
1 tablespoon flour
½ teaspoon salt
½ teaspoon basil
½ teaspoon oregano
¼ teaspoon pepper
1¾ cups milk

1 cup (4 ounces)
Sargento® Shredded *or*
Fancy Shredded
Mozzarella Cheese
1 cup (8 ounces) Sargento®
Ricotta Cheese
3 tablespoons chopped
parsley
10 ounces fettuccine *or*
spaghetti

In medium saucepan, melt butter. Add onion and garlic. Cook until tender, about 5 minutes. Stir in flour, salt, basil, oregano, and pepper. Gradually stir in milk. Cook and stir until thick and bubbly. Remove from heat. Add cheeses; stir until melted and thoroughly combined. Stir in parsley; keep warm. Meanwhile, cook fettuccine according to package directions. Toss immediately with cheese sauce.

Hearty Manicotti

Sargento Cheese Company, Inc.

Makes 6 servings

1¼ cups water, divided
1 pound Italian sweet sausage links
1 pound ground beef
1 medium onion, chopped
1 can (15 ounces) tomato purée
1 can (6 ounces) tomato paste
1 teaspoon sugar
½ teaspoon black pepper
1¾ teaspoons basil, divided

1½ teaspoons salt, divided
1 package (12 ounces) manicotti shells
2 cups (15 ounces) Sargento® Ricotta Cheese
2 cups (8 ounces) Sargento® Shredded Low-Moisture Part-Skim Mozzarella Cheese, divided
2 tablespoons chopped parsley
Sargento® Grated Parmesan Cheese (optional)

Preheat oven to 375°F. In 5-quart covered Dutch oven, combine ¼ *cup* water and sausage; cook over medium heat 5 minutes. Uncover and allow sausage to brown well; drain sausage on paper towels.

Brown beef and onion in Dutch oven over medium heat; drain. Stir in tomato purée, tomato paste, sugar, pepper, *1 teaspoon* basil, *1 teaspoon* salt, and *1 cup* water; simmer, covered, 45 minutes.

Cut sausage into bite-size pieces; add to beef mixture. Simmer 15 minutes, stirring occasionally.

Meanwhile, cook manicotti shells according to package directions; rinse and drain well.

In large bowl, combine ricotta and *1 cup* mozzarella cheese, parsley, ¾ *teaspoon* basil, and ½ *teaspoon* salt. Spoon into shells and set aside.

Spoon half of meat sauce into large, shallow baking dish. Arrange cheese-stuffed shells over sauce. Spoon remaining sauce over shells. Sprinkle with remaining mozzarella cheese. Bake 30 minutes. Serve with grated cheese, if desired.

Tangy Asparagus Linguine

Sargento Cheese Company, Inc.

Makes 4 servings

- 5 ounces linguine
- 2 tablespoons light margarine
- ¼ cup finely chopped onion
- 3 cloves garlic, minced
- 8 ounces fresh asparagus, peeled and sliced diagonally into ½-inch pieces
- 2 tablespoons dry white wine
- 2 tablespoons fresh lemon juice
- Freshly ground black pepper
- ¼ cup (1 ounce) Sargento® Grated Parmesan
- ¾ cup (3 ounces) Sargento® Preferred Light® Fancy Shredded Mozzarella Cheese
- Strips of lemon zest (optional)

Chop and measure all ingredients before beginning. Bring water to a boil and cook linguine to al dente (firm to the bite). Drain. Meanwhile, melt margarine over medium heat in a large skillet. Sauté onions and garlic until onions are soft. Add asparagus and continue to sauté for 2 minutes. Add wine and lemon juice and cook an additional minute. Season with pepper to taste. Remove from the heat. Toss with hot pasta and Parmesan cheese. Remove to serving platter and top with mozzarella cheese. Garnish with strips of lemon zest, if desired. Serve immediately.

Vegetable 'n Chicken Alfredo

Sargento Cheese Company, Inc.

Makes 4 servings

4 tablespoons butter *or* margarine, divided
3 tablespoons flour
3 cups milk
¾ cup (3 ounces) Sargento® Grated Parmesan Cheese
½ teaspoon basil
¼ teaspoon salt
¼ teaspoon pepper
1 tablespoon vegetable oil
3 chicken-breast halves, boned, skinned, and cut into thin strips

¼ cup thinly sliced green onions
4 cups sliced fresh vegetables (broccoli, mushrooms, green *or* red bell peppers, celery, green beans, carrots, zucchini)
½ pound pasta, cooked and drained
Additional Sargento® Grated Parmesan Cheese

In medium saucepan, melt 2 tablespoons butter. Add flour and cook over low heat 2 minutes, stirring occasionally. Whisk in milk. Bring to a simmer and cook over medium heat until thickened, stirring constantly. Stir in ¾ *cup* grated cheese, basil, salt, and pepper. Set aside; keep warm.

Heat remaining butter and oil in large frying pan. Add chicken and cook over medium heat, stirring constantly until cooked through. Remove chicken from pan; set aside.

In same pan, cook green onions and other vegetables until crisp-tender, about 5 minutes. Toss vegetables with hot pasta and chicken. Serve with sauce and additional grated cheese.

Garden Vegetable Spaghetti Sauce

Contadina Foods, Inc., Nestlé Food Company

Makes 8 servings, about 7 cups total

3 tablespoons olive oil
1 cup julienne-cut green pepper
1 cup sliced mushrooms
1 cup julienne-cut carrots
1 cup chopped onion
1 cup halved and sliced zucchini
½ cup broccoli florets
2 large cloves garlic, minced
1¾ cups (14½-ounce can) Contadina® Whole Peeled Tomatoes and juice, cut up

1⅓ cups (12-ounce can) Contadina® Tomato Paste
2 cups water
¼ cup red wine *or* beef broth
1 tablespoon capers, rinsed (optional)
1 teaspoon dried basil leaves, crushed
1 teaspoon dried oregano leaves, crushed
¾ teaspoon salt
¼ teaspoon pepper
1 pound (16 ounces) dry spaghetti, cooked and drained

In large saucepan, heat oil; sauté pepper, mushrooms, carrots, onion, zucchini, broccoli, and garlic for 2 to 3 minutes or until onion is translucent. Stir in tomatoes and juice, tomato paste, water, wine, capers (if desired), basil, oregano, salt, and pepper. Bring to a boil; reduce heat and simmer for 20 to 30 minutes, stirring occasionally. Serve over hot spaghetti.

Homestyle Lasagna Rolls

Ragú Foods Co.

Makes 6 servings

1½ pounds ground beef
 1 cup chopped fresh mushrooms
 1 medium onion, finely chopped
 1 small carrot, minced
 1 clove garlic, minced
 ¼ cup dry red wine
 ⅛ teaspoon nutmeg
 ⅛ teaspoon cayenne pepper
 Salt to taste

Pepper to taste
 2 cups (8 ounces) shredded mozzarella cheese
 1 egg, lightly beaten
 ¼ cup grated Parmesan cheese
 1 jar (28 ounces) Ragú® Slow-Cooked Homestyle Spaghetti Sauce
 ¾ package (16-ounce size) lasagna noodles, cooked and drained

Preheat oven to 350°F. In large skillet, thoroughly brown ground beef; drain fat. Add mushrooms, onion, carrot, and garlic; sauté until vegetables are tender. Add wine, nutmeg, cayenne pepper, salt, and pepper; cook until wine is almost evaporated. Remove from heat; allow to cool 10 to 15 minutes. In medium bowl, thoroughly combine meat mixture, mozzarella cheese, egg, and *1 tablespoon* Parmesan cheese. Pour *½ jar* spaghetti sauce in a 13-by-9-inch baking dish. Evenly spread *⅓ cup* meat filling over length of each lasagna noodle. Carefully roll up noodle. Place seam side down in baking dish. Repeat with remaining noodles. Evenly spread remaining sauce over lasagna rolls. Bake, covered, 40 minutes. Uncover; sprinkle with *3 tablespoons* Parmesan cheese. Bake 5 minutes or until bubbly.

Classic Lasagna

Best Foods, a division of CPC International Inc.

Makes 12 servings

- 1 container (15 ounces) ricotta cheese *or* 1 pound cream-style cottage cheese
- 1 egg, beaten slightly
- 1 cup grated Parmesan cheese

Meat Sauce (see below)
- 1 pound Mueller's® Lasagne, cooked, as package directs, and drained
- 12 ounces mozzarella cheese

In bowl stir together ricotta cheese, egg, and ¾ *cup* Parmesan cheese. In 13-by-9-by-2-inch baking dish spread *1½ cups* Meat Sauce. Layer *⅓ cup* cooked lasagna noodles, *2 cups* sauce, one half of ricotta cheese mixture, and one third of mozzarella cheese. Repeat. Top with remaining noodles, sauce, and cheeses. Bake at 350°F for 50 minutes or until bubbly.

Meat Sauce

Makes 7½ cups

- 1 pound ground beef
- 1 chopped onion
- 2 tablespoons Mazola® Corn Oil
- 2 cans (28 ounces each) tomatoes
- 1 can (6 ounces) tomato paste

- 3 cloves garlic, minced
- ½ cup chopped parsley
- 2 teaspoons sugar
- 1½ teaspoons salt
- 2 teaspoons dried basil
- 1 teaspoon dried oregano
- ¼ teaspoon pepper

In 5-quart Dutch oven heat corn oil over medium heat. Add ground beef, onion, garlic, and parsley. Stirring frequently, cook about 10 minutes or until beef is browned. Place tomatoes in blender container; cover. Blend on high speed 30 seconds or until finely chopped. Add to beef mixture. Stir in tomato paste, sugar, basil, salt, oregano, and pepper. Bring to a boil. Reduce heat and simmer, stirring occasionally, 45 minutes.

Colorful Pasta Bake

Kellogg Company

Makes 8 servings

- 1 package (8 ounces) uncooked spaghetti
- 8 ounces lean ground turkey
- 8 ounces lean ground beef
- 1 clove garlic, finely chopped
- ½ cup sliced onions
- 2 cans (8 ounces each) tomato sauce
- 1 can (14.5 ounces) diced tomatoes
- 1 beef bouillon cube
- 1 teaspoon Italian seasoning
- ½ teaspoon salt
- 2 cups diced zucchini
- 2 cups *KELLOGG'S® RICE KRISPIES®* cereal
- ⅓ cup Parmesan cheese
- 1 package (4 ounces, 1 cup) shredded Mozzarella cheese
- Vegetable cooking spray

Preheat oven to 350°F. Cook spaghetti according to package directions. Drain well.

While spaghetti cooks, brown meats, garlic, and onions in 3-quart saucepan over medium heat, stirring frequently. Drain juices, if necessary. Add tomato sauce, tomatoes, bouillon cube, Italian seasoning, salt, zucchini, and *KELLOGG'S® RICE KRISPIES®* cereal, mixing until combined. Cover and cook over medium heat until mixture starts to simmer, stirring occasionally. Reduce heat and simmer 5 minutes.

Place half of meat sauce in bottom of shallow 2-quart casserole dish coated with cooking spray. Spread spaghetti evenly over sauce and sprinkle with Parmesan cheese. Spread remaining sauce over spaghetti. Cover casserole.

Bake about 30 minutes or until heated through. Sprinkle with Mozzarella cheese and return to oven uncovered, 5 minutes longer or until cheese melts. Serve hot.

Preparation time: 45 minutes   *Baking time:* 35 minutes

Tortellini and Vegetables

Nabisco Foods Group

Makes 8 to 10 servings

3 (13¾-fluid ounce) cans COLLEGE INN Garden Vegetable Broth

1 (16-ounce) bag frozen mixed vegetables

1 (10-ounce) package frozen chopped spinach, partially thawed

1 (9-ounce) package refrigerated tortellini
Crushed red pepper flakes

In 3-quart saucepan, over high heat, heat broth to a boil. Add frozen mixed vegetables and spinach; return mixture to a boil. Reduce heat; simmer for 5 minutes. Add tortellini; simmer 3 to 4 minutes or until tortellini is tender. Serve warm, sprinkled with crushed red pepper.

Penńe with Arrabiatta Sauce

©1996 Reckitt & Colman Inc.

Makes 4 servings (3 cups sauce)

- 8 whole cloves garlic
- 1 can (28 ounces) crushed tomatoes in puree
- 3 tablespoons FRANK'S® Original REDHOT® Cayenne Pepper Sauce
- ¼ cup minced basil
- ¼ cup chopped sun-dried tomatoes in oil
- 8 Kalamata *or* Greek olives, pitted and chopped
- 1 tablespoon capers
- 4 cups hot cooked penne pasta

Heat *2 tablespoons olive oil* in large skillet; cook and stir garlic until lightly golden. Add remaining ingredients *except* pasta. Bring to a boil. Simmer, stirring, 10 minutes.

In serving bowl, toss pasta with half the sauce. Serve remaining sauce on the side.

Preparation time: 15 minutes   *Cook time:* 20 minutes

Irresistible Pièces de Résistance

Easy Family Favorites

ZESTY ONION MEATLOAF
Reckitt & Colman Inc.
255

CHEESY MEATLOAF
Wyler's® or Steero® Beef-Flavor
Bouillon Granules,
Borden® Process American Cheese
Food
256

SOUPERIOR MEAT LOAF
Lipton
256

APPLE-GLAZED HAM LOAF
Kellogg Company
257

HOT DIGGITY DOGS
Reckitt & Colman Inc.
258

ITALIAN STUFFED PEPPERS
Campbell Soup Company
258

TANGY TUNA AND RICE LOAF
Beatrice Cheese, Inc.
259

TUNA CRUZ MELT
Lawry's Foods, Inc.
260

CHICKEN TOSTADAS
Lindsay International, Inc.
261

KELLOGG'S CORN FLAKES®
ENCHILADAS
Kellogg Company
262

THE MAGIC OF CALIFORNIA DIP
The Story of Lipton Dip
263

CALIFORNIA ENCHILADAS
Lipton
265

TAMALE PIE
Lipton
266

TAOS TACOS
Lawry's Foods, Inc.
267

GARDEN TURKEY BURGER
Reckitt & Colman Inc.
268

BISTRO BURGER WITH
BLUE CHEESE
Reckitt & Colman Inc.
268

TEMPTING TACO BURGERS
Lipton
269

CHILI MUSHROOM BURGERS
JFC International, Inc.
270

FRENCH'S® ONION CRUNCH
BURGER
Reckitt & Colman Inc.
270

OVEN-ROAST PORK HAWAIIAN
Dole Food Company
289

PORK CHOPS WITH CREOLE
SAUCE
Lawry's Foods, Inc.
290

PORK CHOPS IN RAISIN SAUCE
Dole Food Company
290

ORANGE-HONEY GLAZED
PORK CHOPS
Ragú Foods Co.
291

PORK TENDERLOIN WITH
PLUM SAUCE
JFC International, Inc.
292

PORK STIR-FRY WITH
SPICY PLUM SAUCE
JFC International, Inc.
292

CHINA SUN PORK
Dole Food Company
293

TROPIC SUN SPARERIBS
Dole Food Company
294

ROSEMARY'S FINGER-LICKING
RIBS
Specialty Brands
294

COUNTRY GLAZED RIBS
Reckitt & Colman Inc.
295

GLAZED HAM WITH DIJON
PINEAPPLE SAUCE
Nabisco Foods Group
296

JUBILEE HAM WITH
RUM TE DUM SAUCE
Oscar Mayer Foods Corporation
297

OVEN-BARBECUED BEEF BRISKET
Nabisco Foods Group
297

HOT 'N SPICY BROCCOLI BEEF
Lawry's Foods, Inc.
298

STEAK AU POIVRE
WITH DIJON SAUCE
Reckitt & Colman Inc.
299

SIZZLING STEAK FAJITAS
Nabisco Foods Group
299

FRUITED BEEF WITH RICE
Lindsay International, Inc.
300

POPPY BEEF STROGANOFF
Specialty Brands
301

Poultry

Seafood

CLAM FRITTERS
McCormick & Company, Inc.
350

SALMON CURRY WITH MELON
McCormick & Company, Inc.
351

SALMON ORIENTAL
Lawry's Foods, Inc.
352

SPICY SCALLOPS WITH PEA
PODS
JFC International, Inc.
352

FISH STEAKS VERONIQUE
Lawry's Foods, Inc.
354

TUNA NOODLE CASSEROLE
Reckitt & Colman Inc.
355

MEDITERRANEAN BROILED FISH
Sargento Cheese Company, Inc.
355

GARLIC SHRIMP WITH NOODLES
Lipton
356

SHRIMP CREOLE
Lipton
357

CAJUN SPICY SHRIMP
Lawry's Foods, Inc.
358

ORANGE ROUGHY AU GRATIN
Lawry's Foods, Inc.
359

CRAB-STUFFED TROUT
Campbell Soup Company
360

BRAISED SNAPPER WITH SPICY
SAUCE
JFC International, Inc.
361

SOLE WITH VEGETABLES
Sargento Cheese Company, Inc.
362

CRISPY OVEN FISH
ReaLemon® Lemon Juice
from Concentrate
362

FISH ROLLS PRIMAVERA
ReaLemon® Lemon Juice
from Concentrate
363

CRISPY LEMON DILL
FISH FILLETS
Kellogg Company
363

EASY FAMILY FAVORITES

Zesty Onion Meatloaf

©1996 Reckitt & Colman Inc.

Makes 6 servings

1½ pounds ground beef
 1 can (11⅛ ounces)
    CAMPBELL'S® Condensed
    Italian Tomato Soup*
1⅓ cups (2.8 ounce can)
    FRENCH'S® French Fried
    Onions

 2 tablespoons FRENCH'S®
    Worcestershire Sauce
 ¾ teaspoon salt
 ¼ teaspoon pepper
 1 egg

Preheat oven to 350°F. Mix beef, *⅓ cup* soup, *⅔ cup* French Fried Onions, and remaining ingredients. Shape into loaf on baking dish.

Bake 1 hour until done; drain fat.

Spoon remaining soup over meatloaf. Top with *⅔ cup* onions. Bake 5 minutes until onions are golden.

*Or substitute 1 cup spaghetti sauce.

Preparation time: 10 minutes   *Cook time:* about 1 hour

Cheesy Meatloaf

Wyler's® or Steero® Beef-Flavor Bouillon Granules, Borden® Process American Cheese Food

Makes 6 to 8 servings

1½ pounds lean ground beef
2 cups fresh bread crumbs
1 cup tomato juice
⅓ cup chopped onion
2 eggs

2 teaspoons Wyler's® *or* Steero® Beef-Flavor Bouillon Granules
¼ teaspoon pepper
6 slices Borden® Process American Cheese Food

In large bowl, combine all ingredients except cheese food. In shallow baking dish, shape half the mixture into loaf. Cut *4 slices* cheese food into strips; arrange on meat. Top with remaining meat; press edges together to seal. Bake at 350°F for 1 hour or until set. Top with remaining cheese food slices. Refrigerate leftovers.

Souperior Meat Loaf

Lipton

Makes about 8 servings

1 envelope Lipton® Recipe Secrets® Onion Soup Mix
2 pounds ground beef
1½ cups bread crumbs

2 eggs
¾ cup water
⅓ cup ketchup

Preheat oven to 350°F. In large bowl, combine all ingredients. In a 13×9-inch baking or roasting pan, shape into loaf. Bake uncovered 1 hour or until done. Let stand 10 minutes before serving.

Variations: Also terrific with Lipton® Recipe Secrets® Beefy Onion, Onion-Mushroom, Beefy Mushroom, or Savory Herb with Garlic Soup Mix.

Apple-Glazed Ham Loaf

Kellogg Company

Makes 12 servings

- 1 jar (10 ounces) apple jelly
- ¼ cup firmly packed brown sugar
- 3 tablespoons lemon juice
- ½ teaspoon dry mustard
- 2 eggs
- 3 cups *KELLOGG'S CORN FLAKES®* cereal, crushed to ¾ cup
- ¼ cup firmly packed brown sugar
- ¾ cup skim milk
- ⅓ cup finely chopped onion
- ¼ teaspoon pepper
- 1½ teaspoons dry mustard
- 1 pound ground cooked ham
- 1 pound ground pork
- Vegetable Cooking Spray

Preheat oven to 350°F. To make glaze, stir together jelly, ¼ cup sugar, lemon juice, and the ½ teaspoon mustard in small saucepan. Cook over low heat, stirring frequently, until jelly melts. Bring to a boil, cooking 1 minute longer, stirring constantly. Remove from heat. Cool to room temperature. In large mixing bowl, beat eggs slightly. Add *KELLOGG'S CORN FLAKES®* cereal, ¼ cup sugar, milk, onion, pepper, and 1½ teaspoons mustard. Beat well. Add ham and pork. Mix until combined. Shape into loaf and place in shallow baking pan coated with cooking spray. Bake about 1 hour and 15 minutes or until well browned. Brush loaf with glaze 2 to 3 times during last 30 minutes of baking. Serve with remaining glaze.

Hot Diggity Dogs

©1996 Reckitt & Colman Inc.

Makes 10 servings and 2½ cups onion topping

2 tablespoons butter *or* margarine
2 large (1 pound) sweet onions, thinly sliced
½ cup FRENCH'S® Classic Yellow® Mustard
½ cup ketchup
10 frankfurters
10 frankfurter buns

Melt butter in medium skillet over medium heat. Cook onion for 10 minutes until very tender, stirring often. Stir in mustard and ketchup. Cook over low heat for 2 minutes, stirring often.

Place frankfurters and buns on grid. Grill over medium heat until frankfurters are browned and buns are toasted.

To serve: Spoon onion mixture into buns; top with frankfurters.

Tip: Serve onion topping on hamburgers or smoked sausage heros, too

Preparation time: 5 minutes   *Cook time:* 20 minutes

Italian Stuffed Peppers

Campbell Soup Company

Makes 8 servings

5 large green *or* sweet red peppers
1 pound ground beef
½ pound sweet Italian sausage, casing removed
½ cup chopped onion
2 large cloves garlic, minced
1 teaspoon dried oregano leaves, crushed
1 can (10¼ ounces) Franco-American® Beef Gravy
2 tablespoons tomato paste
½ cup diced mozzarella cheese
¼ cup grated Parmesan cheese (or more, if desired)
Hot cooked rice

Preheat oven to 350°F. Cut 4 peppers in half lengthwise; discard seed and membranes. Chop remaining pepper; reserve. In 10-inch skillet in ¾ inch boiling water, place pepper halves, cut side down, overlapping to fit. Reduce heat to low. Cover; simmer 5 minutes. Remove from heat. Drain peppers on paper towels. Empty water from skillet; dry skillet. In same skillet, over medium-high heat, cook beef, sausage, reserved chopped pepper, and onion with garlic and oregano until meat is browned and vegetables are tender, stirring to separate meat. Spoon off fat. Stir in gravy and tomato paste. Heat to boiling. Reduce heat to low; simmer 5 minutes. Remove from heat. Stir in cheeses. Spoon meat mixture into pepper shells. In 13-by-9-inch baking dish, arrange stuffed peppers. Cover with foil. Bake 25 minutes or until hot. Serve over rice with additional Parmesan cheese, if desired.

Tangy Tuna and Rice Loaf

Beatrice Cheese, Inc.

Makes 4 to 6 servings

- 2 envelopes unflavored gelatin
- ½ cup cold water
- 1 can (8 ounces) tomato sauce
- 1 cup cooked rice
- ¼ cup chopped green pepper
- 1 cup grated County Line® Medium Sharp Cheddar Cheese
- ½ cup sour cream
- Few drops hot pepper sauce
- ½ teaspoon salt
- ½ teaspoon onion salt
- 1 teaspoon Worcestershire sauce
- 1 can (6½ ounces) flaked tuna

Soften gelatin in cold water. In saucepan, heat tomato sauce; add gelatin and stir until dissolved. Add remaining ingredients. Blend well, and pour into greased 9-by-

5-inch loaf pan. Chill until set. Unmold and slice. Garnish with egg slices and fresh parsley.

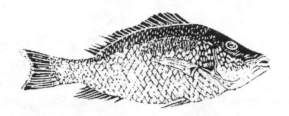

Tuna Cruz Melt

Lawry's Foods, Inc.

Makes 4 servings

- 1 can (12½ ounces) water-packed white tuna, drained
- 1 can (4 ounces) diced green chilies, drained
- 1 can (2.2 ounces) sliced pitted ripe olives, drained
- ¼ cup mayonnaise
- ½ teaspoon Lawry's® Seasoned Salt
- 4 flour tortillas
- 1 cup (4 ounces) grated Cheddar cheese
- 1 green onion with top, chopped
- Parsley for garnish

In medium bowl, flake tuna. Add chilies, olives, mayonnaise, and seasoned salt; blend well. Spoon ¼ of mixture onto each tortilla. Top with equal portions of Cheddar cheese. Place on broiler pan and broil, 4 inches from heat, until cheese is hot and bubbly. Sprinkle each tortilla with green onion. Garnish each serving with parsley. Serve open-faced, or fold over soft-taco style.

Chicken Tostadas

Lindsay International, Inc.

Makes 6 servings

6 (6-inch) tortillas
Cooking oil
2 whole medium chicken
   breasts, skinned, boned,
   and cut into thin strips
¼ cup sliced green onions
2 tablespoons butter *or*
   margarine
1 can (8 ounces) tomato
   sauce

½ teaspoon garlic salt
¼ teaspoon ground cumin
2 cups shredded lettuce
1 cup (4 ounces) shredded
   Monterey Jack cheese
1 large avocado, seeded,
   peeled, and sliced
½ cup Lindsay® Jumbo
   Pitted Ripe Olives,
   drained and sliced

Preheat oven to 250°F. In small skillet, cook tortillas one at a time, in ¼ inch hot oil for 20 to 40 seconds on each side, until crisp and golden. Drain on paper towels; keep warm in foil in oven. In medium skillet, cook chicken and onion in butter until chicken is done and onion is tender. Add tomato sauce, garlic salt, and cumin. Reduce heat; simmer, covered, about 15 minutes. Atop each tortilla, layer lettuce, chicken, cheese, avocado, and olives.

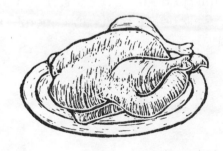

Kellogg's Corn Flakes® Enchiladas

Kellogg Company

Makes 6 servings

1½ cups tomato paste
4 cups water
1 teaspoon salt
4 teaspoons chili powder
½ teaspoon ground cumin
2 garlic cloves, finely chopped
1 pound lean ground beef

1 medium onion, finely chopped
2 cups (8 ounces) shredded Cheddar cheese
1 cup *KELLOGG'S CORN FLAKES®* cereal, crushed to ½ cup
½ cup sliced ripe olives
12 (7-inch) corn tortillas

Preheat oven to 350°F. In medium-size saucepan, stir together tomato paste, water, salt, chili powder, cumin, and garlic. Bring to a boil. Reduce heat and simmer, uncovered, 20 minutes. Remove from heat. In large saucepan, brown ground beef with onion. Drain. Stir in 1 cup tomato mixture, 1 cup cheese, *KELLOGG'S CORN FLAKES®* cereal, and olives. Pour remaining tomato mixture into 13-by-9-by-2-inch baking pan. Spoon 2 measuring-tablespoons of beef mixture onto center of each tortilla. Roll up tortilla and place in pan, seam side down. Top filled tortillas with remaining beef mixture. Bake 15 minutes. Sprinkle remaining cheese over top. Bake about 5 minutes longer or until cheese melts and enchiladas are thoroughly heated.

THE MAGIC OF CALIFORNIA DIP

The Story of Lipton Dip

In 1954, the Lipton company noticed a dramatic surge in Los Angeles sales of its onion soup mix. After investigating, marketing personnel determined the reason: A food writer had raved about a housewife's amazing new recipe for a party dip. The recipe called for only two ingredients: Lipton® Onion Recipe Soup Mix and sour cream.

Some testing in The Lipton Kitchens was necessary to find the best proportions of the ingredients before the company would widely publicize the popular dip. At first the recipe called for one cup of Lipton mix to one cup of sour cream, "enough to blow your head off," as the home economist in The Lipton Kitchens put it. The many months of experiments created an onion and sour-cream shortage in the New Jersey area of Englewood Cliffs, home of Lipton's headquarters. In the end, Lipton decided on one envelope of Lipton Onion Soup Mix to one sixteen-ounce container of sour cream. The final recipe, and others created with California Dip, as the blend came to be called, quickly changed the party scene. Tiny tidbits on limp toast triangles and other drooping canapés were replaced throughout the social scene, from intimate gatherings to major charity balls, with potato chips and California Dip.

Until the dip was introduced, sour cream had been little known, used mostly by people of middle European descent; now it enjoyed an explosion in popularity.

People discovered other uses for California Dip as well, like atop baked potatoes. Potato chips also enjoyed an unprecedented increase in sales.

California Dip established a completely new cooking concept: the use of dried soup mixes as ingredients in all types of recipes. A year after the introduction of the new dip, head of The Lipton Kitchens Dorothy Ebbott bundled up in thermal containers a pot roast, veal, birds in sauce, fish fillets, and a vegetable casserole, all prepared with onion soup mix. She took them to one of the most influential food writers in the country, Clementine Paddleford of the *New York Herald-Tribune*. Paddleford extolled the virtues of cooking with soup mixes, the ease of preparation, the good taste, and the uniqueness of the recipes.

The large volume of Lipton Onion Soup Mix sold throughout the country has made Lipton one of the biggest users of onions in the United States. This tremendous demand encouraged California growers to develop a special onion hybrid containing a higher content of solids and less water than in other onions. The *Lipton cut,* a precise manner of cutting, was developed for the special blend of white and toasted sliced onions. Mature onions are harvested for the soup mix because younger onions have a higher sugar content; sugar caramelizes and causes burning.

Today this simple dip ranks as one of the most famous recipes of the twentieth century. Everybody knows about the Lipton California Dip, including those who will never learn to use another recipe.

California Enchiladas

Lipton

Makes 6 servings

1 can (15 ounces) tomato sauce

1½ teaspoons hot pepper sauce

½ teaspoon garlic powder

2 cups (about 6 ounces) shredded Monterey Jack *or* Muenster cheese

1½ cups cut-up cooked chicken

1 cup Lipton® California Dip (see below)

1 can (4 ounces) chopped green chilies, drained

12 corn tortillas, softened

1 large green bell pepper, cut into 12 thin strips

Preheat oven to 375°. In small saucepan, combine tomato sauce, *½ teaspoon* pepper sauce, and garlic powder. Simmer, stirring occasionally, 15 minutes.

In medium bowl, combine *1½ cups* cheese, chicken, California Dip, chilies, and remaining pepper sauce. Spread *2½ tablespoons* mixture on each tortilla; roll up and place seam side down in lightly greased 2-quart oblong baking dish. Top each tortilla with *1 tablespoon* prepared sauce, remaining cheese, and green-pepper strip. Bake 15 minutes or until cheese is melted. Serve with remaining heated sauce.

Lipton® California Dip

Makes about 2 cups

1 envelope Lipton® Recipe Secrets® Onion Soup Mix

1 container (16 ounces) sour cream

Blend together and chill.

Tamale Pie

Lipton

Makes about 6 servings

- 1 tablespoon olive *or* vegetable oil
- 1 small onion, chopped
- 1 pound ground beef
- 1 envelope Lipton® Recipe Secrets® Fiesta Herb with Red Pepper Soup Mix
- 1 can (14½ ounces) stewed tomatoes, undrained
- ½ cup water
- 1 can (15 to 19 ounces) red kidney beans, rinsed and drained
- 1 package (8½ ounces) corn muffin mix

Preheat oven to 400°. In 12-inch skillet, heat oil over medium heat and cook onion, stirring occasionally, 3 minutes or until tender. Stir in ground beef and cook until browned. Stir in fiesta herb with red pepper soup mix blended with tomatoes and water. Bring to a boil over high heat, stirring with spoon to crush tomatoes. Reduce heat to low; stir in beans. Simmer uncovered, stirring occasionally, 10 minutes. Turn into 2-quart casserole.

Prepare corn muffin mix according to package directions. Spoon evenly over casserole. Bake uncovered 15 minutes or until corn topping is golden and filling is hot.

Variations: Also terrific with Lipton® Recipe Secrets® Onion, Onion-Mushroom, Beefy Onion, or Beefy Mushroom Soup Mix. For extra zip, add 1 can (4 ounces) chopped green chilies, undrained, to skillet with soup mix.

Preparation time: 5 minutes   *Cook time:* 35 minutes

Taos Tacos

Lawry's Foods, Inc.

Makes 6 servings

- 1 pound lean ground beef
- 1 package (1.25 ounces) Lawry's® Taco Spices and Seasonings
- ½ cup beer
- ¼ cup water
- 1 can (15¼ ounces) kidney beans, drained
- 1 medium tomato, chopped
- ¼ cup thinly sliced green onions
- 1 tablespoon chopped cilantro *or* parsley
- Flour tortillas, taco shells, *or* pita breads
- Grated Cheddar *or* Monterey Jack cheese for garnish
- Guacamole for garnish
- Salsa for garnish
- Dairy sour cream for garnish

In large skillet, brown ground beef, stirring until cooked through; drain fat. Add taco spices and seasonings, beer, and water; blend well. Bring to a boil; reduce heat and simmer, uncovered, 10 minutes. Add kidney beans, tomato, green onions, and cilantro; blend well. Simmer 5 minutes. Serve in tortillas, taco shells, or pita breads. Garnish each serving with your choice of grated Cheddar or Monterey Jack cheese, guacamole, salsa, and dairy sour cream.

Variation: Use ¾ cup water instead of ½ cup beer and ¼ cup water.

Garden Turkey Burger

©1996 Reckitt & Colman Inc.

Makes 4 servings

1 pound ground turkey
⅓ cup *each* shredded carrots, minced onion, and celery
¾ cup seasoned dry bread crumbs

1 egg white *or* 1 whole egg
¼ cup FRENCH'S® Worcestershire Sauce
FRENCH'S® Signature Steak Sauce (recipe follows)

With fork, gently mix turkey, vegetables, bread crumbs, egg white, and Worcestershire. Shape into 4 patties.

Broil or grill burgers 15 minutes on well-oiled rack until no longer pink in center. Serve on rolls with lettuce and tomato. Spoon FRENCH'S® Signature Steak Sauce on top.

Preparation time: 15 minutes   *Cook time:* 15 minutes

FRENCH'S® Signature Steak Sauce

Makes ¾ cup

½ cup ketchup
¼ cup FRENCH'S® Worcestershire Sauce

1 tablespoon FRANK'S® Original REDHOT® Cayenne Pepper Sauce
¼ teaspoon garlic powder

In small bowl, combine all ingredients.

Bistro Burger with Blue Cheese

©1996 Reckitt & Colman Inc.

Makes 4 servings

1 pound ground turkey *or* beef
2 tablespoons FRENCH'S® Dijon mustard
¼ cup chopped fresh parsley
2 tablespoons minced chives

¼ teaspoon dried thyme leaves
2 ounces blue cheese, cut into 4 squares (each about 1½-by-¼-inch thick)
4 crusty rolls, split in half
Lettuce and tomato slices

In large bowl, gently mix meat, mustard, and herbs. Divide meat evenly into 8 portions. Press each into a thin patty, about 3 inches in diameter. Place 1 piece cheese between 2 patties, firmly pressing edges together to seal.

Place patties on oiled grid. Grill over medium-high heat 15 minutes until no longer pink. Arrange lettuce and tomatoes on bottom half of rolls. Top with burgers. Serve with additional mustard, if desired.

Preparation time: 15 minutes   *Cook time:* 15 minutes

Tempting Taco Burgers

Lipton

Makes about 4 servings

1 envelope Lipton® Recipe Secrets® Onion-Mushroom Soup Mix	¼ cup finely chopped green bell pepper
1 pound ground beef	1 to 2 teaspoons chili powder
½ cup chopped tomato	¼ cup water

In large bowl, combine all ingredients; shape into 4 patties. Grill or broil until done. Serve, if desired, on hamburger rolls, and top with shredded lettuce and Cheddar cheese.

Variations: Also terrific with Lipton® Recipe Secrets® Onion, Beefy Onion, *or* Beefy Mushroom Soup Mix.

Chili Mushroom Burgers

JFC International, Inc.

Makes 4 servings

1   pound lean ground beef
¼   pound mushrooms, finely chopped
½   cup Dynasty® Panko
¼   cup minced onion
¼   cup Dynasty® Chinese Stir-Fry Sauce
1   tablespoon Dynasty® Szechwan Chili Sauce

Combine beef, mushrooms, panko, onion, and stir-fry and chili sauces; mix well. Form mixture into 4 equal-size patties. Grill or broil, 4 to 5 inches from heat, 8 to 10 minutes on each side, or until desired degree of doneness is reached. Serve plain or on buns with condiments, as desired.

French's® Onion Crunch Burger

©1996 Reckitt & Colman Inc.

Makes 6 servings

1½   pounds ground beef
1⅓   cups (2.8 ounce can) FRENCH'S® French Fried Onions
¾   teaspoon salt
¼   teaspoon pepper
6   rolls

Mix beef, ⅔ *cup* French Fried Onions, and seasonings; shape into 6 burgers.

Grill or broil 10 minutes or until no longer pink in center, turning once.

Serve on rolls and top with ⅔ *cup* onions.

Tip: Add 2 tablespoons FRENCH'S® Classic Yellow® Mustard to ground beef for zestier flavor.

Preparation time: 10 minutes   *Cook time:* 10 minutes

Onion Burger Variations

Tangy Western Burger: Top each burger with 1 tablespoon barbecue sauce and 1 strip crisp bacon before adding French Fried Onions.

California Burger: Combine 2 tablespoons *each* mayonnaise, sour cream, and FRENCH'S® Dijon mustard; spoon on top of burgers. Top each burger with sprouts, avocado slices, and French Fried Onions.

Luscious Oniony Cheeseburger: Place 1 slice cheese on each burger before topping with French Fried Onions.

Salisbury Steak Burger: Prepare 1 package brown gravy mix according to directions. Stir in 1 can (4 ounces) drained sliced mushrooms. Spoon over burgers and top with French Fried Onions.

Pizza Burger: Top each burger with pizza sauce, mozzarella cheese, and French Fried Onions.

Chili Burger: Combine 1 can (15 ounces) chili without beans, 2 tablespoons FRANK'S® Original REDHOT® Cayenne Pepper Sauce, and 2 teaspoons *each* chili powder and ground cumin. Cook until heated through. Spoon over burgers and top with French Fried Onions.

Calico Meatball Stew

Campbell Soup Company

Makes 8 servings, 8½ cups total

1 pound ground beef
½ pound bulk pork sausage
1 cup soft bread crumbs
½ teaspoon dried oregano leaves, crushed
1 egg
¼ cup vegetable oil
2 cans (10¼ ounces each) Franco-American® Beef Gravy
1 can (about 14½ ounces) stewed tomatoes
3½ cups potatoes, peeled and cut in 1-inch cubes
1½ cups diagonally sliced carrots
½ cup chopped onion
1 large bay leaf
¼ teaspoon pepper
1 cup frozen peas, thawed

In medium bowl, mix *thoroughly* beef, sausage, bread crumbs, oregano, and egg. Shape into 24 meatballs. In 6-quart Dutch oven over medium heat, in hot oil, cook meatballs until browned on all sides. Spoon off fat. Add gravy, tomatoes, potatoes, carrots, onion, bay leaf, and pepper. Heat to boiling, stirring occasionally. Reduce heat to low. Cover; simmer 25 minutes. Stir in peas. Cook uncovered, 5 minutes more. Discard bay leaf.

Steak Pot Pie

Nabisco Foods Group

Makes 4 servings

1 cup chopped onion
2 tablespoons FLEISCHMAN'S Margarine
2 tablespoons all-purpose flour
1½ cups COLLEGE INN Beef Broth
½ cup A.1.® Steak Sauce
3 cups (about 1½ pounds) diced cooked steak
2 cups frozen peas and carrots, thawed
Prepared pastry for 2-crust pie

Preheat oven to 400°F. In 2-quart saucepan, over medium-high heat, cook onion in margarine until tender. Blend in flour; cook 1 minute. Add beef broth and steak sauce; cook and stir until mixture thickens and begins to boil. Stir in steak and peas and carrots. Spoon mixture evenly into four 16-ounce ovenproof individual casseroles. Roll out and cut pastry crust to fit over casseroles. Seal crust to edge of casseroles. Slit tops of crusts to vent. Bake 25 minutes or until golden brown. Serve warm.

Preparation time: 15 minutes   *Total time:* 50 minutes

THE FIRST PACKAGED BAKING MIX

The Story of Bisquick

The last thing on Carl Smith's mind that cold night in November 1930 was discovering a product concept to alter the way America bakes. Smith had climbed aboard the Southern Pacific car for the late-night run from Portland to San Francisco and just wanted something to eat. He didn't expect much, really. Not at that late hour in a dining car.

What a pleasant surprise to be presented with hot biscuits in no time at all! His naturally curious salesman's mind was intrigued.

"Oh, I always make biscuits right from the oven in the blink of an eye," explained the ingenious chef. "No trouble at all." Before leaving Portland he had blended a mixture of lard, flour, baking powder, and salt that he kept stored in the ice chest.

Smith, a sales executive for General Mills, couldn't wait for morning, when he could take this idea to Charles Kress, head chemist, whose life-long search had been "for the secret hidden in the heart of the wheat kernel."

Before that fateful encounter, homemakers needed time to locate recipes; to scoop flour, shortening, and other ingredients from large bulk containers; and to measure ingredients precisely. The new concept of a baking mixture would streamline the process of making cakes, muffins, and biscuits. Baking became much easier and the results more predictable.

But stumbling blocks had to be overcome before this concept could successfully be brought to market. First, the oil must maintain its sweetness in the package during the many weeks between manufacturer and consumer. Also, the portion of the mixture contacting the wrapping paper must not turn rancid when exposed to the air filtering through the paper. Parchment paper, like the paper used to wrap butter, proved to be the solution to this problem. Finally, the discovery that the ingredients should not be mixed completely in the package foolproofed baking results. Lumps of oil interspersed with layers of flour perfected the product.

General Mills introduced this baking mix in 1931 under the trademark Bisquick. Other manufacturers jumped into the baking market soon after the introduction of Bisquick, but Bisquick grabbed the major share of the business and has remained the leader ever since.

Impossible Cheeseburger Pie

General Mills, Inc.

Makes 6 to 8 servings

1 pound ground beef	3 eggs
1½ cups chopped onion	¾ cup Bisquick® Baking Mix
½ teaspoon salt	2 tomatoes, sliced
¼ teaspoon pepper	1 cup shredded Cheddar *or*
1½ cups milk	process American cheese

Preheat oven to 400°F. Grease pie plate, 10-by-1½ inches, or square baking dish, 8-by-8-by-2 inches, or six 10-ounce custard cups. Cook and stir ground beef and onion in 10-inch skillet over medium heat until beef is brown; drain. Stir in salt and pepper. Spread in pie plate. Beat milk, eggs, and baking mix 15 seconds in blender on high, or 1 minute with hand beater or wire whisk, until smooth. Pour into pie plate. Bake 25 minutes. Top with tomatoes; sprinkle with cheese. Bake 5 to 8 minutes or until knife inserted in center comes out clean. Cool 5 minutes.

To microwave: Crumble ground beef into ungreased microwave-safe pie plate, 10-by-1½ inches; add onion. Cover with waxed paper and microwave on HIGH 6 to 7 minutes, stirring after 3 minutes, until beef is done; drain. Continue as directed—except place pie plate on inverted microwave-safe dinner plate in microwave oven. Microwave, uncovered, on MEDIUM-HIGH 12 to 18 minutes, rotating pie plate a quarter turn every 6 minutes, until knife inserted in center comes out clean. Top with tomatoes and cheese. Microwave, uncovered, 6 to 8 minutes, rotating pie plate a quarter turn every 3 minutes, until cheese is melted. Let stand on flat, heatproof surface (not on wire rack) 5 minutes.

Variations

Impossible California Cheeseburger Pie: Just before serving, top with 1½ cups shredded lettuce and 12 to 16 dill-pickle slices.

Impossible Bacon-Cheeseburger Pie: Arrange 6 slices crisply cooked bacon on pie after baking.

Sloppy Joes

Kellogg Company

Makes 8 servings

1 pound lean ground beef	1 teaspoon salt
1 can (16 ounces, 2 cups) diced tomatoes, undrained	¼ teaspoon pepper
½ cup chopped green pepper	1 tablespoon Worcestershire sauce
½ cup chopped onions	8 hamburger buns, sliced and toasted
2 cups *KELLOGG'S CORN FLAKES®* cereal	

In large frypan, brown ground beef and drain.

Stir in tomatoes, green pepper, onions, *KELLOGG'S CORN FLAKES®* cereal, salt, pepper, and Worcestershire sauce. Stir to combine.

Cover and cook over low heat 15 minutes, stirring occasionally. Serve on hamburger buns.

Turkey Joes

Oscar Mayer Foods Corporation

Makes 6 servings

- 1 package (1 pound) Louis Rich® Ground Turkey
- 1 medium onion, chopped
- 1 cup barbecue sauce
- 1 tablespoon sweet pickle relish
- 6 hamburger buns

Place turkey and onion in skillet. Cook over medium heat 8 to 10 minutes or until turkey is no longer pink, stirring and separating turkey as it cooks. Stir in barbecue sauce and relish. Cook 2 to 3 minutes more. Serve in buns.

To microwave: Crumble turkey in 2-quart casserole; add onion. Cover with waxed paper. Microwave at HIGH 3 minutes. Stir cooked portions from outside to center. Cover. Microwave 3 minutes more. Add barbecue sauce and relish. Microwave 1 minute more.

Pizza Provençal

Ragú Foods Co.

Makes 6 servings

- 1 long loaf French bread, split lengthwise
- 1 jar (14 ounces) Ragú® Pizza Quick Sauce
- 1 cup thinly sliced yellow pepper
- 1 cup thinly sliced red pepper
- 1 cup thinly sliced zucchini
- ½ cup sliced black olives
- 1 package (12 ounces) shredded mozzarella cheese
- 2 tablespoons minced fresh parsley

Preheat oven to 375°F. Place French bread halves on baking sheet. Evenly top each with pizza sauce. Layer yellow and red peppers, zucchini, and black olives.

Sprinkle with mozzarella cheese and parsley. Bake 20 to 25 minutes or until cheese is bubbly.

Frank's® Buffalo-Style Chicken Pizza

©1996 Reckitt & Colman Inc.

Makes 8 servings

2 large (12 inches *each*) prebaked pizza crust shells	6 tablespoons FRANK'S® Original REDHOT® Cayenne Pepper Sauce
1 cup pizza sauce *or* barbecue sauce	2 tablespoons butter, melted
½ cup thinly sliced celery	2 cups (8 ounces) shredded mozzarella cheese
3 cups cooked, sliced chicken (see note)	⅔ cup (3 ounces) gorgonzola or blue cheese, crumbled

Place pizza shells on disposable foil pizza pans or on top of heavy-duty aluminum foil. Spread shells with pizza sauce and sprinkle with celery.

Place chicken in large bowl. Add RedHot® sauce and butter; toss well to coat. Arrange chicken on top of pizzas. Sprinkle with the cheeses.

Grill* pizza over medium-high heat 15 minutes or until crust is crispy and cheese melts. Cut into wedges to serve.

*Or bake in a 400°F oven for 15 minutes.

Note: To cook chicken—Grill 1 pound boneless chicken over high heat 10 minutes or until no longer pink in center. You may also cook chicken quickly in the microwave. Microwave, loosely covered, 7 minutes.

Preparation time: 20 minutes   *Cook time:* 15 minutes

Impossible Pizza Pie

General Mills, Inc.

Makes 6 to 8 servings

⅔ cup chopped onion

⅓ cup grated Parmesan cheese

1½ cups milk

3 eggs

¾ cup Bisquick® Baking Mix

Sauce (see page 280)

¼ cup grated Parmesan cheese

1 package (3½ ounces) sliced pepperoni

⅓ cup chopped onion

½ cup chopped green bell pepper

1 to 1½ cups shredded mozzarella cheese

Preheat oven to 425°F. Grease pie plate, 10-by-1½ inches. Sprinkle ⅔ *cup* onion and ⅓ *cup* Parmesan cheese in plate. Beat milk, eggs, and baking mix 15 seconds in blender on high, or 1 minute with hand beater, until smooth. Pour into pie plate. Bake 20 minutes. Spread Sauce over top. Layer remaining ingredients on Sauce. Bake 15 to 20 minutes or until cheese is light brown. Cool 5 minutes.

To microwave: Sprinkle ⅔ *cup* onion and ⅓ *cup* Parmesan cheese in greased microwave-safe pie plate, 10-by-1½ inches. Continue as directed except place pie plate on inverted microwave-safe dinner plate in microwave oven. Microwave, uncovered, MEDIUM-HIGH 12 to 16 minutes, rotating pie plate a quarter turn every 6 minutes, until knife inserted in center comes out clean. Spread Sauce over top. Layer remaining ingredients on Sauce. Microwave, uncovered, 5 to 9 minutes, rotating pie plate a quarter turn every 3 minutes, until cheese is melted and bubbly. Let stand on flat, heatproof surface (not on wire rack) 5 minutes.

Sauce

1 can (6 ounces) tomato paste	½ teaspoon garlic salt
¼ cup water	½ teaspoon dried basil
1 teaspoon dried oregano	¼ teaspoon pepper

Mix together.

Variation: Substitute ½ pound ground beef *or* bulk Italian sausage, cooked and drained, for the pepperoni.

Spicy Sicilian Seafood Stew

Classico® di Sicilia Pasta Sauce

Makes 8 servings

2 pounds small baking potatoes, unpared, baked or boiled until tender and cut into ¼-inch thick rounds

1 pound carrots, pared, cut into ½-inch slices and cooked

3 cloves garlic, chopped

½ cup olive oil

⅓ cup dry white vermouth or wine

1 (26-ounce) jar Classico® di Sicilia (Mushrooms & Ripe Olives) Pasta Sauce

1 (9-ounce) package frozen artichoke hearts, thawed

1½ teaspoons ground turmeric

¾ teaspoon salt

½ teaspoon cayenne pepper

1 pound sea scallops

1 pound raw medium shrimp, peeled, leaving tails on if desired, and deveined

In large kettle, over medium-high heat, cook and stir carrots and garlic in *¼ cup* oil until carrots begin to brown. Add vermouth; bring to a boil. Boil 3 minutes. Stir in pasta sauce, artichokes, *1 teaspoon* turmeric, *½ teaspoon* salt, and *¼ teaspoon* cayenne pepper.

Bring to a boil; reduce heat and simmer covered 15 minutes. Stir in scallops and shrimp; cover and simmer 10 minutes or until scallops are opaque and shrimp are pink. In small bowl, combine remaining ½ *teaspoon* turmeric, ¼ *teaspoon* salt, and ¼ *teaspoon* cayenne pepper. In large skillet, over medium-high heat, brown potatoes in remaining ¼ *cup* oil; sprinkle with turmeric mixture. Serve with seafood stew. Refrigerate leftovers.

A.1.® Texas Chili

Nabisco Foods Group

Makes 6 servings

2 pounds round *or* chuck steak, cut into ¼-inch cubes	2 cans (16 ounces each) peeled tomatoes, coarsely chopped
1 tablespoon FLEISCH-MANN'S Margarine	½ cup A.1.® Steak Sauce
1 cup chopped onion	¼ to ⅓ cup chili powder
	30 PREMIUM Saltine Crackers

In large saucepan, over medium-high heat, brown steak, in batches, in margarine. Add onion; cook until tender. Add tomatoes with liquid, steak sauce, and chili powder. Heat to a boil; reduce heat. Cover and simmer 1¼ to 1½ hours, stirring occasionally. Serve with crackers

Mushroom Frittata

Lawry's Foods, Inc.

Makes 4 servings

1 teaspoon butter *or* margarine
1 medium zucchini, shredded
1 medium tomato, chopped
1 can (4 ounces) sliced mushrooms, drained
6 eggs, beaten
¼ cup milk
2 teaspoons Dijon mustard
½ teaspoon Lawry's® Seasoned Salt
½ teaspoon Lawry's® Seasoned Pepper
2 cups (8 ounces) grated Swiss cheese

In large, ovenproof skillet, melt butter and sauté zucchini, tomato, and mushrooms 1 minute. In large bowl, combine remaining ingredients; blend well. Pour egg mixture into skillet; cook 10 minutes over low heat. To brown top, place skillet under broiler 2 to 3 minutes. Serve directly from skillet or remove frittata to serving dish.

Serve with additional Swiss cheese and fresh fruit.

Variation: Try serving frittata with prepared Lawry's® Spaghetti Sauce Seasoning. Blend with imported mushrooms.

Three-Alarm Chili

©1996 Reckitt & Colman Inc.

Makes 6 to 8 servings

2 pounds coarse ground beef for chili

1 medium onion, chopped

3 cloves garlic, minced

1 can (16 ounces) whole tomatoes, cut up

1 can (8 ounces) tomato sauce

1 cup water

½ cup FRANK'S® Original REDHOT® Cayenne Pepper Sauce

1 tablespoon chili powder

1 teaspoon dried oregano

1 teaspoon paprika

In Dutch oven or 5-quart pot, cook beef, onion, and garlic, until beef is browned, stirring to separate meat. Pour off fat.

Stir in remaining ingredients. Bring to a boil. Reduce heat to medium-low. Simmer, covered, 1 hour until thickened and flavors are blended; stirring occasionally. Serve with rice and shredded cheese, if desired.

Preparation time: 15 minutes   *Cook time:* 1 hour 10 minutes

CLASSIC MEAT MAIN DISHES

Lamb Chops with Horseradish-Pecan Sauce

McCormick & Company, Inc.

Makes 6 lamb chops

6   slices bacon
6   boneless lamb loin chops, cut 1½ inches thick
1   tablespoon olive oil
1   tablespoon soy sauce
1   tablespoon lemon juice
⅛   teaspoon McCormick/ Schilling® Instant Garlic Powder
⅛   teaspoon McCormick/ Schilling® Instant Onion Powder
Horseradish-Pecan Sauce (see page 285)
Fresh mint for garnish (optional)

Cook bacon over low heat until cooked but not crisp. Shape lamb chops into rounds. Wrap each chop with 1 piece bacon. Secure with wooden toothpick. Place lamb chops on broiler pan. Combine next 5 ingredients. Brush chops with mixture. Broil 4 inches from heat 10 minutes or until desired doneness. Turn chops once and brush with marinade occasionally while cooking.

Serve on Horseradish-Pecan Sauce. Garnish with fresh mint, if desired.

Horseradish-Pecan Sauce

Makes 1 cup sauce

1 tablespoon olive oil
1 tablespoon flour
⅛ teaspoon McCormick/ Schilling® ground White Pepper
1 teaspoon McCormick/ Schilling Bon Appétit®
⅛ teaspoon McCormick Schilling® Instant Minced Garlic
1 cup half-and-half
1 tablespoon horseradish sauce
¼ cup chopped pecans

Combine olive oil and flour in small saucepan. Add white pepper, McCormick/ Schilling Bon Appétit®, and minced garlic. Heat until bubbly. Gradually add half-and-half, stirring constantly. Add horseradish sauce and chopped pecans. Cook over medium heat, stirring constantly until mixture thickens.

Spanish Lamb

Lindsay International, Inc.

Makes 4 servings

1 pound boneless lamb, cut into ½-inch cubes
1 cup finely chopped onion
2 cloves garlic, minced
2 tablespoons salad oil
1 can (16 ounces) tomatoes, cut up, undrained
1 can (8 ounces) tomato sauce
1 can (3 ounces) whole mushrooms, undrained
1 bay leaf
1 teaspoon dried basil, crushed
½ cup Lindsay® Salad-Style Green Olives, drained
Cooked brown rice
Grated Parmesan cheese

In saucepan, cook the lamb, onion, and garlic in hot oil until meat is brown and onion is tender. Stir in *undrained* tomatoes, tomato sauce, *undrained* mushrooms, bay leaf, and basil. Simmer, uncovered, 20 minutes. Stir in olives; simmer 10 minutes more or until mixture is desired consistency. Discard bay leaf. Serve lamb mixture over rice; sprinkle Parmesan cheese on top.

Lamb Kabobs with Duck Sauce

JFC International, Inc.

Makes 4 servings, 2 skewers each

1½ pounds lean, boneless lamb *or* beef, cut into 1-inch chunks

3 tablespoons Dynasty® Oriental Marinade

2 medium zucchini, cut crosswise into ½-inch widths

1 medium red bell pepper, seeded and cut into 1-inch squares

½ cup Dynasty® Duck Sauce

Coat lamb with marinade; cover and refrigerate 2 hours. Thread lamb, zucchini, and pepper alternately onto eight 9-inch bamboo or metal skewers. Arrange threaded skewers, in single layer, on broiler pan or baking rack in baking pan. Brush top sides of skewers with half the Duck Sauce. Broil 3 to 4 inches from heat, 8 to 10 minutes. Turn skewers over; brush with remaining Duck Sauce. Broil 8 to 10 minutes longer, or until desired degree of doneness.

Variation: Substitute 2 yellow crookneck squash for zucchini and 1 green bell pepper for red bell pepper.

Beef and Bacon Kabobs

Nabisco Foods Group

Makes 4 servings

½ cup A.1.® Steak Sauce
¼ cup REGINA Sherry
  Cooking Wine
2 tablespoons honey
1½ pounds sirloin beef cubes

½ pound bacon slices, halved
Onion wedges
Green *or* red pepper squares
Whole mushroom caps

Blend steak sauce, sherry, and honey. In nonmetal dish, pour marinade over steak cubes. Cover; chill 2 hours, stirring occasionally. Drain beef; reserve marinade. Wrap half bacon slice around each steak cube. On 4 skewers, thread steak, onion wedges, pepper squares, and mushroom caps. Grill or broil 4 inches from heat source for 8 to 10 minutes or until desired doneness, turning occasionally and brushing with reserved marinade. Serve garnished as desired.

Preparation time: 15 minutes   *Total time:* 25 minutes

Skewered Beef with Horseradish Sauce

Ragú Foods Co.

Makes 6 servings

6 ounces cream cheese,
  softened
¼ cup sour cream
1 tablespoon prepared
  horseradish
2 teaspoons Dijon mustard
1 package Adolph's® Meat
  Marinade

⅓ cup white vinegar
⅓ cup water
2 teaspoons Worcestershire
  sauce
1½ pounds beef top round
  steak, cut into cubes for
  kabobs

Preheat grill or broiler. In small bowl, thoroughly combine cream cheese, sour cream, horseradish, and mustard. Refrigerate until ready to serve.

In medium bowl, thoroughly combine contents of marinade package with vinegar, water, and Worcestershire sauce. Place beef cubes in marinade; pierce deeply with a fork. Marinate 15 minutes, turning occasionally. Thread small skewers with meat. Grill or broil beef 5 to 6 inches from heat, 8 minutes per side for medium. Baste with remaining marinade. Serve beef with horseradish sauce.

Pork and Shrimp Kabobs

McCormick & Company, Inc.

Makes 4 servings, 1 skewer each

- ¼ cup lime juice
- ½ cup cream of coconut
- 1 teaspoon McCormick/Schilling® Freeze-Dried Shallots
- ⅛ teaspoon McCormick/Schilling® ground Nutmeg
- ⅛ teaspoon McCormick/Schilling® ground Cloves
- 1 McCormick/Schilling® Bay Leaf
- 1 teaspoon McCormick/Schilling® Cracked Black Pepper
- 1 tablespoon soy sauce
- 12 (2-inch) cubes lean pork
- 1 red bell pepper
- 1 green bell pepper
- 12 jumbo shrimp, shelled and deveined

Preheat oven to 325°F. Mix first 8 ingredients. Put pork cubes in shallow glass or enamel baking dish. Pour marinade over pork. Bake, covered, 45 minutes. Cool, covered. Remove meat from marinade. Save marinade. Seed bell peppers and cut in bite-size pieces. Thread pork, peppers, and shrimp on 4 skewers. Broil 5 to 6 minutes, brushing frequently with reserved marinade.

Oven-Roast Pork Hawaiian

Dole Food Company

Makes 12 servings

2 cans (20 ounces each) Dole® Crushed Pineapple, undrained	Pepper
	3 large cloves garlic, pressed
2 cups Dole® Golden Raisins	½ cup pineapple-apricot jam
1 center-cut pork loin roast (6 pounds) *or* 2 pork loin roasts (3 pounds each)	¼ cup minced crystalized ginger
Salt	¾ cup Dole® Pineapple Juice
	1 tablespoon cornstarch

Preheat oven to 350°F. Combine *1 cup* undrained pineapple with *1 cup* raisins. Cover roasting pan with heavy-duty foil. Place pork on foil. Make slit lengthwise through center of roast. Fill with raisin mixture. Sprinkle with salt and pepper; rub with garlic. Tie pork with string. Wrap tightly with foil. Roast 2 hours.

For sauce, combine jam, ginger, and remaining undrained pineapple and raisins. Cook 15 minutes. Uncover roast; baste with drippings. Spoon ¾ *cup* pineapple mixture over roast. Bake, uncovered, 15 to 20 minutes. Mix pineapple juice with cornstarch; add to pineapple mixture. Cook until sauce boils and thickens. Serve sauce with pork roast.

Pork Chops with Creole Sauce

Lawry's Foods, Inc.

Makes 4 to 6 servings

- 1 package (1.5 ounces) Lawry's® Extra Rich and Thick Spaghetti Sauce Seasoning Blend
- 1 can (6 ounces) tomato paste
- 1¾ cups water
- 2 tablespoons butter *or* vegetable oil
- 1 can (4 ounces) sliced mushrooms, finely chopped
- 1 green bell pepper, finely chopped
- ½ to 1 teaspoon hot red pepper sauce
- ¼ teaspoon celery seed
- 4 to 6 pork chops (about 4 ounces each)

In medium saucepan, prepare spaghetti sauce seasoning blend according to package directions with tomato paste, water, and butter. Add mushrooms, green pepper, pepper sauce, and celery seed. In large, nonstick skillet, pan-fry pork chops 10 to 12 minutes, depending on thickness of chops, until pork is no longer pink. Top with prepared sauce. Serve with oven-browned potatoes and steamed sliced zucchini.

Pork Chops in Raisin Sauce

Dole Food Company

Makes 2 servings

- 2 pork chops, thick cut
- Salt (optional)
- Pepper (optional)
- 1 large clove garlic, pressed
- 1 tablespoon olive oil
- ½ teaspoon thyme, crumbled
- ¼ teaspoon sage
- 1 cup orange juice
- 2 teaspoons cornstarch
- ½ cup Dole® Raisins

Sprinkle pork chops with salt and pepper if desired. Rub with garlic. In skillet, brown chops in oil. Cover skillet and shake occasionally during browning. Add thyme and sage; stir into pan juices. Mix 3 *tablespoons* juice with cornstarch. Set aside. Add remaining juice to skillet. Cover; simmer 10 minutes. Stir in cornstarch mixture until blended. Add raisins. Cook, stirring, until sauce boils and thickens.

Serve with green and yellow vegetables.

Orange-Honey Glazed Pork Chops

Ragú Foods Co.

Makes 6 servings

- ¾ cup orange juice
- 3 tablespoons honey
- 2 tablespoons soy sauce
- 2 tablespoons apple cider vinegar
- 4 teaspoons cornstarch
- 1 tablespoon Dijon mustard
- 2 teaspoons Worcestershire sauce
- 1 clove garlic, minced
- ½ teaspoon dill weed
- 6 center-cut 1-inch-thick pork chops (about 3 pounds total)
- 2 teaspoons Adolph's® 100% Natural Tenderizer—Unseasoned

Preheat broiler or grill. In medium saucepan, combine first 9 ingredients. Simmer over low heat until thickened; set aside and keep warm.

Moisten meat with water. Evenly sprinkle both sides with tenderizer and pierce deeply with a fork. (*Do Not Add Salt.*) Broil or grill pork chops 4 to 6 inches from heat 12 to 14 minutes per side or until thoroughly cooked. Baste occasionally with sauce. Serve pork chops with remaining heated sauce.

Pork Tenderloin with Plum Sauce

JFC International, Inc.

Makes about 3 dozen appetizers or 4 to 6 main-dish servings

½ cup Dynasty® Golden Plum Sauce

3 tablespoons Dynasty® Chinese Soy Sauce

¾ teaspoon Dynasty® Chinese Five Spices

1½ to 2 pounds boneless pork tenderloin

Preheat oven to 375°F. Combine plum and soy sauces and five spices; mix well. Place pork tenderloin on baking rack in baking pan or on broiler pan. Add enough water to cover bottom of pan without touching pork. Generously brush some plum mixture over pork to glaze. Bake, uncovered, 1 hour and 20 minutes, or until internal temperature registers 165°F on meat thermometer. Brush with remaining plum mixture every 20 minutes during cooking. Remove from oven; slice crosswise into ¼-inch-thick slices.

Pork Stir-Fry with Spicy Plum Sauce

JFC International, Inc.

Makes 2 to 3 servings

1 pound boneless lean pork, cut into thin strips

2 tablespoons Dynasty® Oriental Marinade

2 tablespoons Dynasty® Chinese Stir-Fry Oil, divided

1 small onion, cut into thin wedges

1 green bell pepper, seeded and thinly sliced

2 tablespoons Dynasty® Plum Sauce

1 tablespoon Dynasty® Chinese Soy Sauce

1 teaspoon Dynasty® Hot Chili Oil

Coat pork with marinade; let stand 20 minutes. Heat wok or large frying pan over high heat. Add *1 tablespoon* oil;

coat wok. Add half the pork mixture; stir-fry 1 to 2 minutes, or until lightly browned. Remove from wok with slotted spoon. Reheat wok over high heat 1 minute. Add remaining half pork; stir-fry 1 to 2 minutes, or until lightly browned. Remove from wok. Heat remaining *1 tablespoon* oil in same wok. Add onion and green pepper; stir-fry 2 to 3 minutes, or until tender-crisp. Return pork to wok; add plum and soy sauces. Cook and stir 1 minute, or until heated through. Remove from heat; stir in chili oil. Serve while hot.

China Sun Pork

Dole Food Company

Makes 4 servings

1 can (20 ounces) Dole® Pineapple Chunks	2 large cloves garlic, pressed
½ cup water	2 tablespoons minced ginger root *or* 1 teaspoon ground ginger
3 tablespoons soy sauce	
1 tablespoon cornstarch	
1 teaspoon white vinegar	1 onion, cut in wedges
¼ teaspoon hot red pepper flakes	2 medium Dole® Carrots, slivered
1 pound boneless pork loin	1 Dole® Green *or* Red Bell Pepper, slivered
1 tablespoon vegetable oil	2 cups Dole® Sugar Peas

Drain pineapple and reserve *3 tablespoons* juice. Mix reserved juice with water, soy sauce, cornstarch, vinegar, and pepper flakes; set aside. Cut pork in strips. In skillet, brown pork in hot oil. Add garlic and ginger; cook 1 minute. Add onion and carrots; cook 1 minute. Stir sauce; add to skillet with pineapple, bell pepper, and sugar peas. Cook until sauce boils and thickens.

Tropic Sun Spareribs

Dole Food Company

Makes 4 to 6 servings

3½ to 4 pounds spareribs *or* country-style ribs
3 large cloves garlic, pressed
Salt
Pepper
1 large onion, sliced

1 can (20 ounces) Dole® Crushed Pineapple, undrained
1 bottle (12 ounces) chili sauce
½ cup brown sugar, packed
1 teaspoon ground ginger
½ teaspoon dry mustard

Preheat oven to 350°F. Rub ribs with garlic. Sprinkle with salt and pepper. Arrange onion in large baking pan. Place ribs on top. Add ¼ *cup* water to pan. Cover with foil. Bake 30 minutes. Combine remaining ingredients. Spoon over ribs. Bake, uncovered, 1 hour longer.

Rosemary's Finger-Licking Ribs

Specialty Brands

Makes about 4 servings

½ cup orange marmalade
1 teaspoon soy sauce
1 teaspoon Durkee® Rosemary, crushed
½ teaspoon Durkee® Garlic Powder

½ teaspoon Durkee® Thyme Leaves *or* ¼ teaspoon Durkee® Ground Thyme
¾ teaspoon seasoned salt
2 pounds lean pork ribs

In small bowl, combine orange marmalade, soy sauce, rosemary, garlic powder, thyme, and ¼ *teaspoon* seasoned salt; mix well. Rub ½ *teaspoon* seasoned salt into both sides of ribs. Broil or grill ribs over medium-high heat for 20 minutes, turning frequently. Baste both sides with marmalade sauce. Cook 10 more minutes, or until no longer pink inside.

Country Glazed Ribs

©1996 Reckitt & Colman Inc.

Makes 4 to 6 servings

3 to 4 pounds pork baby back ribs, split

½ cup FRENCH'S® Deli Brown Mustard

½ cup packed brown sugar

½ cup finely chopped onion

¼ cup FRENCH'S® Worcestershire Sauce

¼ cup cider vinegar

1 tablespoon mustard seed

1 teaspoon ground allspice

Honey Mustard Dip (recipe follows)

Place ribs in shallow non-metal baking pan or large plastic bag. Stir together mustard, sugar, onion, Worcestershire, vinegar, mustard seed, and allspice. Pour marinade over ribs, turning to coat all sides. Cover and marinate in refrigerator for 1 hour or overnight.

Place ribs on oiled grid. Grill over medium heat 45 minutes or until meat is no longer pink near bone, turning and basting often. (DO NOT baste during last 10 minutes of cooking.)

Serve with Honey Mustard Dip.

Preparation time: 10 minutes   *Marinate time:* 1 hour
Cook time: 45 minutes

Honey Mustard Dip

Makes 1 cup

½ cup FRENCH'S® Deli Brown Mustard

½ cup honey

Stir together mustard and honey.

Glazed Ham with Dijon Pineapple Sauce

Nabisco Foods Group

Makes 20 servings

1 precooked boneless ham (5 pounds)

Whole cloves

Large maraschino cherries, halved (optional)

1 cup firmly packed dark brown sugar

½ cup maple-flavored syrup

¼ cup GREY POUPON Dijon *or* COUNTRY DIJON Mustard

1 tablespoon cornstarch

1 can (20 ounces) crushed pineapple in its own juice

Score ham; stud with cloves and cherries. Place on rack in shallow baking pan. Bake at 350°F for 2 hours.

Meanwhile, combine brown sugar, syrup, and mustard; use *¾ cup* glaze mixture to baste ham every 10 minutes during last 35 to 40 minutes of baking. In saucepan, blend remaining glaze mixture, cornstarch, and pineapple with juice. Over medium-high heat, cook and stir until sauce thickens and begins to boil. Slice and serve ham with sauce.

Jubilee Ham with Rum Te Dum Sauce

Oscar Mayer Foods Corporation

Makes 12 servings

- 1 can (3 pounds) Oscar Mayer® Ham
- 1 can (8¼ ounces) crushed pineapple, with liquid
- ½ cup orange juice
- ½ cup brown sugar
- ¼ cup raisins
- 1 tablespoon cornstarch
- 1 teaspoon dry mustard
- ¼ teaspoon ground ginger
- ⅛ teaspoon ground cloves
- ⅛ teaspoon ground nutmeg
- 2 tablespoons rum

Heat ham according to label directions. Combine remaining ingredients except rum in saucepan. Bring to a boil. Turn down heat. Simmer 5 minutes until thickened, stirring occasionally. Stir in rum. Brush on ham last 30 minutes of heating. Serve remainder as sauce.

Oven-Barbecued Beef Brisket

Nabisco Foods Group

Makes 10 to 12 servings

- 1 beef brisket (5 to 6 pounds)
- 2 cans (15 ounces each) tomato sauce
- ½ cup firmly packed light brown sugar
- 1 bottle (3.5 ounces) WRIGHT'S Concentrate Natural Hickory Seasoning
- ¼ cup A.1.® Steak Sauce
- 2 tablespoons lemon juice
- ½ teaspoon liquid hot pepper seasoning

Preheat oven to 350°F. Place brisket, fat side up, in large roasting pan; set aside.

Blend tomato sauce, brown sugar, hickory seasoning, steak sauce, lemon juice, and hot pepper seasoning; pour over brisket. Bake, covered, 4 to 5 hours or until tender, basting occasionally. If necessary, thicken cooking liquid with flour; serve with sliced meat.

Hot 'n Spicy Broccoli Beef

Lawry's Foods, Inc.

Makes 4 servings

3 tablespoons vegetable oil
1 flank *or* round steak (about 1 pound), cut into thin strips
3 cups broccoli florets
½ cup water
1 teaspoon crushed red pepper
¼ teaspoon Lawry's® Garlic Powder with Parsley
¼ cup ketchup
1 to 2 tablespoons soy sauce
1½ teaspoons cornstarch
½ teaspoon ground ginger
Scallions for garnish

In large skillet, heat oil and stir-fry steak until just browned. Remove steak and set aside. In same skillet, add broccoli, ¼ *cup* water, red pepper, and garlic powder with parsley. Cover and cook 5 minutes. Meanwhile, in small bowl, combine remaining ingredients except scallions; blend well. Return meat to skillet; blend in ketchup mixture. Bring to a boil. Cook until sauce thickens and glaze develops. Garnish with scallions. Serve over chow mein noodles with sliced cucumbers and carrot sticks on the side.

Steak au Poivre with Dijon Sauce

©1996 Reckitt & Colman Inc.

Makes 4 servings

- 4 beef tenderloin steaks, cut 1½ inches thick (about 1½ pounds)
- 1 tablespoon FRENCH'S® Worcestershire Sauce
- Crushed black pepper
- ⅓ cup FRENCH'S® Dijon Mustard

- ⅓ cup mayonnaise
- 3 tablespoons dry red wine
- 2 tablespoons minced red *or* green onion
- 2 tablespoons minced parsley
- 1 clove garlic, minced

Brush steaks with Worcestershire and sprinkle with pepper to taste; set aside. Prepare Dijon Sauce: Stir together mustard, mayonnaise, wine, onion, parsley, and garlic.

Place steaks on grid. Grill steaks over high heat 15 minutes for medium rare or to desired doneness, turning often. Serve with Dijon sauce.

Note: Dijon sauce is also good with grilled salmon and swordfish. To serve with fish, substitute white wine for the red wine, and minced dill for the parsley.

Preparation time: 10 minutes   *Cook time:* 15 minutes

Sizzling Steak Fajitas

Nabisco Foods Group

Makes 4 servings

- ½ cup A.1.® Steak Sauce
- ½ cup mild, medium, *or* hot prepared salsa
- 1 (1-pound) beef flank *or* bottom round steak, thinly sliced
- 1 medium onion, thinly sliced

- 1 medium green pepper, cut into strips
- 1 tablespoon FLEISCHMANN'S Margarine
- 8 (6½-inch) flour tortillas, warmed

Blend steak sauce and salsa. Place steak in glass dish; coat with ¼ *cup* salsa mixture. Cover; chill for 15 minutes to 1 hour, stirring occasionally.

In large skillet, over medium-high heat, cook onion and pepper in margarine for 3 minutes or until tender. Remove with slotted spoon; reserve. In same skillet, cook and stir steak for 5 minutes or until done. Add *remaining* marinade, onion, and pepper; cook until heated through. Serve with tortillas and your favorite fajita toppings if desired.

Fruited Beef with Rice

Lindsay International, Inc.

Makes 6 servings

1 pound beef stew meat, cut in 1-inch cubes
1 tablespoon cooking oil
1 cup dry red wine
1 can (8 ounces) tomatoes, cut up
1 large onion, sliced ¼-inch thick
1 green pepper, cut in strips
¼ cup raisins
¼ cup dried apricots, halved
1 clove garlic, minced
1 teaspoon dried basil, crushed
1 teaspoon dried thyme, crushed
1 teaspoon dried tarragon, crushed
1 bay leaf
½ teaspoon salt
⅛ teaspoon pepper
½ cup sliced fresh mushrooms
½ cup Lindsay® Medium Pitted Ripe Olives, drained
1 cup cold water
1 tablespoon all-purpose flour
Hot cooked rice

In 10-inch skillet, brown beef in hot oil. Stir in wine, tomatoes, onion, green pepper, raisins, apricots, garlic, basil, thyme, tarragon, bay leaf, salt, and pepper. Simmer, covered, 1 hour. Stir in mushrooms and olives; simmer, covered, 30 minutes more. Discard bay leaf. Stir water into flour; stir into stew. Cook and stir until thickened and bubbly. Cook and stir 1 minute more. Serve over rice.

Poppy Beef Stroganoff

Specialty Brands

Makes about 6 servings

- 2 tablespoons vegetable oil
- 2 pounds sirloin *or* round steak, cut in 1-inch cubes
- 1 tablespoon Durkee® Poppy Seed
- 1 tablespoon Durkee® Instant Chopped Onion
- 1 teaspoon Durkee® Paprika
- 1 teaspoon Durkee® Garlic Powder
- ¼ teaspoon Durkee® Ground Black Pepper
- 1 can (10½ ounces) condensed beef broth
- 2 tablespoons all-purpose flour
- ½ cup sour cream

In large skillet, heat oil on high; add meat and spices. Cook meat about 5 minutes or until browned, stirring frequently. Add broth and flour; stir until flour is blended. Simmer, covered, about 30 to 40 minutes or until meat is tender. Stir in sour cream and heat about 5 minutes.

Serve over noodles or spaghetti squash, if desired.

Boeuf en Daube

Lindsay International, Inc.

Makes 8 servings

2 slices bacon, cut up
2 to 2½ pounds beef stew meat, cut into 1-inch cubes
2 cups dry red wine
1 medium onion, chopped
2 cloves garlic, minced
1 tablespoon vinegar
½ teaspoon instant beef bouillon granules
½ teaspoon dried rosemary, crushed
½ teaspoon dried thyme, crushed

½ teaspoon finely shredded orange peel
½ cup water
¼ teaspoon pepper
6 carrots, bias-sliced into 1-inch pieces
3 medium onions, quartered
1 can 6 ounces; 1½ cups Lindsay® Large Pitted Ripe Olives, drained
2 tablespoons cold water
2 tablespoons cornstarch

In Dutch oven, cook bacon until crisp. Add beef; brown. Stir in next 8 ingredients, *½ cup* water, and pepper. Bring to a boil. Reduce heat. Cover; simmer 1 hour. Stir in carrots, onions, and olives. Simmer, covered, about 35 minutes or until tender. Combine cornstarch and *2 tablespoons* cold water; stir into meat mixture. Cook and stir until thickened and bubbly. Cook and stir 2 minutes more.

Italian Braciole

Lindsay International, Inc.

Makes 6 servings

2 pounds beef round steak, cut ½-inch thick
Salt

1 teaspoon sugar
1 teaspoon Worcestershire sauce

Pepper
½ cup chopped onion
¼ cup chili sauce
¼ cup condensed beef broth
1 can (3 ounces) sliced mushrooms, undrained
2 tablespoons chopped green pepper
½ cup Lindsay® Salad-Style Green Olives, drained and sliced

¼ teaspoon dried oregano, crushed
⅛ teaspoon garlic powder
⅛ teaspoon pepper
Hot cooked spaghetti
½ cup cold water
3 tablespoons all-purpose flour

Preheat oven to 350°F. Cut steak into 6 rectangular pieces; pound each piece to ¼-inch thickness. Season with a little salt and pepper. Spread onion over meat to within ½ inch of edge. Roll up each piece jelly-roll style; secure with wooden toothpicks. Place meat rolls, seam side down, in a 10-by-6-by-2-inch baking dish.

Combine chili sauce, beef broth, undrained mushrooms, green pepper, olives, sugar, Worcestershire sauce, oregano, garlic powder, and ⅛ *teaspoon* pepper. Pour over meat rolls. Bake, covered, 1¼ to 1½ hours or until meat is tender.

Arrange meat rolls atop spaghetti on serving platter; keep warm. Pour pan juices into measuring cup; skim off excess fat. Add enough water to juices to make 1½ cups; pour into saucepan. Blend ½ *cup* cold water with flour; add to juices. Cook and stir until thickened and bubbly. Spoon some sauce over meat; pass remaining sauce.

Thai Beef and Noodle Toss

Nabisco Foods Group

Makes 4 servings

1 pound beef round tip steaks, cut ⅛ to ¼-inch thick	1 cup diagonally sliced carrots
1 jalapeño pepper, minced*	½ cup chopped green onion
2 cloves garlic, minced	½ cup A.1.® THICK & HEARTY Steak Sauce
2 tablespoons sesame oil	¼ cup water
1 (3-ounce) package beef-flavored instant ramen noodles	¼ cup PLANTERS® Dry Roasted Unsalted Peanuts
	2 tablespoons chopped cilantro *or* parsley

Cut beef steaks crosswise into 1-inch-wide strips; cut each strip in half. Toss beef, jalapeño peppers, and garlic with 1 tablespoon oil. Break noodles into 3 to 4 pieces; reserve seasoning packet. Cook noodles according to package directions; drain and rinse. Meanwhile heat large skillet over medium-high heat; stir-fry beef in batches for 30 to 60 seconds. Remove beef from pan; keep warm. In same skillet, in remaining oil, stir-fry carrot and green onion until tender. Add cooked noodles, steak sauce, water, peanuts, and cilantro; sprinkle with reserved seasoning packet. Heat mixture until hot, stirring occasionally. Return beef to skillet; mix lightly. Serve immediately.

*Remove interior ribs and seeds if a milder flavor is desired.

Frank's® Southwest Steak

©1996 Reckitt & Colman Inc.

Makes 6 to 8 servings

¾ cup Italian salad dressing
½ cup minced fresh parsley
⅓ cup FRANK'S® Original REDHOT® Cayenne Pepper Sauce

3 tablespoons lime juice
1 tablespoon FRENCH'S® Worcestershire Sauce
2 pounds boneless sirloin (1½ inches thick)

Place first 5 ingredients in blender or food processor. Cover; process until smooth. Reserve ¾ cup.

Pour remaining sauce over steak in deep dish. Cover; refrigerate 30 minutes.

Grill or broil steak 10 minutes per side for medium-rare or to desired doneness. Let steak stand 5 minutes. Slice steak and serve with reserved sauce mixture.

Preparation time: 10 minutes   *Marinate time:* 30 minutes

Cook time: 20 minutes

FROM HUMBLE BEGINNINGS

The Story of Pepperidge Farm

What good cook hasn't fantasized about introducing a prized recipe to the marketplace and later seeing the product made from it on supermarket shelves nationwide? Margaret Rudkin, a Fairfield, Connecticut, mother of three sons, had this fortune, starting in 1937, when homemakers hardly ventured from their hearths.

Rudkin didn't start out to build a major company. In fact, her success began with dismal news. "We've tried everything known to medical science," the doctors told her, regarding her youngest son, who suffered from severe asthma attacks. "There's nothing more we can do for his allergic condition."

Intuitively, Rudkin knew that there must be something to make her son better. She wondered if a more nutritious diet, starting with better bread, might help her son to breathe more easily. Self-evident as it seems today, few people in 1937 associated good nutrition with good health. The popular, commercially available white bread contained additives and preservatives even then.

Rudkin bought whole-wheat grain from a feed dealer and tracked down an old-time gristmill to stone-grind it. Describing her result years later, she said, "My first loaf of whole wheat tasted like a relic from the Stone Age!" But Rudkin was determined to make the best loaf of bread possible.

After tasting her perfected recipe, her son's doctors insisted on ordering some of the bread to send to other allergic patients. Her Fairfield neighbors started purchasing it at the local grocery. Rudkin could hardly produce enough to meet the ever-increasing local demand.

A natural saleswoman, Rudkin convinced a New York store manager to take on her fledgling product. Already she had enough confidence in her bread to charge twenty-five cents a loaf when the going price was ten cents. But with success came a whole new set of problems. How could she meet deliveries with no real bakery, no distribution network, no bakery trucks?

To the amusement of her stockbroker husband, she set up shop in the garage of their Fairfield home, naming the business after the pepperidge sour gum trees that grew on the property. Praising and criticizing, she taught a few local women to knead and bake bread her way.

With no other means to get the bread into the city, Rudkin prevailed upon her husband, who commuted, to take two "small" twenty-five-pound packages of fresh-baked loaves with him into Grand Central Station each morning. The first official Pepperidge Farm distributor was a railway porter who delivered the packages to a food specialty shop across the street.

By 1938, regular shipments of bread were being distributed to area stores in Dodge panel trucks. Rail express now carried fresh bread to New York specialty food shops. Three short years later, the Pepperidge Farm business outgrew the farm and moved into a rented bakery in Norwalk, Connecticut.

New products were introduced. New bread varieties led to stuffing. Exquisite cookies were modeled after the most delicious varieties the Rudkins had discovered during their trips to Europe.

Ground was broken for plants in Pennsylvania and Illinois, and by 1957, Pepperidge Farm had entered the modern era as a national company. Today, it employs more than five thousand people and makes more than two hundred products in its eight bakeries nationwide—far from its humble beginnings.

Beef Wellington

Pepperidge Farm, Inc.

Makes 6 servings

2½ pounds filet of beef
 1 sheet Pepperidge Farm®
    Frozen Puff Pastry, thawed
    20 minutes
1½ cups liver pâté

1 egg beaten with
   1 tablespoon water
1 cup homemade *or* canned
   beef gravy

Preheat oven to 425°F. Roast filet 20 minutes; cool thoroughly. On a lightly floured surface, roll out pastry to a rectangle approximately 4 inches wider and longer than the filet. Spread half the pâté in center of pastry. Place meat on pastry and spread with remaining pâté. Completely enclose the meat in the pastry, sealing the edges. If desired, make decorative designs from pastry scraps and place on top. Brush with egg; place on an ungreased baking sheet seam side down. Bake 25 minutes, or until pastry is browned. Let stand 5 minutes before slicing. Serve with heated gravy.

Bold Beef Stroganoff

Nabisco Foods Group

Makes 6 servings

1 cup thinly sliced onions
3 tablespoons margarine
3 cups thinly sliced
   mushrooms
1½ pounds beef flank steak,
    thinly sliced across the
    grain

¾ cup A.1.® ORIGINAL *or* A.1.®
   BOLD Steak Sauce
½ cup dairy sour cream
Hot cooked noodles
Chopped parsley, for garnish

In large skillet, over medium-high heat, cook onions in
1 tablespoon margarine for 2 to 3 minutes. Add mushrooms; cook just until tender. Remove from skillet.

In same skillet, brown meat in batches in remaining
margarine. Return meat and vegetables to skillet. Stir in
steak sauce. Heat to boil; reduce heat to low. Simmer for
15 minutes. Stir in sour cream. Serve immediately over
noodles, garnished with parsley.

Bistro Steak au Poivre

©1996 Reckitt & Colman Inc.

Makes 6 servings

1½ to 2 pounds boneless
   sirloin steak, 1½-inches
   thick
  2 cups sliced mushrooms
  1 can (10¾ ounces) condensed
   golden mushroom soup

½ cup dry red wine or beef
   broth
3 tablespoons FRENCH'S®
   Worcestershire Sauce

Rub sides of steak with ¼ teaspoon pepper. Heat 1 tablespoon oil over medium-high heat in nonstick skillet. Cook
steak about 5 minutes per side for medium rare or to
desired doneness. Transfer steak to platter.

Stir-fry mushrooms in 1 tablespoon oil until browned.
Stir in soup, wine, Worcestershire, and ¼ cup water. Bring
to a boil. Simmer, stirring, for 3 minutes. Return steak and
juices to skillet. Cook until heated through. Serve with
mashed potatoes, if desired.

Preperation time: 10 minutes   Cook time: 20 minutes

Burgundy Beef

Campbell Soup Company

Makes 4 servings, about 3½ cups total

1 tablespoon butter *or* margarine

½ cup chopped onion

1 large clove garlic, minced

1 pound beef for stew, cut into ½-inch pieces

1 can (10¼ ounces) Franco-American® Beef Gravy

1 cup thinly sliced carrots

¼ cup Burgundy *or* other dry red wine

¼ cup tomato paste

Hot cooked noodles

In 2-quart microwave-safe casserole, combine butter, onion, and garlic. Cover with lid; microwave on HIGH 3 minutes or until onion is tender, stirring once during cooking. Stir in beef. Cover; microwave on HIGH 5 minutes or until beef is no longer pink, stirring once during cooking. Stir in gravy, carrots, wine, and tomato paste. Cover; microwave on HIGH 5 minutes or until boiling. Stir. Reduce to MEDIUM (50% Power). Cover; microwave 30 minutes or until meat is tender, stirring twice during cooking. Let stand, covered, 5 minutes. Serve over noodles.

Southwest Barbecue Kabobs

Nabisco Foods Group

Makes 6 servings

1 cup beer

¾ cup A.1.® Steak Sauce

2 cloves garlic, crushed

2 teaspoons chili powder

1 teaspoon ground cumin

1½ pounds round steaks, cut into ½-inch strips

3 small red *or* green peppers, cut into 1-inch pieces

1 teaspoon cornstarch

Blend beer, steak sauce, garlic, chili powder, and cumin. In nonmetal dish, pour marinade over sliced steak. Cover; chill 2 hours, stirring occasionally.

Remove steak from marinade; reserve marinade. Thread steak and pepper pieces on 6 skewers. Heat reserved marinade and cornstarch to a boil. Grill or broil kabobs 4 inches from heat source for 15 minutes or until done, turning and brushing with marinade often. Heat remaining marinade to a boil; serve with kabobs.

Veal Cutlets Trentino with Fettuccine

Classico® di Firenze Pasta Sauce

Makes 4 to 6 servings

2 eggs
2 tablespoons water
½ teaspoon salt
1½ cups dry bread crumbs
⅓ cup butter *or* margarine
3 tablespoons olive oil
4 to 6 (4-ounce) veal cutlets, each cut in half
¾ cup chopped onion

2 cloves garlic, chopped
2 (26-ounce) jars Classico® di Firenze (Florentine Spinach & Cheese) Pasta Sauce
1 (1-pound) package fettuccine, cooked as package directs and drained

In bowl, beat eggs, water, and salt. Dip veal in egg mixture, then in crumbs. In large skillet, over medium heat, melt butter with *2 tablespoons* oil; brown veal on both sides. Drain. In medium saucepan, cook onion and garlic in remaining *1 tablespoon* oil until tender. Add pasta sauce; heat through. Place hot cooked fettuccine on plate; top with sauce, then veal and additional sauce if desired. Refrigerate leftovers.

Florentine Veal Roast

Specialty Brands

Makes 8 to 10 servings

4 pounds boneless breast of veal	1 teaspoon salt
¼ teaspoon Durkee® Ground Black Pepper	2 cups (8 ounces) shredded mozzarella cheese
2 teaspoons Durkee® Poultry Seasoning	1 red *or* yellow pepper, chopped
2 teaspoons Durkee® Basil	2 tablespoons olive oil
1½ teaspoons Durkee® Garlic Powder	1 can (13¾ ounces) chicken broth
2 packages (10 ounces *each*) frozen chopped spinach, thawed and drained	¼ cup dry white wine *or* water
	3 tablespoons cornstarch

Preheat oven to 350°F. Season outside of meat with black pepper and *½ teaspoon each* poultry seasoning, basil, and garlic powder; turn meat over. Combine spinach, salt, cheese, and red or yellow pepper with remaining *1½ teaspoons each* poultry seasoning and basil and with *1 teaspoon* garlic powder. Spread evenly over meat. Tightly roll up meat; tie with string at 1-inch intervals. Heat oil in Dutch oven or heavy roasting pan; brown roast on all sides. Pour broth on top. Cover tightly; roast for 1½ hours or until 165°F internal temperature. Remove roast to carving board; keep warm. Strain liquid and skim fat. Combine wine and cornstarch; stir into liquid. Bring to a boil; simmer 5 minutes, stirring, until thickened. Serve with roast.

Zesty Marinated Beef Kabobs

©1996 Reckitt & Colman Inc.

Makes 8 servings

¼ cup olive oil

¼ cup FRENCH'S® Worcestershire Sauce

¼ cup FRENCH'S® Classic Yellow® Mustard

1½ teaspoons oregano leaves

1 teaspoon seasoned salt

2 pounds boneless sirloin or top round steak, cut into 1-inch cubes

2 red *or* green peppers, cut into chunks

1 package (10 ounces) baby mushrooms

Combine oil, Worcestershire, mustard, and seasonings. Pour marinade over steak cubes in deep dish. Cover; marinate in refrigerator 30 minutes.

Alternately thread meat and vegetables on metal skewers. Broil or grill about 10 minutes or until done, basting frequently.

Preparation time: 15 minutes   *Marinate time:* 30 minutes

Cook time: 10 minutes

Beef Stew Poupon

Nabisco Foods Group

Makes 4 to 6 servings

1½ pounds beef cubes

2 tablespoons all-purpose flour

1 tablespoon vegetable oil

1 (13¾-fluid-ounce) can COLLEGE INN Beef Broth

2 cups onion slices (2 medium onions)

1½ cups sliced carrots

1 (10-ounce) package frozen peas

½ cup GREY POUPON Horseradish Specialty Mustard

4 cups hot cooked noodles

Coat beef cubes with flour, shaking off excess; set aside. In large heavy pot, over medium-high heat, brown beef in oil. Add broth and onion; heat to a boil. Cover; reduce heat and simmer for 45 minutes. Uncover; stir in carrots and peas. Simmer for 30 minutes or until beef is tender. Stir in mustard; heat through. Serve over noodles.

Marinated Sizzle Steak

©1996 Reckitt & Colman Inc.

Makes 6 to 8 servings

- ¼ cup FRENCH'S® Worcestershire Sauce
- ¼ cup red wine vinegar
- ¼ cup FRENCH'S® Dijon Mustard
- 2 tablespoons olive oil
- 1 teaspoon onion powder
- 1 teaspoon garlic powder
- 2 pounds boneless sirloin *or* top round steak (1½-inches thick)

Combine Worcestershire, vinegar, mustard, oil, and seasonings; mix well. Pour marinade over steak in deep dish. Cover; marinate in refrigerator 30 minutes.

Grill or broil steak 8 minutes per side for medium-rare or to desired doneness. Let steak stand 5 minutes before slicing. Serve with reserved sauce.

Preparation time: 5 minutes   *Marinate time:* 30 minutes
Cook time: 20 minutes

POULTRY

Chicken in a Skillet

Lipton

Makes 4 servings

2 tablespoons oil

2½ to 3 pounds chicken, cut into serving pieces

1 can (14½ ounces) whole peeled tomatoes, undrained and chopped

1 envelope Lipton® Recipe Secrets® Onion Soup Mix

⅓ cup water

In 12-inch skillet, heat oil over medium-high heat and brown chicken; drain. Add tomatoes, then onion soup mix blended with water. Simmer covered, stirring occasionally, 45 minutes or until chicken is no longer pink.

Herbed Chicken and Potatoes

Lipton

Makes 4 servings

1 pound all-purpose potatoes, thinly sliced

4 bone-in chicken breast halves (about 2 pounds)

8 Lemon slices (optional)

1 envelope Lipton® Recipe Secrets® Savory Herb with Garlic Soup Mix

⅓ cup water

1 tablespoon olive *or* vegetable oil

Preheat oven to 375°. In 13-by-9-inch baking or roasting pan, add potatoes and lemon; arrange chicken on top. Pour savory herb with garlic soup mix blended with water and oil over chicken and potatoes.

Bake uncovered 50 minutes or until chicken is no longer pink and potatoes are tender.

Variations: Also delicious substituting 1 (2½ to 3-pound) chicken, cut into serving pieces, for chicken breast halves.

Also terrific with Lipton® Recipe Secrets® Golden Herb with Lemon Soup Mix.

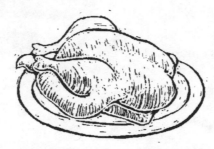

Chicken with Mustard-Dill Sauce

Ragú Foods Co.

Makes 4 servings

1 package Adolph's® Chicken Marinade
½ cup water
¼ cup lemon juice
1 pound boneless chicken breasts, pounded thin

1 tablespoon vegetable oil
1 tablespoon chopped fresh dill
1 teaspoon Dijon mustard
¼ cup light cream
6 slices bacon, cooked and crumbled

In shallow pan, combine marinade mix with water and lemon juice. Place chicken in marinade; pierce deeply with a fork. Marinate 15 minutes, turning chicken occasionally. Remove chicken; reserve ¼ cup marinade. In large skillet, thoroughly brown chicken on both sides in hot oil. Cover and cook 15 minutes over low heat. Add reserved marinade, dill, mustard, cream, and bacon. Mix thoroughly; heat through. Serve sauce over chicken.

Classic Herbed Chicken

Lipton

Makes 4 servings

1 envelope Lipton® Recipe Secrets® Savory Herb with Garlic Soup Mix
⅓ cup mayonnaise

2 tablespoons water
4 boneless, skinless chicken breast halves (about 1¼ pounds)

Preheat oven to 425°. In small bowl, blend savory herb with garlic soup mix, mayonnaise, and water.

In 13-by-9-inch baking or roasting pan sprayed with nonstick cooking spray, arrange chicken; brush with ½ of the soup mixture.

Bake uncovered, turning once and brushing with remaining soup mixture, 25 minutes or until chicken is no longer pink.

Variation: Also terrific with Lipton® Recipe Secrets® Golden Herb with Lemon Soup Mix.

Onion-Roasted Chicken and Vegetables

Lipton

Makes about 4 servings

1 envelope Lipton® Recipe Secrets® Onion Soup Mix
¼ cup olive *or* vegetable oil
½ teaspoon garlic powder
4 bone-in chicken breast halves (about 2 pounds)

1 pound all-purpose potatoes, cut into small chunks
2 carrots, sliced

Preheat oven to 450°. In large plastic bag or bowl, add all ingredients. Close bag and shake, or toss in bowl, until chicken and vegetables are evenly coated.

In 13-by-9-inch baking or roasting pan, arrange chicken, breast side up, and vegetables; discard bag.

Bake uncovered, basting halfway through, 45 minutes or until chicken is no longer pink and vegetables are done.

Variation: Also terrific with Lipton® Recipe Secrets® Onion-Mushroom, Golden Onion, or Savory Herb with Garlic Soup Mix.

Citrus Glazed Chicken

Ragú Foods Co.

Makes 4 servings

1 package Adolph's® Marinade in Minutes— Lemon-Pepper Flavor
⅔ cup orange juice
1 tablespoon Dijon mustard
1 teaspoon Worcestershire sauce
1 chicken (about 3½ to 4 pounds), quartered

Preheat oven to 350°F. In medium bowl, thoroughly combine contents of marinade package with orange juice, Dijon mustard, and Worcestershire sauce. Place chicken in marinade; pierce deeply with a fork. Marinate 15 minutes, turning chicken occasionally. Remove chicken from marinade. Place on baking sheet. Bake 1 hour and 10 minutes or until thoroughly cooked. Baste occasionally with remaining marinade.

Chicken Fanfare

Oscar Mayer Foods Corporation

Makes 8 servings
8 boneless chicken-breast halves

Stuffing
1 package (6 ounces)
   chicken-flavored stuffing
   mix
1½ cups water
¼ cup butter, melted
1 cup raisins

Topping
1 cup ground pecans
Grated rind from 2 oranges *or*
   2 tablespoons dried
   orange peel
2 tablespoons sugar
1 package (12 ounces)
   Oscar Mayer®
   Center-Cut Bacon

Preheat oven to 350°F. Remove skin from chicken; pound between 2 pieces of waxed paper to ¼-inch thick. Remove waxed paper. In large bowl, combine stuffing ingredients; mix thoroughly. Place ⅓ cup stuffing mixture on each pounded chicken breast. Fold ends of chicken over stuffing. Wrap chicken bundle with 3 slices of bacon. Combine topping ingredients in pie plate. Roll chicken bundle in nut mixture. Place seam side down in shallow baking sheet. Sprinkle with remaining nut mixture. Bake 40 to 45 minutes.

Stuffed Chicken Breasts

Lawry's Foods, Inc.

Makes 6 to 8 servings

1½ to 2 pounds boneless chicken-breast halves, with skin

1 package (10 ounces) frozen chopped spinach, thawed

1 cup (4 ounces) grated fontina *or* Monterey Jack cheese

1 cup (4 ounces) grated Parmesan cheese

½ cup shredded carrot

¼ cup sliced green onions

2 tablespoons minced fresh basil *or* 2 teaspoons dried basil, crushed

½ teaspoon Lawry's® Garlic Powder with Parsley

½ teaspoon Lawry's® Seasoned Pepper

Imperial® Margarine, melted

Preheat oven to 375°F. Rinse chicken thoroughly; pat dry. Place spinach in strainer; press with back of spoon to remove excess liquid. In medium bowl, combine all ingredients except chicken and margarine. Using fingers, carefully stuff thin layer of spinach mixture under skin of chicken. Pat top with paper towel; brush with margarine. Place stuffed chicken pieces in shallow baking dish. Bake 25 to 30 minutes or until chicken is golden brown. Let stand 5 minutes.

Slice chicken crosswise and serve with rice pilaf. Garnish with lemon slices and fresh basil.

Variation: To prepare recipe using skinless chicken, slit 1 side of chicken breast to create a "pocket." Place stuffing mixture in "pocket," brush with margarine, and bake as above.

Vegetable Confetti Stuffed Chicken

Lawry's Foods, Inc.

Makes 6 servings

1½ pounds boneless chicken breasts, skinned

1 tablespoon vegetable oil

1 carrot, cut into julienne strips

1 zucchini, cut into julienne strips

1 red bell pepper, cut into julienne strips

½ teaspoon Lawry's® Seasoned Salt

¼ teaspoon Lawry's® Garlic Powder with Parsley

4 ounces Cheddar cheese, thinly sliced

½ cup dry white wine *or* chicken broth

Lawry's® Seasoned Salt

Lawry's® Lemon Pepper Seasoning

To microwave: Place chicken breasts between 2 sheets of waxed paper; pound with meat mallet or rolling pin to flatten to ¼-inch thickness. In medium skillet, heat oil and sauté carrot, zucchini, and red pepper with *½ teaspoon* seasoned salt and with garlic powder with parsley. On each chicken breast, place 1 slice of Cheddar cheese. Divide vegetable mixture evenly among chicken breasts. Roll up each breast and secure with wooden toothpicks. Place chicken rolls in microwave-safe dish; pour wine over rolls. Cover with vented plastic wrap and microwave on HIGH 8 to 12 minutes or until chicken is cooked through. Let stand 5 minutes. Drain off excess liquid. Sprinkle with seasoned salt and lemon pepper seasoning to taste.

Slice chicken rolls into ¼-inch slices. Serve with seasoned rice and garnish with tomato rose.

Caribbean Chicken

Kellogg Company

Makes 4 servings

4 split chicken breasts (without *or* with skin), rinsed and dried
1 egg, slightly beaten
2 cups *KELLOGG'S CORN FLAKES®* cereal, crushed to ½ cup
¼ cup firmly packed brown sugar
1 tablespoon cornstarch
Water
1 can (10 ounce) mandarin oranges, drained, reserving juice
2 tablespoons frozen orange juice concentrate, thawed
2 tablespoons margarine (optional)
Vegetable cooking spray

Preheat oven to 350°F. Dip chicken in beaten egg and coat with *KELLOGG'S CORN FLAKES®* cereal. Place in single layer in shallow baking pan coated with cooking spray.

Bake about 1 hour or until chicken is tender, no longer pink, and juices run clear. Do not cover pan or turn chicken while baking.

In medium-size saucepan, combine sugar and cornstarch. Add enough water to reserved mandarin orange juice to measure ¾ cup. Stir into cornstarch mixture along with orange juice concentrate. Cook over medium heat, stirring constantly, until mixture boils. Continue cooking and stirring 3 minutes longer. Stir in margarine, if desired, and mandarin oranges. Serve hot over chicken.

Drunken Chicken

McCormick & Company, Inc.

Makes 4 servings

- 4 half chicken breasts, boneless and skinless
- ¼ cup light rum
- ¼ teaspoon McCormick/Schilling® ground Nutmeg
- 1 tablespoon soy sauce
- 1 tablespoon lime juice
- 1 tablespoon brown sugar
- ¾ teaspoon McCormick/Schilling Bon Appétit®
- ¼ teaspoon McCormick/Schilling ® Crushed Red Pepper
- ⅛ teaspoon McCormick/Schilling® ground Ginger
- 2 tablespoons butter
- 2 cups sliced mushrooms
- 1 cup dairy sour cream

Additional McCormick/Schilling ® ground Nutmeg (optional)

Carrot strips for garnish

Celery strips for garnish

Pound chicken breasts to ½-inch thickness. Pierce several times using tines of a fork. Place in single layer in shallow glass dish. Set aside. Combine next 8 ingredients. Mix well. Pour liquid over chicken. Marinate at room temperature 30 minutes, turning once. Melt butter in skillet over medium heat. Reserving marinade, remove chicken and sauté in butter. Remove chicken. Keep warm. Sauté mushrooms. Reduce heat and add marinade. Gradually add sour cream. Stir to blend. Cook, covered, over low heat 5 minutes. Serve sauce over chicken breasts. Sprinkle with additional nutmeg if desired. Garnish with thin strips of carrots and celery.

Mustard Crusted Chicken Cutlets

©1996 Reckitt & Colman Inc.

Makes 4 servings

- ¼ cup FRENCH'S® Deli Brown Mustard
- ¼ cup finely chopped green onion
- ½ teaspoon dried tarragon leaves
- ¼ teaspoon ground black pepper
- ¼ cup plain dry bread crumbs
- 4 boneless, skinless chicken breast halves, patted dry
- 2 tablespoons vegetable oil

Combine mustard, onion, tarragon, and black pepper in small bowl. Sprinkle bread crumbs onto sheet of waxed paper. Brush chicken with mustard mixture. Dip into bread crumbs to coat completely.

Heat oil in large nonstick skillet over medium heat. Add chicken; cook 10 to 15 minutes until chicken is browned on outside and no longer pink in center, turning halfway during cooking.

To serve, cut chicken into strips and serve over tossed salad greens or on a hero with desired dressing.

Preparation time: 15 minutes   *Cook time:* 10 minutes

Chicken Italienne

Kellogg Company

Makes 6 servings

- 1 cup (8 ounce can) tomato sauce
- ½ teaspoon garlic salt
- ½ teaspoon sweet basil
- ¼ teaspoon oregano
- 3 pounds broiler chicken pieces (without *or* with skin), rinsed and dried
- 5 cups *KELLOGG'S CORN FLAKES®* cereal, crushed to 2½ cups
- Vegetable cooking spray

Preheat oven to 350°F. Combine tomato sauce and seasonings. Dip chicken pieces into tomato sauce mixture, then roll in *KELLOGG'S CORN FLAKES*® cereal. Place chicken pieces, skin side up, in shallow pan coated with cooking spray. Do not crowd.

Bake about 1 hour or until tender, no longer pink, and juices run clear. Do not cover pan or turn chicken while baking.

South Seas Chicken

Specialty Brands

Makes 6 servings

2 tablespoons vegetable oil

1½ pounds boneless, skinless chicken breasts, cut into cubes

½ cup chopped onion

3 cups assorted vegetables (red pepper, carrots, and snow peas), cut in bite-size pieces

1 can (20 ounces) pineapple chunks, drained, with juice reserved

2 tablespoons soy sauce

1 tablespoon cornstarch

1 teaspoon Durkee® Ground Cumin

¼ teaspoon Durkee® Garlic Powder

¼ teaspoon Durkee® Ground Ginger

In large skillet, heat oil. Stir-fry chicken and onion 5 minutes or until chicken is done. Add vegetables and pineapple; stir-fry 2 minutes. In small bowl, combine reserved pineapple juice and remaining ingredients; mix until smooth and stir into chicken mixture. Cook and stir until sauce is thickened and bubbly, about 2 minutes.

Serve over rice.

Easy Chicken and Vegetable Stir-Fry

©1996 Reckitt & Colman Inc.

Makes 6 servings

- 1 pound chicken strips
- 1 package (21 ounces) teriyaki stir-fry frozen vegetable combination*
- 1⅓ cups (2.8 ounce can) FRENCH'S® French Fried Onions

In nonstick skillet, in *1 tablespoon hot oil,* stir-fry chicken until browned.

Add vegetables and contents of sauce packet. Stir-fry until crisp-tender.

Microwave French Fried Onions 1 minute. Sprinkle over stir-fry. If desired, serve with rice.

*Or use 4 cups frozen vegetables and ¾ cup teriyaki stir-fry sauce.

Preparation time: 5 minutes   *Cook time:* 10 minutes

Sunburst Stir-Fry

Dole Food Company

Makes 4 servings

- 1 can (20 ounces) Dole® Pineapple Chunks, drained, with ⅓ cup juice reserved
- 2 chicken breast halves, skinned and boned
- 2 large cloves garlic, pressed
- 2 tablespoons minced ginger root *or* 1 teaspoon ground ginger
- 2 tablespoons vegetable oil
- 2 medium Dole® Carrots, sliced
- 1 Dole® Green Bell Pepper, slivered
- 4 ounces cooked thin spaghetti
- ⅓ cup soy sauce
- 1 tablespoon cornstarch
- 1 tablespoon sesame oil
- 3 Dole® Green Onions, chunked

Drain pineapple, reserving ⅓ cup juice for sauce. Chunk chicken. In large skillet, stir-fry chicken with garlic and ginger in oil 2 minutes. Add pineapple, carrots, and bell pepper. Cover; steam 2 to 3 minutes until vegetables are tender-crisp. Stir in spaghetti.

To make sauce; stir together reserved pineapple juice, soy sauce, cornstarch, and sesame oil. Pour into skillet along with green onions. Toss until ingredients are thoroughly mixed and heated through.

Chicken Curry

Dole Food Company

Makes 4 to 6 servings

1 can (20 ounces) Dole® Pineapple Chunks, drained, with juice reserved
2 chicken bouillon cubes
4 boneless, skinless chicken breast halves, cubed
1 cup chopped onion
2 tablespoons margarine
2 teaspoons curry powder
1 cup long-grain rice, uncooked
½ cup Dole® Raisins
2 tablespoons chopped parsley
2 tablespoons Dole® Blanched Slivered Almonds, toasted

Add enough water to reserved pineapple juice to make 2 cups liquid. Heat. Add bouillon to dissolve. Sauté chicken and onion in margarine. Stir in curry powder. Add rice and juice mixture. Bring to a boil. Reduce heat. Simmer, covered, 25 minutes. Stir in pineapple, raisins, parsley, and almonds just before serving.

To toast almonds: Preheat oven to 350°F. Place almonds in a shallow pan and bake for 10 minutes. Toasting time will vary depending on the size of the almonds.

Teriyaki Chicken

Dole Food Company

Makes 12 buffet servings

8 chicken breast halves, boned
2 cups Dole® Pineapple Juice
1 cup soy sauce
3 tablespoons honey
2 pounds quartered mushrooms
¼ cup cornstarch

Preheat oven to 450°F. Place chicken in 3-quart shallow baking dish. Combine juice, soy sauce, and honey. Pour over chicken. Marinate 1 hour or overnight in refrigerator.

Add mushrooms to chicken and coat with marinade. Bake 20 minutes. Spoon ½ *cup* pan juices into small bowl. Stir in cornstarch. Pour back into pan, spooning sauce over chicken and mushrooms. Return to oven and bake 20 minutes longer or until chicken is tender. Cut chicken in slices.

General Tso's Chicken

JFC International, Inc.

Makes 2 to 3 servings

1½ chicken breasts, skinned, boned, and cut into ¾-inch pieces
1 tablespoon Dynasty® Oriental Marinade
2 tablespoons Dynasty® Hoisin Sauce
2 tablespoons Dynasty® Black Bean Sauce
1 tablespoon dry sherry *or* water
1 tablespoon Dynasty® Chinese Stir-Fry Oil
1 green onion and top, halved lengthwise and cut into ¾-inch lengths
½ cup roasted, salted peanuts
1 teaspoon Dynasty® Hot Chili Oil

Coat chicken with marinade; let stand 20 minutes. Combine hoisin and black bean sauces with sherry; mix well.

Heat wok or large frying pan over high heat. Add oil; coat wok. Add chicken; stir-fry 3 to 4 minutes or until lightly browned. Add hoisin sauce mixture and green onion; cook and stir 1 minute or until heated through. Remove from heat; stir in peanuts and chili oil. Serve immediately with hot cooked rice, as desired.

Hot and Spicy Peanut Chicken

JFC International, Inc.

Makes 3 to 4 servings

- 2 whole chicken breasts, skinned, boned, and cut into ¾-inch pieces
- 2 tablespoons Dynasty® Oriental Marinade
- 2 tablespoons Dynasty® Chinese Stir-Fry Oil
- 2 medium zucchini, halved lengthwise and cut crosswise into ½ inch widths
- ¼ cup Dynasty® Spicy Kung Pao Sauce
- 1 can (8 ounces) Dynasty® Whole Water Chestnuts, drained and halved vertically
- ⅓ cup roasted, salted peanuts

Coat chicken with marinade; let stand 20 minutes. Heat wok or large frying pan over high heat. Add oil; coat wok. Add chicken; stir-fry 2 to 3 minutes or until lightly browned. Add zucchini; stir-fry 1 minute. Stir in Kung Pao sauce. Bring to a boil. Cover wok and cook 2 minutes. Add water chestnuts; stir-fry 1 minute, or until sauce is slightly thickened and zucchini is tender-crisp. Remove from heat; stir in peanuts. Serve immediately.

THE PEANUT PRESCRIPTION

The Story of Peanuts and Peanut Butter

Not really a nut at all, the peanut, like a pea, is a seed in a pod, actually a legume, a member of the bean family. The peanut plant is a botanical oddity because it produces its fruit by growing downward instead of upward. After the flower of the plant is fertilized, it withers and drops off. An elongated stalk appears in its place to grow downward and bury itself in the ground. Once covered with soil, the tip of the stalk develops into a peanut pod.

For many years peanuts were thought to have entered the Americas from Africa via slave ships, but actually they are among the many important foods discovered nearly five hundred years ago in the New World. The peanuts found in ancient Peruvian tombs and related legume plants growing wildly in Brazil have confirmed that peanuts are South American natives. Early Portuguese traders exchanged peanuts for ivory and spices on the African coast. From there, the legumes sailed back to the New World with African slaves. At first Southeasterners grew them mainly to feed chickens and pigs; only slaves and poor Southern families ate the "goobers," as they were called.

Seventeenth-century colonists found Indians growing peanuts in Virginia when they arrived there. Virginia landowners began to enjoy eating the seed from shells. Some decided to dedicate fields to raising them. By the middle of the nineteenth century, Georgia was called the Goober State because of its colossal peanut crops. Former President Jimmy Carter is the most famous peanut farmer in the Goober State.

Peanuts were a welcome surprise for hungry Civil War Union soldiers, who developed a taste for the crunchy roasted seed. "Peanut porridge" became a staple of the Union army. The soldiers carried the plants back home to the North, but the seed remained no more than a curiosity there until P. T. Barnum began selling nickel peanut bags at his circuses in the 1880s.

In 1890 a diligent St. Louis physician seeking an easily digestible source of protein for his elderly patients ground peanuts with salt in his kitchen grinder. His peanut-spread prescription became so popular that in 1893 he decided to introduce Chicago World's Fair visitors to the peanutty treat. A decade later, commercially produced peanut butter was on the market, and by 1914 there were several dozen brands.

First sold in 1933, Skippy® Peanut Butter boasted "fuller flavor; smooth as satin" on the package. Skippy® Peanut Butter is now so popular that someone in the United States buys a jar every few seconds. Enough peanut butter is consumed in the United States today to make 10 billion peanut butter and jelly sandwiches annually.

Chicken Saté with Peanut Butter Sauce

Best Foods, a division of CPC International Inc.

Makes 4 servings

3 tablespoons soy sauce
2 tablespoons Mazola®
  Corn Oil
1 tablespoon lemon juice
½ teaspoon curry powder

1 clove garlic, minced or
  pressed
1 pound chicken breasts,
  boned, skinned, and cut
  into 1-inch cubes
Peanut Butter Sauce
  (see below)

In small bowl, stir together soy sauce, corn oil, lemon juice, curry powder, and garlic. Add chicken; toss to coat well. Cover; refrigerate at least 2 hours. Drain; reserve marinade. Rinse bamboo skewers in water; thread with chicken cubes. Broil about 6 inches from source of heat, turning and basting frequently with reserved marinade, about 5 minutes or until tender. Serve with Peanut Butter Sauce.

Peanut Butter Sauce

Makes about 1½ cups

1 teaspoon Mazola®
  Corn Oil
¼ cup sliced green onions
1 teaspoon minced ginger
  root
¼ to ½ teaspoon red
  pepper flakes

½ cup Skippy® Creamy *or*
  Super Chunk® Peanut
  Butter
1 cup water
1 tablespoon soy
  sauce

In 1-quart saucepan, heat corn oil over medium heat. Add green onions, ginger root, and red pepper flakes. Stirring frequently, cook 1 minute. Stirring constantly, add peanut butter. Gradually stir in water and soy sauce until well blended. While stirring constantly, bring to a boil until mixture thickens. Serve hot or at room temperature with chicken kabobs.

Chicken Paella

Lindsay International, Inc.

Makes 4 servings

6 ounces chorizo *or* Italian sausage, sliced
1 medium onion, chopped
1 small sweet red *or* green pepper, cut into chunks
1 clove garlic, minced
3 chicken breasts, halved
Salt
Pepper
¾ cup long-grain rice
1½ teaspoons instant chicken bouillon granules

¼ teaspoon ground turmeric
3 cups hot water
4 baby carrots *or* 3-inch carrot chunks
1 package (10 ounces) frozen peas
1 package (9 ounces) frozen artichoke hearts
1 cup Lindsay® Large Pitted Ripe Olives, drained
6 cherry tomatoes, halved

In 12-inch skillet or Dutch oven, cook sausage, onion, pepper, and garlic until sausage is brown and onion and pepper are tender. Drain, reserving drippings in pan; set sausage mixture aside. Season chicken with salt and pepper. Brown in reserved drippings; remove from skillet. Stir in uncooked rice, bouillon granules, turmeric, and water; bring to a boil. Add sausage mixture and carrots. Arrange chicken atop. Reduce heat; cover and simmer 20 minutes.

Meanwhile, rinse peas and artichoke hearts under hot tap water to separate. Arrange atop chicken. Cover and cook 15 to 17 minutes more or until rice and chicken are tender. Add olives and tomatoes; heat through.

Venetian Chicken in Spicy Tomato Cream

Classico® di Roma Arrabiata and di Sorrento Pasta Sauces

Makes 4 to 6 servings

1 pound skinned boneless chicken breast halves, cut in 1-inch pieces and seasoned lightly with salt and pepper

3 tablespoons chopped fresh *or* 1 teaspoon dried basil leaves

2 tablespoons olive oil

1 (26-ounce) jar Classico® di Roma Arrabbiata (Spicy Red Pepper) *or* di Sorrento (Roasted Garlic) Pasta Sauce

½ cup whipping cream *or* evaporated skim milk

2 tablespoons chopped fresh parsley

1 (1-pound) package penne rigate, cooked as package directs and drained

Italian parsley

In Dutch oven, over medium-high heat, cook and stir chicken and basil in oil until chicken is no longer pink. Stir in pasta sauce, cream, and parsley. Bring to a boil; reduce heat and simmer, covered, 10 minutes. Serve with hot cooked penne and garnish with parsley. Refrigerate leftovers.

Lemon Chicken and Pasta

Nabisco Foods Group

Makes 4 servings

¼ cup (½ stick) BLUE BONNET 53% Vegetable Oil Spread

2 (4-ounce) boneless, skinless chicken breasts, cut into strips

2 cloves garlic, minced

1 tablespoon each chopped chives, parsley, and thyme

½ cup fresh squeezed lemon juice

½ pound angel hair pasta, cooked

Grated Parmesan cheese

In large skillet, over medium-high heat, melt spread. Add chicken and garlic; cook and stir for 2 to 3 minutes or until chicken is done. Add herbs and lemon juice; heat through. Pour over hot cooked pasta; toss and serve immediately with cheese.

Chicken Cordon Bleu

Sargento Cheese Company, Inc.

Makes 4 servings

4 large chicken breast halves, boned and skinned

1 tablespoon Dijon mustard

½ teaspoon dried thyme

4 slices (4 ounces) lean cooked ham

2 slices (1½ ounces) Sargento® Preferred Light® Sliced Swiss Cheese

¼ cup seasoned bread crumbs

1 tablespoon Sargento® Grated Parmesan

4 teaspoons melted light margarine

Preheat oven to 400°F. Place chicken breast between 2 pieces of waxed paper. Pound to ¼-inch thickness. Divide mustard and spread down center of chicken. Sprinkle with thyme. Top each chicken breast with a slice of ham and half a slice of Swiss cheese. Roll up jelly-roll style, tucking in sides of ham and chicken to seal. Secure with skewers or large sandwich picks. Combine bread crumbs and Parmesan cheese. Brush chicken with melted margarine and roll in crumb mixture. Place on a 9-by-9-inch baking pan. Bake 10 minutes. Reduce heat to 350°F and continue baking 20 to 25 minutes or until chicken is done. Remove picks. Serve immediately.

Chicken Taquitos

Lawry's Foods, Inc.

Makes 6 servings

12 corn tortillas	½ cup minced green onions
1 pound chicken breasts, boneless and skinless, cooked and shredded	¼ teaspoon Lawry's® Garlic Powder with Parsley
1 package (1.25 ounces) Lawry's® Taco Spices and Seasonings	1 cup finely chopped tomatoes
	Vegetable oil for frying
	Lettuce, shredded
½ cup hot water	Guacamole for garnish
	Red onion, sliced, for garnish

Preheat oven to 200°F. Sprinkle tortillas lightly with water; wrap in aluminum foil and place in oven 10 minutes to soften. Leave in foil until ready to use. In skillet, combine chicken, spices and seasonings, water, onions, and garlic powder with parsley; blend well. Bring to a boil, reduce heat, and simmer 10 minutes. Stir in tomatoes. Place 2 *tablespoons* chicken mixture down center of each warmed tortilla. Roll up tortillas tightly; secure with toothpicks. In deep, large saucepan, heat oil to 375°F. Fry rolled tortillas in oil until golden brown and crisp. Drain well on paper towels. Keep warm in oven; remove toothpicks before serving. Serve on shredded lettuce. Garnish with guacamole and sliced red onion.

To microwave: Sprinkle tortillas lightly with water; wrap in plastic wrap and microwave on HIGH 30 seconds to soften. Leave in plastic until ready to use. In large micro-wave-safe dish, combine chicken, spices and seasonings, water, onions, and garlic powder with parsley; blend well. Cover and microwave on HIGH 5 to 6 minutes, stirring after 4 minutes. Stir in tomatoes. Fill and roll tortillas and fry as above.

Rosemary's Chicken

©1996 Reckitt & Colman Inc.

Makes 4 servings

4 large (2 pounds) boneless, skinless chicken breast halves

¼ cup FRENCH'S® Classic Yellow® Mustard

¼ cup orange juice concentrate (undiluted)

2 tablespoons cider vinegar

2 teaspoons rosemary leaves, crushed

4 strips thick sliced bacon

Place chicken into plastic bag or bowl. Stir together mustard, orange juice concentrate, vinegar, and rosemary. Pour over chicken. Seal bag and marinate in refrigerator 30 minutes.

Wrap 1 strip of bacon around each piece of chicken; secure with toothpicks.

Place chicken on oiled grid. Grill chicken over medium heat 25 minutes or until chicken is no longer pink, turning and basting often. DO NOT BASTE chicken during last 10 minutes of cooking. Remove toothpicks before serving.

Preparation time: 15 minutes   *Marinate time:* 30 minutes

Cook time: 25 minutes

Chicken Risotto

Sargento Cheese Company, Inc.

Makes 6 servings

6 tablespoons butter *or* margarine, divided

1 pound chicken breasts, boned, skinned, and cut into thin strips

1½ cups rice

1 clove garlic, minced

¼ pound mushrooms, sliced

3 green onions, thinly sliced

3 cups chicken broth

1 teaspoon basil

1 cup (4 ounces) Sargento® Fancy Shredded Cheddar Cheese

In large skillet, melt *2 tablespoons* butter. Add chicken and cook over medium heat, stirring constantly, until browned, about 5 minutes. Remove chicken from skillet. Add *remaining* butter, rice, and garlic to skillet and cook, stirring constantly, until rice is lightly browned, about 5 minutes. Add mushrooms and green onions. Continue cooking, stirring occasionally, until mushrooms are tender, about 2 minutes. Stir in chicken broth and basil. Bring to a boil; cover and simmer 15 minutes. Gently stir in chicken. Continue simmering until chicken is heated through and rice is tender, about 5 minutes. Top with cheese and serve immediately.

Lemon Herb Roasted Chicken

**ReaLemon® Lemon Juice from Concentrate
Wyler's® or Steero® Chicken-Flavor Bouillon
Granules**

Makes 4 servings

4 skinless, boneless chicken breast halves

¼ cup ReaLemon® Lemon Juice from Concentrate

1 tablespoon Wyler's® *or* Steero® Chicken-Flavor Bouillon Granules *or* 3 Chicken-Flavor Bouillon Cubes

1 teaspoon oregano leaves

Preheat oven to 350°F. Place chicken in shallow baking dish. In small bowl, combine remaining ingredients and ¼ *cup water*, pour over chicken. Bake 30 to 40 minutes or until chicken is tender, basting frequently. Refrigerate leftovers.

Sweet 'n Spicy Baked Chicken

Specialty Brands

Makes 4 servings

2½ to 3 pounds cut-up chicken, skinned if desired
1 tablespoon dehydrated minced onion
1 cup ketchup
⅓ cup packed brown sugar
¼ cup red wine vinegar *or* white distilled vinegar
¼ teaspoon Durkee® Ground Cloves
¼ teaspoon Durkee® Ground Black Pepper

Preheat oven to 350°F. Arrange chicken pieces meaty side up, in single layer, in shallow 9-by-13-inch baking dish. Combine remaining ingredients and pour over chicken. Bake, uncovered, 45 to 50 minutes, basting halfway through.

Chicken Stir-Fry Dijon

Nabisco Foods Group

Makes 4 servings

1 cup COLLEGE INN Chicken Broth
1 tablespoon soy sauce
2 teaspoons cornstarch
4 cups cut-up assorted vegetables (carrots, pepper, onion, broccoli)
1 clove garlic, crushed
1 tablespoon vegetable oil
1 pound boneless, skinless chicken breasts, cut into strips
½ cup GREY POUPON COUNTRY DIJON Mustard *or* GREY POUPON Dijon Mustard
Hot cooked rice

In small bowl, combine broth, soy sauce, and cornstarch; set aside.

In large skillet, over medium-high heat, sauté vegetables and garlic in oil until tender-crisp. Remove from pan; keep warm. In same skillet, sauté chicken strips until no longer pink, about 3 to 5 minutes. Return vegetables to pan. Stir in broth mixture; heat to boil. Reduce heat; simmer 5 minutes or until mixture thickens slightly. Stir in mustard; heat through. Serve over rice.

Creamy Chicken & Pasta

©1996 Reckitt & Colman Inc.

Makes 6 servings

1½ pounds boneless, skinless chicken, cut into cubes

1 can (10¾ ounces) CAMPBELL'S® Condensed Cream of Chicken Soup

1½ cups milk

⅓ cup grated Parmesan cheese

1⅓ cups (2.8 ounce can) FRENCH'S® French Fried Onions

3 cups hot cooked noodles

Heat *1 tablespoon oil* in nonstick skillet; cook chicken 5 minutes until browned.

Stir in soup, milk, cheese, ⅔ *cup* French Fried Onions, and noodles. Simmer, stirring, until hot.

Microwave ⅔ *cup* onions 1 minute. Sprinkle over noodles. If desired, garnish with chopped parsley and tomatoes.

Preparation time: 10 minutes   *Cook time:* 11 minutes

RECKITT & COLMAN ADDS "SPICE OF LIFE" TO AMERICA'S RECIPES FOR 100 YEARS

From dressing up the world's first hot dog at the 1904 St. Louis World's Fair, to being the key ingredient used to create the first Buffalo chicken wings and unleashing a national chicken wing flurry, when it comes to adding zest to life's favorite foods, Reckitt & Colman has been there for more than a century.

Committed to developing quality products that enhance and enliven various foods, the family of Reckitt & Colman fine quality products include FRENCH'S® Classic Yellow®, FRENCH'S Deli Brown Mustard and FRENCH'S Dijon Mustard, FRENCH'S French Fried Onions, FRENCH'S Potato Sticks, FRENCH'S Worcestershire Sauce and FRANK'S® Original REDHOT® Cayenne Pepper Sauce.

These extraordinary products have become a significant and historic part of America's food celebrations and are now standard fare at dinner tables and family gatherings. On their own or as part of a recipe, these products add just the right flavor to one's favorite dishes and have become synonymous with great taste.

A true American favorite, FRENCH'S CLASSIC YELLOW Mustard, with its mild, delicious taste, has been making the difference on hot dogs, sandwiches and in family recipes for more than 90 years. Now joined by mild FRENCH'S Dijon Mustard and hearty Deli Brown Mustard, FRENCH'S offers a delectable enhancement to a host of recipes featured in this book.

FRANK'S Original REDHOT Cayenne Pepper Sauce dates back to a 1920's recipe offering a unique blend of tang and spice to enhance all kinds of foods. If you're in the mood for a snack with a bit of a kick, try the famous Buffalo Chicken Wing recipe.

And speaking of classics, who hasn't delighted in the traditional holiday favorite, Green Bean Casserole, found on thousands of Thanksgiving tables every year. For that special oniony taste and crispy crunch, nothing beats FRENCH'S French Fried Onions. They make a difference, in those quick and easy meals, that your family will notice. FRENCH'S Potato Sticks are another way to add crispy, crunchy texture to specific recipes.

For more than 100 years, steak has not been steak without being marinated in FRENCH'S Worcestershire Sauce. An important component of some of the world's best recipes, this flavorful product uses only the finest blend of spices and ingredients, guaranteeing a delicious taste.

A tradition of the finest flavors and enhancers can now be part of your special occasion. These recipes are perfect for entertaining or as part of a barbecue or family gathering. We hope you enjoy these exciting new recipes.

Carolina-Style Barbecue Chicken
©1996 Reckitt & Colman Inc.

Makes 8 servings

- 2 pounds boneless, skinless chicken breast halves or thighs
- ¾ cup FRENCH'S® Classic Yellow® Mustard
- ½ cup cider vinegar
- ¾ cup packed light brown sugar
- ¼ cup FRANK'S® Original REDHOT® Cayenne Pepper Sauce
- 2 tablespoons vegetable oil
- 2 tablespoons FRENCH'S® Worcestershire Sauce
- ½ teaspoon salt
- ¼ teaspoon ground black pepper

Place chicken into large resealable plastic food storage bag or glass bowl. In 1 cup measure, combine mustard, vinegar, ½ *cup* brown sugar, RedHot® sauce, oil, Worcestershire, salt, and pepper; mix well. Pour *1 cup* mixture over chicken. Seal bag; marinate in refrigerator 1 hour or overnight.

Pour remaining mustard mixture into small saucepan. Stir in remaining ¼ *cup* sugar.

Bring to a boil. Reduce heat; simmer 5 minutes until sugar is dissolved and mixture thickens slightly, stirring often. Reserve for serving sauce.

Place chicken on well-oiled grid, reserving marinade. Grill over high heat 10 to 15 minutes or until chicken is no longer pink in center, turning and basting once with marinade. (*Do not baste during last 5 minutes of cooking.*) Serve chicken with reserved sauce.

Preparation time: 15 minutes   *Marinate time:* 1 hour

Cook time: 15 minutes

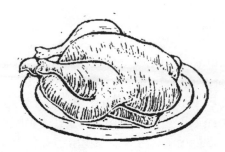

Broccoli-Olive Stuffed Cornish Hens

Lindsay International, Inc.

Make 4 servings

1 package (10 ounces) frozen chopped broccoli	2 tablespoons butter *or* margarine, melted
¼ cup chopped onion	¼ teaspoon salt
1 cup cooked long-grain rice	Dash pepper
½ cup (2 ounces) shredded process Swiss cheese	4 Cornish game hens 1 to 1½ pounds each
½ cup Lindsay® Medium Pitted Ripe Olives, drained and sliced	Melted butter *or* margarine ⅓ cup orange marmalade

Preheat oven to 375°F. For stuffing, cook chopped broccoli according to package directions except omit salt and add chopped onion; drain well. Combine with cooked rice, cheese, olives, *2 tablespoons* butter, salt, and pepper.

Rinse Cornish hens; pat dry with paper towels. Lightly salt cavities. Stuff cavities with stuffing mixture. (Reserve some stuffing mixture to serve separately.) Secure neck skin to back with small skewers. Tie legs to tail. Twist wing tips under back.

Place stuffed hens on a rack in a large roasting pan. Brush with a little melted butter. Cover loosely with foil and roast 30 minutes. Uncover; roast about 1 hour more or until done, brushing with additional melted butter every ½ hour. In saucepan, melt marmalade. Brush hens with marmalade during last 5 minutes of roasting. Just before serving, cook and stir reserved stuffing mixture in a saucepan until heated through.

Duck with Cranberry–Wild Rice Stuffing

Campbell Soup Company

Makes 4 servings

1 can (14 ounces) chicken broth

½ cup regular rice, uncooked

¼ cup regular wild rice, uncooked

2 tablespoons butter *or* margarine

1 package (12 ounces) Campbell's® Fresh Mushrooms, coarsely chopped (about 2½ cups)

¼ cup finely chopped green onions

1 cup whole cranberry sauce

¼ teaspoon salt

⅛ teaspoon pepper

1 duckling (4 to 5 pounds)

¼ cup orange marmalade

1 tablespoon lemon juice

Lemon leaves for garnish

Campbell's® Fresh Mushrooms, fluted, for garnish

Lemon peel twist for garnish

To make stuffing: In 1½-quart saucepan, combine broth, regular rice, and wild rice. Over high heat bring to a boil. Reduce heat to low; simmer, covered, 30 minutes or until rice is tender and all liquid is absorbed, stirring occasionally. In 10-inch skillet over medium heat, in hot butter, cook chopped mushrooms and onions until tender and liquid has evaporated, stirring occasionally. Remove from heat. Stir in cooked rice, cranberry sauce, salt, and pepper.

Remove neck and giblets from inside bird. Remove excess fat. Cut off and discard neck skin. Rinse duck with cold running water; drain well. Spoon stuffing loosely into body cavity. Fold skin over stuffing; secure with skewer. With breast side up, lift wings toward neck, then fold tips under back of bird to balance. Tie legs. With fork, prick skin in several places.

To make glaze: In small saucepan, combine marmalade and lemon juice. Over low, heat until marmalade is melted, stirring constantly.

To grill: Arrange preheated coals around drip pan; test for medium heat above pan. Insert a meat thermometer into thickest part of meat between breast and thigh, without touching fat or bone. On grill rack, place duck, breast side up, over pan but not over coals. Grill, covered, 1¼ to 1½ hours or until well done, or 180°F. Adjust vents and add more charcoal as necessary. Brush often with glaze during the last 30 minutes. Garnish with lemon leaves, mushrooms, and lemon peel twist.

To roast: Preheat oven to 350°F. Place stuffed bird, breast side up, on rack in roasting pan. Roast, uncovered, 2 hours or until well done, or 180°F. Brush often with glaze during the last 30 minutes.

Turkey with Fruit Stuffing

McCormick & Company, Inc.

Makes 12 generous servings

- 2 turkey-breast halves, boneless
- 1 package (10 ounces) pitted dates
- 1 package (6 ounces) dried apricot halves
- 1 cup walnut pieces
- 2 cups water
- ¼ teaspoon McCormick/ Schilling® Ginger
- ½ teaspoon McCormick/ Schilling® ground Cinnamon
- ¼ teaspoon McCormick/ Schilling ground Black Pepper
- ¼ teaspoon McCormick/ Schilling® Nutmeg
- ¼ teaspoon McCormick/ Schilling® ground Cloves

Preheat oven to 325°F. Cut 3 parallel, lengthwise, 1-inch-deep slits in each turkey-breast half. Place turkey-breast halves flat in a buttered roasting pan. Cut dates in thirds. Cut apricot halves in fourths. Combine dates, apricots, and remaining ingredients in saucepan. Heat, stirring constantly. Simmer 2 minutes, stirring. Cool slightly. Fill slits in turkey with fruit mixture. Cook 2 hours. Cut each half breast in 6 slices.

Turkey Oscar

Oscar Mayer Foods Corporation

Makes 4 servings

- 2 tablespoons margarine
- 1 package (about 1 pound) Louis Rich® Fresh Turkey Breast Slices
- 1 can (8½ ounces) asparagus tips, drained
- 1 can (6½ ounces) crabmeat, drained
- 1 package (⅞ ounces) hollandaise sauce mix, prepared according to package directions

Melt *1 tablespoon* margarine in skillet on medium heat. When margarine begins to brown, add half the turkey: Cook 3 minutes, turn. Top with half the asparagus and crabmeat. Cover. Cook 2 minutes more. Place on platter; cover to keep warm. Repeat with *remaining* margarine, turkey, asparagus, and crabmeat. Top with warm hollandaise sauce.

Turkey en Croûte

Oscar Mayer Foods Corporation

Makes 2 to 4 servings

- 1 package (about 1 pound) Louis Rich® Fresh Turkey Breast Tenderloins
- 1 tablespoon margarine
- 1 package (17½ ounces) frozen puff pastry, thawed

Sauce

- 1¼ cups half-and-half
- 1 tablespoon cornstarch
- ½ teaspoon dill weed
- ⅛ teaspoon dried basil leaves
- ⅛ teaspoon pepper
- ⅛ teaspoon onion powder

Preheat oven to 375°F. Cook turkey in margarine in skillet on medium-high 5 minutes, turning to brown. Remove turkey and allow to cool slightly. Cut pastry in half; wrap each half around a tenderloin, gently stretching pastry to cover turkey. Pinch edges of pastry together to seal. Decorate with additional pastry. Place seam side down on ungreased baking sheet. Bake 25 to 30 minutes until golden brown.

Meanwhile, combine sauce ingredients in skillet used to brown turkey. Cook on medium, stirring constantly until thickened. Serve with turkey.

Turkey Slices Provençal

Lawry's Foods, Inc.

Makes 4 servings

- 1 tablespoon olive *or* vegetable oil
- 1¼ pounds turkey-breast slices
- 1 cup sliced onions
- ¾ cup sliced fresh mushrooms
- 1 cup water
- ½ cup chicken broth
- ¼ cup dry red wine
- 1 package (1.5 ounces) Lawry's® Extra Rich and Thick Spaghetti Sauce Spices and Seasonings
- 1 can (6 ounces) tomato paste
- 1 can (3¼ ounces) ripe olives, drained and sliced

Parsley for garnish

In large skillet, heat oil and sauté turkey 2 minutes on each side. Remove and keep warm. To skillet, add onions and mushrooms; sauté 3 minutes or until tender. Stir in water, broth, wine, spaghetti sauce spices and seasonings, and tomato paste. Bring to a boil; reduce heat and simmer, uncovered, 10 minutes, stirring occasionally. Add turkey slices and olives. Heat through.

Serve over cooked egg noodles. Garnish with parsley.

SEAFOOD

Clam Fritters

McCormick & Company, Inc.

Makes 40 fritters

2 cups sifted flour
1 tablespoon baking powder
1 teaspoon McCormick/ Schilling® Bon Appétit®
½ teaspoon McCormick/ Schilling® ground Black Pepper
1 teaspoon McCormick/ Schilling® Instant Onion Powder
1½ teaspoons McCormick/ Schilling® Chesapeake Bay Style Seafood Seasoning

1 tablespoon sugar
4 egg yolks, beaten
⅔ cup milk
2 tablespoons melted butter
4 egg whites, beaten
2 cups drained, coarsely chopped clams (or 4 cans, 6½ ounces each, minced clams, drained)
Vegetable oil for deep-fat frying
Orange-Dijon Dipping Sauce (see below)

Sift together flour and baking powder. Mix with next 5 ingredients. Mix beaten egg yolks with milk and butter. Stir into flour mixture. Fold in beaten egg whites, lightly but thoroughly. Stir in clams. Drop by spoonfuls into deep, hot vegetable oil, 350°F. Fry until brown on 1 side. Turn and brown other side. Drain on paper towels. Keep hot. Serve with Orange-Dijon Dipping Sauce.

Orange-Dijon Dipping Sauce

Makes ¾ cup

¾ cup orange marmalade
2 teaspoons Dijon mustard

1 tablespoon orange juice
Dash ground McCormick/ Schilling® Mace

Combine all ingredients. Mix well. Serve at room temperature.

Salmon Curry with Melon

McCormick & Company, Inc.

Makes 6 servings, ½ cup each

- 1 can (1 pound) red salmon (*or* 1 pound fresh salmon, poached and separated into bite-size pieces)
- 1⅔ cups water
- 1 teaspoon McCormick/ Schilling® Chicken Flavor Base
- 1 tablespoon butter
- 1 teaspoon McCormick/ Schilling® Seasoning Salt
- ¼ teaspoon McCormick/ Schilling® Dill Weed
- 1 tablespoon McCormick/ Schilling® Madras Curry Powder, *or* to taste
- 1 teaspoon McCormick/ Schilling® Instant Minced Onion
- 1 tablespoon cornstarch
- 1 tablespoon cold water
- 1 cup sliced water chestnuts
- Cooked rice
- Melon Garnish (see below)

Drain salmon, saving ⅓ *cup* of the liquid. Break salmon in bite-size pieces, removing skin and bones. Combine liquid from salmon with next 7 ingredients. Heat to a boil. Mix cornstarch with water. Stir into curry sauce. Stir until slightly thickened. Add salmon and water chestnuts. Heat 2 to 3 minutes over low heat without stirring. Serve over rice with Melon Garnish.

Melon Garnish

- Cantaloupe
- Honeydew
- 1 tablespoon honey
- 2 tablespoons gin
- ¼ teaspoon McCormick/ Schilling® Orange Extract
- 1 sprig fresh mint

Cut melon balls from cantaloupe and honeydew. Mix honey with gin and orange extract. Toss with melon balls; cover and chill. Arrange several melon balls at one side of plate. Add a sprig of fresh mint.

Salmon Oriental

Lawry's Foods, Inc.

Makes 4 servings

½ cup soy sauce
¼ cup rice vinegar
3 tablespoons sesame *or* vegetable oil
2 tablespoons chopped green onion
1½ tablespoons minced fresh ginger

1 tablespoon brown sugar
½ teaspoon Lawry's® Garlic Powder with Parsley
¾ teaspoon Lawry's® Lemon Pepper Seasoning
1½ pounds salmon fillets

In medium bowl, combine all ingredients except fish; blend well. Place fish in marinade. Marinate in refrigerator 30 minutes. Grill or broil 5 to 7 minutes on each side or until fish flakes easily.

Serve with grilled or steamed vegetables and a rice side dish.

Variation: Substitute chicken breasts for salmon fillets.

Spicy Scallops with Pea Pods

JFC International, Inc.

Makes 2 to 3 servings

1 pound scallops
1 tablespoon Dynasty® Oriental Marinade
2 tablespoons Dynasty® Chinese Stir-Fry Oil, divided

1 small onion, cut into thin wedges
½ pound Chinese pea pods
2 tablespoons Dynasty® Black Bean Sauce
1 teaspoon Dynasty® Hot Chili Oil

Coat scallops with marinade; let stand 20 minutes. Heat wok or large frying pan over high heat. Add *1 tablespoon* oil; coat wok. Add scallops; stir-fry 1 to 2 minutes or until cooked through. Remove from wok. Heat remaining *1 tablespoon* oil in same wok. Add onion and pea pods; stir-fry 2 to 3 minutes, or until tender-crisp. Return scallops to wok along with black bean sauce; cook and stir 1 minute, or until heated through. Remove from heat; stir in chili oil. Serve immediately with hot, cooked rice, as desired.

Variation: If pea pods are unavailable, substitute 1 package (6 ounces) frozen Chinese pea pods, thawed and drained. Stir-fry onion only and add pea pods with black bean sauce. Continue as directed.

Fish Steaks Veronique

Lawry's Foods, Inc.

Makes 2 servings

12 ounces orange roughy *or* halibut steaks	¼ teaspoon dried rosemary, crushed
2 tablespoons Imperial® Margarine	⅛ teaspoon dried thyme, crushed
2 tablespoons dry white wine	¼ cup milk
½ teaspoon Lawry's® Seasoned Salt	1 teaspoon all-purpose flour
	½ cup seedless green grapes, halved

In medium skillet, sauté fish in margarine 8 to 10 minutes or until almost done. Add wine, seasoned salt, rosemary, and thyme. Simmer, covered, about 5 minutes or until fish flakes easily. Remove fish from skillet; keep warm. Bring pan juices to a boil; boil 1 minute. In 1-cup measure, combine milk and flour; blend well. Add to skillet; bring just to a boil. Reduce heat and cook, stirring, until thickened. Stir grapes into cream mixture; heat through. Spoon sauce over fish steaks.

Serve with wild rice pilaf.

Variation: Substitute 2 tablespoons water for white wine.

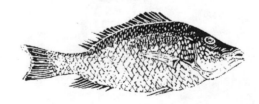

Tuna Noodle Casserole

©1996 Reckitt & Colman Inc.

Makes 6 servings

1 can (10¾ ounces) CAMPBELL'S® Condensed Cream of Mushroom Soup

1¼ cups milk

3 cups hot cooked rotini pasta

1 can (12.5 ounces) tuna, drained and flaked

1⅓ cups (2.8 ounce can) FRENCH'S® French Fried Onions

1 package (10 ounces) frozen peas and carrots

In 2-quart microwave dish, mix soup and milk. Stir in pasta, tuna, ⅔ *cup* French Fried Onions, and vegetables.

Cover; microwave 10 minutes or until hot, stirring once. Top with ⅔ *cup* onions. Microwave 1 minute.

Conventional Directions: Prepare as above. Bake, uncovered, at 350°F for 30 to 35 minutes or until hot, stirring once. Top with remaining onions; bake 5 minutes until onions are golden.

Preparation time: 10 minutes   *Cook time:* 11 minutes

Mediterranean Broiled Fish

Sargento Cheese Company, Inc.

Makes 4 servings

¼ cup light mayonnaise

¼ cup (1 ounce) Sargento® Preferred Light Fancy Shredded Cheddar Cheese

1 tablespoon Sargento® Grated Parmesan Cheese

1 small clove garlic, minced

5 pitted ripe olives, sliced

2 tablespoons minced green onion

4 Orange Roughy *or* Sole fillets (about 5 ounces each)

Paprika

Combine all ingredients except fish and paprika. Set aside. Place fish fillets on a broiler pan that has been coated with a nonstick vegetable spray. Sprinkle fish with paprika. Broil 4 to 5 inches from heat until fish begins to flake with a fork, 5 to 7 minutes. Divide cheese mixture and spread evenly over each fillet. Broil until topping puffs and cheese melts, 2 to 3 minutes. Serve immediately.

Garlic Shrimp with Noodles

Lipton

Makes about 4 servings

- 4 tablespoons butter
- ¼ cup finely chopped onion
- 2 cups water
- 1 package Lipton® Noodles & Sauce—Butter & Herb
- 2 tablespoons olive oil
- 1 tablespoon finely chopped garlic
- 1 pound uncooked medium shrimp, cleaned
- 1 can (14 ounces) artichoke hearts, drained and halved
- ¼ cup finely chopped fresh parsley
- Pepper to taste

In medium saucepan, melt *2 tablespoons* butter and cook onion until tender. Add water and bring to a boil. Stir in Noodles & Sauce–Butter & Herb and continue boiling over medium heat, stirring occasionally, 8 minutes or until noodles are tender.

Meanwhile, in 12-inch skillet, heat remaining *2 tablespoons* butter with olive oil and cook garlic over medium heat 30 seconds. Add shrimp and artichokes and cook, stirring occasionally, 3 minutes or until shrimp turn pink. Stir in parsley and pepper. To serve, combine shrimp mixture with hot noodles. Garnish, if desired, with watercress.

To microwave: In 2-quart microwave-safe casserole, microwave *2 tablespoons* butter with onions, uncovered, at HIGH

(Full Power) 2 minutes or until tender. Stir in water and Noodles & Sauce—Butter & Herb and microwave 11 minutes or until noodles are tender. Stir; then cover and set aside.

In 1-quart microwave-safe casserole or 9-inch glass pie plate, microwave remaining *2 tablespoons* butter, olive oil, and garlic at HIGH (Full Power) 2 minutes. Stir in shrimp and artichokes and microwave 3 minutes or until shrimp are almost pink, stirring once; stir in parsley and pepper. Combine shrimp mixture with noodles and microwave, covered, 1 minute or until heated through. Let stand, covered, 2 minutes.

Shrimp Creole

Lipton

Makes about 4 servings

½ cup Wish-Bone® Italian Dressing

1 medium green bell pepper, cut into chunks

1 medium onion, sliced

1 can (14½ ounces) whole peeled tomatoes, undrained and chopped

1 pound uncooked medium shrimp, cleaned

⅛ teaspoon crushed red pepper

2 cups hot cooked rice

In 10-inch skillet, heat Italian dressing over medium heat and cook green pepper and onion, stirring occasionally, 5 minutes or until tender. Stir in tomatoes and simmer, covered, 15 minutes. Add shrimp and red pepper and simmer, covered, an additional 5 minutes or until shrimp turn pink. To serve, arrange shrimp mixture over hot rice.

Variation: Also terrific with Wish-Bone® Robusto Italian *or* Lite Italian Dressing.

Cajun Spicy Shrimp

Lawry's Foods, Inc.

Makes 4 to 6 servings

¼ cup butter *or* margarine
¼ cup dry white wine
1 teaspoon Lawry's® Garlic Salt
½ teaspoon rosemary, crushed
½ teaspoon paprika
¼ teaspoon basil
¼ to ½ teaspoon cayenne pepper
⅛ teaspoon oregano, crushed
1 pound fresh large shrimp, peeled, deveined, and butterflied, with tails left on

In large skillet, melt butter and add white wine and spices. Bring to a boil; reduce heat, and simmer, uncovered, 5 minutes. Wash shrimp and pat dry. Add to skillet and sauté until shrimp is pink and edges curl.

Serve on a bed of rice.

Orange Roughy au Gratin

Lawry's Foods, Inc.

Makes 4 servings

4 orange roughy fillets (about 1 pound)

1 tablespoon butter *or* margarine

2 tablespoons diced celery

4 green onions, cut into ½-inch pieces

2 teaspoons all-purpose flour

½ teaspoon Lawry's® Seasoned Salt

½ teaspoon Lawry's® Seasoned Pepper

⅓ cup milk

½ cup (2 ounces) grated Swiss cheese

Parsley, chopped, for garnish

Preheat oven to 350°F. Wash fillets; pat dry with paper towels. Place fillets in 10-by-6-by-2–inch greased baking dish. In small skillet, melt butter and sauté celery and onions 5 minutes. Stir in flour, seasoned salt, and seasoned pepper; cook 1 minute. Gradually blend in milk and cheese. Cook until cheese is melted. Pour mixture over fillets. Cover and bake 25 minutes or until fish begins to flake when tested with a fork. Carefully drain off excess liquid.

Garnish with chopped parsley. Serve with boiled potatoes.

To microwave: Place fillets in microwave-safe 10-by-6-by-2-inch baking dish. Microwave on HIGH 4 minutes; drain. Prepare sauce as directed; pour over fillets. Cover with vented plastic wrap and microwave on HIGH 3 to 5 minutes longer or until fish begins to flake when tested with a fork. Carefully drain off excess liquid.

Crab-Stuffed Trout

Campbell Soup Company

Makes 6 servings

⅓ cup butter *or* margarine,
2 cups chopped Campbell's® Fresh Mushrooms
½ cup finely chopped onion
½ cup shredded carrot
1 cup crabmeat, flaked
¼ cup fine dry bread crumbs
3 tablespoons chopped fresh parsley, divided
1 tablespoon white wine Worcestershire sauce
6 brook trout *or* salmon (8 ounces each), pan-dressed
2 teaspoons lemon juice
Arugula for garnish
Cherry tomatoes for garnish

To make filling: In 10-inch skillet over medium heat, in *3 tablespoons* hot butter, cook mushrooms, onion, and carrot until tender and liquid has evaporated, stirring occasionally. In medium bowl, combine onion mixture, crabmeat, bread crumbs, *2 tablespoons* parsley, and Worcestershire sauce; toss gently to coat. Spoon ½ cup filling loosely into each fish cavity; secure with toothpicks.

Arrange fish in oiled grill basket. In covered grill, arrange preheated coals around drip pan; test for hot coals above pan. On grill rack, place grill basket over pan but not over coals. Cover, grill 16 to 20 minutes or until fish begins to flake when tested with fork, turning once.

To make sauce: In 1-quart saucepan, combine *remaining* butter, *remaining* parsley, and lemon juice. Over medium heat, melt butter, stirring occasionally.

To serve, garnish with arugula and tomatoes. Serve with sauce.

To broil: Arrange fish on rack in broiler pan. Broil 6 inches from heat 16 to 20 minutes or until fish begins to flake when tested with fork, turning once.

Braised Snapper with Spicy Sauce

JFC International, Inc.

Makes 4 servings

1½ pounds red snapper *or* sea bass fillets

1 tablespoon Dynasty® Chinese Stir-Fry Oil

2 tablespoons Dynasty® Chinese Barbecue Sauce

1 tablespoon Dynasty® Chinese Soy Sauce

½ teaspoon Dynasty® Hot Chili Oil

½ green onion and top, slivered

Cut fillets into serving pieces. Heat large frying pan over high heat. Add oil; coat pan. Add fillets in single layer. Cook, uncovered, 1 to 2 minutes on each side. Meanwhile, combine barbecue and soy sauces. Spoon over fillets. Reduce heat; cover and simmer 3 to 5 minutes, or until fish flakes easily with fork. Lift fillets from pan to serving platter; keep warm. Remove frying pan from heat. Stir chili oil into sauce in pan. Spoon over fillets and sprinkle with green onion to serve.

To microwave: Omit stir-fry oil. Cut fillets into serving pieces. Place in single layer in microwave-safe 9-inch pie plate or shallow baking dish. Cover with waxed paper. Microwave on HIGH 5 to 8 minutes, or until fish flakes easily with fork. Drain well. Combine barbecue sauce, soy sauce, and chili oil; mix well. Spoon over fillets; sprinkle with green onion. Cover and microwave on HIGH 1 minute, or until heated through. Remove from microwave and serve immediately.

Sole with Vegetables

Sargento Cheese Company, Inc.

Makes 4 servings

4 sole fillets, about
4 ounces each

½ teaspoon salt

¼ teaspoon pepper

1 cup sliced mushrooms

1 medium tomato, seeded
and chopped

1 cup (4 ounces) Sargento®
Shredded *or* Fancy
Shredded Mozzarella
Cheese

½ cup (2 ounces) Sargento®
Grated Parmesan Cheese

Preheat oven to 325°F. Place fish fillets in lightly greased 13-by-9-inch baking dish. Sprinkle with salt and pepper. Sprinkle mushrooms and tomatoes equally over fillets. Bake, covered, 20 to 25 minutes or until fish is cooked through. Uncover; sprinkle with cheeses. Broil 4 inches from heat source until cheese is melted and top is lightly browned, about 3 minutes.

Crispy Oven Fish

ReaLemon® Lemon Juice from Concentrate

Makes 4 servings

2½ cups finely crushed potato
chips

½ cup grated Parmesan
cheese

2 tablespoons chopped
parsley

½ cup mayonnaise *or* salad
dressing

4 tablespoons ReaLemon®
Lemon Juice from
Concentrate

1 pound fish fillets, fresh or
frozen, thawed

Preheat oven to 400°F. Combine chips, cheese, and parsley. In small bowl, combine mayonnaise and *2 table-spoons* ReaLemon®. Dip fish in remaining *2 tablespoons* ReaLemon®, then mayonnaise mixture, then chip mixture.

Arrange in oiled baking dish. Bake 5 to 10 minutes or until fish flakes with fork. Refrigerate leftovers.

Fish Rolls Primavera

ReaLemon® Lemon Juice from Concentrate

Makes 4 servings

- 1 cup shredded carrots
- 1 cup shredded zucchini
- 2 tablespoons finely chopped onion
- ½ cup fresh bread crumbs (1 slice bread)
- ⅛ teaspoon thyme leaves
- ¼ cup margarine *or* butter, melted
- ¼ cup ReaLemon® Lemon Juice from Concentrate
- 4 fish fillets, fresh *or* frozen, thawed (about 1 pound)

Preheat oven to 375°F. In medium bowl, combine vegetables, bread crumbs, and thyme. Combine margarine and ReaLemon®; add ¼ *cup* to vegetable mixture. In shallow baking dish, place equal amounts of vegetable mixture on fillets; roll up. Pour *remaining* margarine mixture over fillets. Bake 15 minutes or until fish flakes with fork. Refrigerate leftovers.

Crispy Lemon Dill Fish Fillets

Kellogg Company

Makes 6 servings

- 2 pounds fish fillets, fresh *or* frozen, thawed
- 4 cups *KELLOGG'S CORN FLAKES®* cereal, crushed to 2 cups
- ½ teaspoon salt
- ½ teaspoon dill weed
- ¼ cup light margarine, *melted*
- 1 teaspoon grated lemon peel

Preheat oven to 375°F. Rinse and pat dry fish. Cut into 6 pieces. Set aside.

Combine *KELLOGG'S CORN FLAKES®* cereal, salt, and dill weed in shallow dish or pan. Set aside.

In second shallow dish or pan, stir together margarine and lemon peel. Dip fish in margarine mixture. Coat with cereal mixture. Place in single layer on foil-lined shallow baking pan, coated with cooking spray.

Bake about 25 minutes or until fish flakes easily when tested with fork. Do not cover pan or turn fish while baking.

Condiments & Sauces

Soy Marinade

ReaLemon® Lemon Juice from Concentrate

Makes about 1½ cups

½ cup ReaLemon® Lemon
Juice from Concentrate
½ cup *each* soy sauce and
vegetable oil

3 tablespoons ketchup
3 cloves garlic, finely
chopped
¼ teaspoon pepper

Combine ingredients; mix well. Reserve ½ *cup* marinade; cover and chill. In shallow dish or plastic bag, pour marinade over meat.* Cover; marinate in refrigerator 4 hours or overnight. Remove meat from marinade. Grill or broil until tender, basting frequently with *reserved* marinade. Refrigerate leftover meat.

*1½ to 2 pounds chicken, pork, or beef may be used.

Sweet 'n Spicy Onion Glaze

Lipton

Makes 2½ cups glaze

1 envelope Lipton® Recipe
Secrets® Onion Soup Mix
1 jar (20 ounces) apricot
preserves

1 cup Wish-Bone® Sweet 'n
Spicy French Dressing

In small bowl, blend all ingredients. Remove amount of glaze you need for chicken, spareribs, kabobs, hamburgers, or frankfurters. Brush on during last half of grilling, broiling, or baking. Remainder of glaze can be stored covered in refrigerator up to 2 weeks.

NOTE: Recipe can be doubled.

Variation: Also terrific with Wish-Bone® Fat Free Sweet 'n Spicy French-Style, or Russian Dressing.

Garlic Mayonnaise Sauce

Lawry's Foods, Inc.

Makes 1½ cups

1 cup mayonnaise	1 teaspoon lemon juice
¼ cup milk	½ teaspoon Lawry's®
1 teaspoon Lawry's® Garlic	Seasoned Pepper
Powder with Parsley	

In blender or food processor, combine all ingredients; process until well blended. Cover and refrigerate. Use as a sandwich spread or as a sauce for vegetables or grilled steak.

Variation: For a low-cal version, use reduced-calorie mayonnaise and skim milk *or* plain nonfat yogurt; omit lemon juice if using yogurt.

Wright's® Tangy Barbecue Sauce

Nabisco Foods Group

Makes 4½ cups

3 medium onions, finely chopped
3 cloves garlic, minced
3 tablespoons vegetable oil
3 cups ketchup
½ cup firmly packed light brown sugar
⅓ cup REGINA White Wine Vinegar
3 tablespoons WRIGHT'S Concentrated Natural Hickory Seasoning
2 tablespoons GREY POUPON Dijon Mustard
1 teaspoon liquid hot pepper seasoning

In large saucepan, over medium-high heat, cook onions and garlic in oil until tender. Stir in ketchup, brown sugar, vinegar, hickory seasoning, mustard, and hot pepper seasoning. Heat to a boil; reduce heat. Simmer 10 minutes. Use as a barbecue sauce when cooking poultry, beef, or pork. Cover and store in refrigerator for up to 2 weeks.

AN A.1. SAUCE, FIT FOR A KING

The Story of A.1. Steak Sauce

An extravagant and self-indulgent epicure, King George IV of England, circa 1820, was a ceaseless challenge to his royal chef, Brand, who was expected to produce a continual stream of culinary delights. One of Brand's original recipes, a blend of soy, vinegar, shallots, and anchovies, particularly titillated his majesty's finely tuned palate. "This is an A-one sauce!" he is reported to have raved.

The expression, A-one, was commonly used as a slang term during George IV's reign to denote first class or top of the line, as in an A-one theater production. The saying originated with businessmen familiar with Lloyd's of London's terms for rating ships for insurance purposes, capital letter A, number 1 being the top rating.

After the king's death, Brand resigned from his royal kitchen duties to commercially produce his masterpiece blend. For many years the Brand Company marketed A.1. exclusively in Great Britain. The condiment was introduced in the United States in 1906 when the Heublein Company, a spirits-making concern, became an agent for distribution.

When World War I interrupted the flow of supplies from England, Heublein acquired all U.S. rights to the recipe. Manufacturing began at the Heublein plant in Hartford, Connecticut, with slight alteration of ingredients to suit U.S. tastes. A.1. Steak Sauce has since become one of the fine Nabisco Foods Group products.

Quick Barbecue Basting Sauce

Nabisco Foods Group

Makes 1 cup

½ cup A.1.® Steak Sauce
½ cup ketchup

½ teaspoon liquid hot pepper seasoning

In small bowl, combine all ingredients. Use as a basting sauce while grilling beef, ribs, or poultry.

Stir-Fry Sauce Mix

Best Foods, a division of CPC International Inc.

Makes 4 cups
- ½ cup Argo® *or* Kingsford's® Corn Starch
- ¼ cup firmly packed brown sugar
- 1½ tablespoons minced fresh ginger
- 4 large cloves garlic, minced
- ¼ teaspoon ground red pepper
- ⅔ cup soy sauce
- ⅓ cup cider vinegar
- 1 can (13¾ or 14½ ounces) chicken *or* beef broth
- ⅔ cup dry sherry

In 1-quart jar, combine cornstarch, brown sugar, ginger, garlic, and red pepper. Add soy sauce and vinegar; shake until blended. Add broth and sherry; shake well. Store covered in refrigerator up to 2 weeks; shake before using. Mix may be frozen in tightly covered containers in 1-cup portions; thaw and shake before using.

Old-Fashioned Corn Relish

©1996 Reckitt & Colman Inc.

Makes about 3 cups
- ⅓ cup cider vinegar
- 2 tablespoons sugar
- 1 tablespoon cornstarch
- 3 tablespoons FRENCH'S® Classic Yellow® Mustard
- ¼ teaspoon seasoned salt
- 1 package (9 ounces) frozen corn, thawed and drained
- ½ cup chopped celery
- ½ cup chopped red pepper
- ¼ cup minced red onion
- 3 tablespoons sweet pickle relish

In large microwave-safe bowl, mix together vinegar, sugar, and cornstarch; stir until well blended. Add mustard and salt. Microwave, uncovered, on HIGH 1 to 2 minutes or until thickened, stirring once.

Add corn, celery, pepper, onion, and pickle relish; toss well to coat evenly. Cover; refrigerate 30 minutes.

Serve as a relish on hamburgers, hot dogs, or as a side with barbecued meats.

Preparation time: 10 minutes   *Cook time:* 2 minutes

Chill time: 30 minutes

Zesty Salsa Ole

©1996 Reckitt & Colman Inc.

Makes 3 cups

2 cans (4 ounces each) chopped green chilies, drained

6 ripe plum tomatoes, chopped

2 green onions, chopped

¼ cup minced cilantro

3 tablespoons Italian salad dressing

2 tablespoons FRENCH'S® Worcestershire Sauce

1 tablespoon FRANK'S® Original REDHOT® Cayenne Pepper Sauce

Combine all ingredients in medium bowl. Cover; refrigerate 1 hour. Serve with tortilla chips. Great also on top of burgers or grilled chicken!

Preparation time: 20 minutes   *Chill time:* 1 hour

Pineapple Salsa

Dole Food Company

Makes 8 servings

1 can (20 ounces) Dole® Crushed Pineapple in Juice

½ cup minced Dole® Red Bell Pepper

¼ cup minced Dole® Green Bell Pepper

1 tablespoon minced Dole® Green Onion

2 teaspoons minced cilantro

2 teaspoons minced jalapeño peppers

1 teaspoon lime zest

Drain ½ cup juice from pineapple. Use drained juice for a beverage. Combine remaining undrained pineapple with all other ingredients. Serve salsa at room temperature or slightly chilled. Salsa is also tasty heated slightly.

Serve over chicken or fish, as a dip with tortilla chips, or spooned over quesadillas or tacos.

America's
Favorite
Desserts

COCONUT-PECAN FILLING
AND FROSTING
Kraft General Foods, Inc.
404

Show-Off Cheesecakes

NORTHWEST CHEESECAKE
SUPREME
Kraft General Foods, Inc.
405

COOKIES AND CREAM
CHEESECAKE
Kraft General Foods, Inc.
406

MARBLE CHEESECAKE
Kraft General Foods, Inc.
407

BEAT-THE-HEAT CHEESECAKE
Nabisco Foods Group
408

PINEAPPLE CHEESECAKE
SQUARES
Dole Food Company
409

Prized Pies

EASY-AS-PIE CRUST
Best Foods, a division of
CPC International Inc.
410

LIGHT 'N LUSCIOUS LEMON PIE
Nestlé Food Company
410

RITZ MOCK APPLE PIE
Nabisco Foods Group
411

REALEMON® MERINGUE PIE
ReaLemon® Lemon
Juice from Concentrate
412

HERSHEY'S® BAVARIAN
CHOCOLATE MINT PIE
Hershey Foods Corporation
413

CHERRY CHEESE PIE
Eagle® Brand
Sweetened Condensed Milk
ReaLemon® Lemon Juice
from Concentrate
414

BANANA CREAM CHEESE PIE
Kellogg Company
414

FUDGE PIE
Nabisco Foods Group
415

CHOCOLATE-PECAN
AND CARAMEL PIE
Nabisco Foods Group
416

NO-BAKE OLD-FASHIONED
COCONUT CREAM PIE
Nabisco Foods Group
417

HONEY APRICOT BISCOTTI
Lipton
467

CARAMEL NUT BITES
Kellogg Company
476

Candy

CALIFORNIA WHITE
CHOCOLATE FUDGE
Kraft General Foods, Inc.
469

MICROWAVE TRUFFLES
McCormick & Company, Inc.
470

FOOLPROOF DARK
CHOCOLATE FUDGE
Eagle® Brand Sweetened
Condensed Milk
470

FANTASY FUDGE
Kraft General Foods, Inc.
471

FIVE-MINUTE FUDGE
Carnation, Nestlé Food Company
473

HERSHEY'S® VANILLA MILK
CHIPS ALMOND FUDGE
Hershey Foods Corporation
474

CHOCOLATE PIZZA
Kraft General Foods, Inc.
474

Easy, Yet Impressive

EASY CHERRIES JUBILEE
Pepperidge Farm, Inc.
477

NAPOLEONS
Pepperidge Farm, Inc.
477

ELEPHANT EARS
Pepperidge Farm, Inc.
478

FRUIT 'N CHEESE
DESSERT SALAD
Sargento Cheese Company, Inc.
479

Toppings

WHIPPED TOPPING
Nestlé Food Company
479

NUTMEG BRANDY SAUCE
Nestlé Food Company
480

CHOCOLATE CAKES AND BROWNIES

Deep Dark Chocolate Cake

Hershey Foods Corporation

Makes 8 to 10 servings

2 cups sugar
1¾ cups all-purpose flour
¾ cup Hershey's® Cocoa
   or Hershey's® Premium
   European-Style Cocoa
1½ teaspoons baking powder
1½ teaspoons baking soda
1 teaspoon salt

2 eggs
1 cup milk
½ cup vegetable oil
2 teaspoons vanilla extract
1 cup boiling water
One-Bowl Buttercream
   Frosting (see page 386)

Heat oven to 350°F. Grease and flour two 9-inch round baking pans or one 13-by-9-by-2-inch baking pan. In large mixer bowl, stir together sugar, flour, cocoa, baking powder, baking soda, and salt. Add eggs, milk, oil, and vanilla; beat on medium speed 2 minutes. Remove from mixer; stir in boiling water (batter will be thin). Pour batter into prepared pans. Bake 30 to 35 minutes for round pans, 35 to 40 minutes for rectangular pan, or until toothpick inserted in center comes out clean. Cool 10 minutes; remove from pans to wire racks. Cool completely. (Cake may be left in rectangular pan, if desired.) Frost with One-Bowl Buttercream Frosting.

One-Bowl Buttercream Frosting

Makes about 2 cups

6 tablespoons butter *or* margarine, softened	⅓ cup milk
2⅔ cups confectioners' sugar	1 teaspoon vanilla extract
½ cup Hershey's Cocoa *or* Hershey's® Premium European-Style Cocoa	

In small mixer bowl, beat butter. Add confectioners' sugar and cocoa alternately with milk; beat to spreading consistency. (Additional milk may be needed.) Blend in vanilla.

THE SAUCE OF MAHON

The Story of Mayonnaise

The origin of mayonnaise is mysterious. One story claims that the sauce was first created in the French town of Bayonne and was called Bayonnaise sauce. A more plausible story is that the chef of the French Duke Richelieu couldn't locate the eggs and cream he needed to prepare a sauce for the victory feast to celebrate the capture of

Port Mahon on the island of Minorca in 1756. Undaunted, the chef blended what was available: raw egg yolks and Spanish olive oil. Duke Richelieu, thrilled with the new taste, called the exotic condiment "The Sauce of Mahon" and brought the recipe back to France. The great French chefs decided the difficult-to-prepare "mahonnaise" sauce, with its exquisite taste, was haute cuisine. They reserved it for the finest meals.

Mayonnaise first crossed the Atlantic Ocean as a silken French sauce, far too sophisticated for standard American fare. "Mayo" wasn't popularized until the turn of the twentieth century, when it debuted in a small Manhattan delicatessen. Richard Hellmann, an ambitious German immigrant, was besieged with compliments from customers on his prepared salads. Deciding the mayonnaise mixed by his wife was the key, the deli operator began to envision the commercial possibilities of producing quality, premixed mayonnaise on a larger scale. He placed two large jars filled with the sauce on his countertop and watched with satisfaction as customers eagerly bought his wife's creation for ten cents per "wooden boat" (a one-pound container he used for weighing butter).

The demand for the mayonnaise was so great that Hellmann started a small production facility in back of the deli and sold what he called his Blue Ribbon formula in large glass jars. He soon bought a truck for deliveries, and before long the truck was part of a fleet. By 1915 he had built his first manufacturing plant in Queens, New York, a facility large enough to satisfy production for an ever-growing list of consumers and retail stores.

Twenty-five years later the now-famous chocolate mayonnaise cake was born. In 1937 the Hellmann's Company managers learned that Mrs. Paul Price, wife of a sales distributor, had created an astonishingly rich cake. The deep, dark chocolate flavor and moist texture were attributed to the addition of an unconventional ingredient: mayonnaise. Today, real, light, and cholesterol-free mayonnaise make three versions of the famous cake possible.

Hellmann's® Real Mayonnaise is still based on the original Blue Ribbon formula. Thanks to Richard Hellmann, the exotic and difficult-to-prepare sauce of the great French chefs is now a common condiment for U.S. tuna salads, potato salads, burgers, and much more.

Chocolate Mayonnaise Cake

Best Foods, a division of CPC International Inc.

Makes one 9-inch layer cake

2 cups unsifted flour *or*	1⅔ cups sugar
2¼ cups unsifted cake flour	1 teaspoon vanilla
⅔ cup unsweetened cocoa	1 cup Hellmann's® Best
1¼ teaspoons baking soda	Foods® Mayonnaise
¼ teaspoon baking powder	1⅓ cups water
3 eggs	

Preheat oven to 350°F. Grease and flour bottoms of two 9-by-1½-inch round cake pans. In medium bowl, stir flour, cocoa, baking soda, and baking powder, set aside. In large bowl with mixer at high speed, beat eggs, sugar, and vanilla, scraping bowl occasionally, 3 minutes or until light and fluffy. Reduce speed to low; beat in real mayonnaise until blended. Add flour mixture in 4 additions alternately with water, beginning and ending with flour. Pour into prepared pans. Bake 30 to 35 minutes or until cake tester inserted in center comes out clean. Cool in pans on wire racks 10 minutes. Remove; cool completely on racks. Frost as desired.

To microwave: Prepare Chocolate Mayonnaise Cake. Line bottoms of two 8-by-2½-inch round glass cake dishes with circles of waxed paper or microwave paper towels. Pour batter into prepared cake dishes. Microwave 1 layer at a time. Place 1 cake dish on inverted pie plate in microwave oven. Microwave on MEDIUM (50% Power) 5 minutes. If cake appears to be rising unevenly, rotate dish. Microwave on HIGH (100% Power) 3 to 5 minutes longer or just until cake begins to set up on the outer edge. Although center may appear to be slightly soft, it will firm up as it cools. Let stand in dish 10 minutes. Remove; let cool completely on rack. Repeat with remaining layer. Frost as desired. Makes one 8-inch layer cake.

German Sweet Chocolate Cake

Kraft General Foods, Inc.

Makes 1 cake

1 package (4 ounces) Baker's® German's® Brand Sweet Chocolate

⅓ cup boiling water

2 cups sifted cake flour *or* 1¾ cups unsifted all-purpose flour

¾ teaspoon baking soda

¼ teaspoon salt

¾ cup Parkay® Margarine

1⅓ cups sugar

3 egg yolks

¾ teaspoon vanilla

¾ cup buttermilk

3 egg whites, stiffly beaten

Coconut-pecan filling and frosting (see page 404)

Preheat oven to 350°F. Melt chocolate in boiling water. Cool. Sift flour with soda and salt (or mix together, if using all-purpose flour). Cream margarine. Gradually beat in sugar and continue beating until light and fluffy. Add egg yolks, 1 at a time, beating after each. Blend in vanilla and chocolate; mix until blended. Add flour mixture alternately with buttermilk, beating after each addition until smooth. Fold in egg whites.

Pour into pans lined on the bottom with waxed paper. Bake until cake springs back when lightly pressed in center: about 35 minutes for two 9-inch layer pans, 45 to 50 minutes for one 13-by-9-inch pan, or 30 to 35 minutes for two 8½-inch heart-shaped pans. Immediately run spatula around sides between cake and pans. Cool in pans 15 minutes. Then remove from pans and finish cooling on racks. Spread coconut-pecan filling and frosting between layers and over top of cake.

Supreme Chocolate Almond Torte

Hershey Foods Corporation

Makes 10 to 12 servings

3 eggs
1¼ cups sugar
1 cup (2 sticks) butter or
   margarine, melted
1 teaspoon vanilla extract
Dash salt
½ cup Hershey's® Premium
   European-Style Cocoa

⅓ cup all-purpose flour
¾ cup toasted almonds,
   very finely chopped
Supreme Cocoa Glaze
   (see below)
Sliced almonds (optional)

Heat oven to 350°F. Line 9-by-1½-inch round baking pan with aluminum foil; butter bottom only. In large mixer bowl, beat eggs, sugar, butter, vanilla, and salt; beat on high speed 3 minutes until smooth and thick, scraping bowl often. Add cocoa and flour; blend well. Stir in almonds. Spread into prepared pan. Bake 35 to 40 minutes or until wooden toothpick inserted in center comes out clean. Cool on wire rack 15 minutes; remove from pan. Carefully peel off foil; cool thoroughly. Place on serving plate. Spread Supreme Cocoa Glaze over top and sides; garnish with sliced almonds, if desired.

Supreme Cocoa Glaze

Makes about ¾ cup

2 tablespoons butter *or*
   margarine
2 tablespoons Hershey's®
   Premium European-Style
   Cocoa

2 tablespoons water
1 cup confectioners' sugar
½ teaspoon vanilla extract

In small saucepan, over low heat, melt butter; add cocoa and water, stirring constantly until mixture thickens. Do not boil. Remove from heat; gradually add confectionery sugar and vanilla, beating with spoon until smooth. Add additional water, ½ teaspoon at a time, until desired consistency.

Microwave Rocky Road Brownies

Kraft General Foods, Inc.

Makes 8 brownies

1 cup sugar
4 squares (1 ounce each) Baker's® Semi-Sweet Chocolate
⅓ cup Miracle Whip® Salad Dressing
2 eggs
½ teaspoon vanilla

1 cup flour
¾ teaspoon Calumet® Baking Powder
½ teaspoon salt
2 cups Kraft® Miniature Marshmallows
½ cup peanuts

Microwave sugar and *3 ounces* chocolate on HIGH 3 minutes. Stir until blended. Beat in salad dressing, eggs, and vanilla. Blend in combined dry ingredients. Pour into 8-inch square baking dish. Cover corners of dish with foil; do not overlap foil. Microwave on HIGH 7 to 8 minutes, turning dish halfway after 4 minutes. Top with marshmallows and peanuts. Microwave on HIGH 30 seconds. Microwave remaining *1 ounce* of chocolate on High 1 to 2 minutes, stirring after 1 minute. Stir until smooth. Drizzle over brownies.

Preparation time: 10 minutes   *Microwave time:* 13 minutes

Note: Since 1976 it has been considered safe to use aluminum foil in the microwave oven. The general guidelines are that the foil should not touch the side of the oven and the proper ratio is ¼ foil to ¾ food. The foil is used as a shielding technique for baking, a method of achieving even cooking. Without foil, the corners of the brownies get too brown.

Chewy Double Chocolate Brownies

Kraft General Foods, Inc.

Makes 24 brownies

2 eggs, beaten
½ cup Miracle Whip®
    Salad Dressing
¼ cup cold water
1 package (21.5 ounces)
    fudge brownie mix

1 cup Baker's® Real Semi-
    Sweet Chocolate Chips
Confectioners' sugar
    (optional)

Preheat oven to 350°F. Mix eggs, salad dressing, and water until well blended. Stir in brownie mix, mixing just until moistened. Add chocolate chips; mix lightly. Pour into greased 13-by-9-inch pan. Bake 25 minutes or until edges begin to pull away from sides of pan. Cool; sprinkle with sifted confectioners' sugar, if desired. Cut into squares.

Variation: Substitute Miracle Whip® Light Reduced Calorie Salad Dressing for regular Salad Dressing.

Preparation time: 5 minutes

Cooking time: 30 minutes, plus cooling

Double Fudge Saucepan Brownies

Hershey Foods Corporation

Makes about 18 brownies

½ cup sugar
2 tablespoons butter *or* margarine
2 tablespoons water
2 cups (12-oz. pkg.) Hershey's Semi-Sweet Chocolate Chips, divided

2 eggs, slightly beaten
1 teaspoon vanilla extract
⅔ cup all-purpose flour
¼ teaspoon baking soda
¼ teaspoon salt
½ cup chopped nuts (optional)

Heat oven to 325°F. Grease 9-inch square baking pan. In medium saucepan over low heat, cook sugar, butter, and water, stirring constantly, until mixture comes to a boil. Remove from heat; immediately add *1 cup* chocolate chips, stirring until melted. Stir in eggs and vanilla until blended. Stir together flour, baking soda, and salt; stir into chocolate mixture. Stir in remaining *1 cup* chips and nuts, if desired. Pour batter into prepared pan. Bake 25 to 30 minutes or until brownies begin to pull away from sides of pan. Cool completely in pan on wire rack; cut into squares.

Chocolate Caramel Brownies

Nestlé Food Company

Makes 48 brownies

1 package (18.25 to 18.5 ounces) devil's food *or* chocolate cake mix
1 cup finely chopped nuts
½ cup butter
½ cup *undiluted* Carnation® Evaporated Milk
35 light caramels (10 ounces)
⅓ cup *undiluted* Carnation® Evaporated Milk
1 cup Nestlé® Toll House® Semi-Sweet Chocolate Morsels (6 ounces)

Preheat oven to 350°F. In large bowl, combine cake mix and nuts; cut in butter. Stir in *½ cup* evaporated milk. Batter will be thick. Spread half of batter in greased 13-by-9-by-2-inch baking pan. Bake 15 minutes. In small saucepan, combine caramels and *⅓ cup* evaporated milk. Cook over low heat, stirring occasionally, until caramels are melted. Sprinkle chocolate pieces over baked layer. Drizzle caramel syrup over chocolate pieces, carefully spreading to cover chocolate layer. Drop remaining half of batter in heaping teaspoons over caramel mixture. Return to oven and bake 20 to 25 minutes longer (top layer will be soft). Cool completely before cutting.

OTHER TREASURED
CAKE RECIPES

Orange Dream Cake

Kraft General Foods, Inc.

Makes 12 servings

¾ cup Miracle Whip®
    Salad Dressing
1 (2-layer) yellow cake mix
1 envelope Dream Whip®
    Whipped Topping Mix
¾ cup orange juice

3 eggs
2 teaspoons grated orange
    peel
1½ cups confectioners' sugar
2 tablespoons milk
1 tablespoon red and green
    sprinkles

Preheat oven to 350°F. Mix together first 6 ingredients at medium speed of electric mixer for 2 minutes. Pour into greased and floured 10-inch fluted tube pan. Bake 35 to 40 minutes or until wooden toothpick inserted near center comes out clean. Let stand 10 minutes; remove from pan. Cool.

Combine confectioners' sugar and milk. Drizzle over cake. Decorate with sprinkles.

Preparation time: 10 minutes   *Cook time:* 40 minutes

THE MYSTERY CAKE

The Story of Chiffon Cake

In 1948, after nearly a year of hushed, behind-closed-doors experimentation and intrigue, Betty Crocker of General Mills finally announced to the country that a totally new cake, the *chiffon* cake, had been created. This was the first important contribution to cake baking since the introduction of baking powder one hundred years earlier and was expected to cause the revision of textbooks on the subject.

Made with a "mystery ingredient," this unique cake had an airiness, moistness, and velvetiness that surpassed the qualities of the two basic cake types then recognized, the butter cake and the angel food (or sponge) cake. It had the melt-in-your-mouth feel of the butter cake, but was higher in volume, richer, and more delicate. It was made with only seven eggs rather than the thirteen required for an angel food cake, yet was more tender. And the easy-to-make chiffon cake required only ten minutes of beating time rather than the twenty-five minutes necessary for angel food perfection—no small matter when you realize that electric beaters were not a standard household appliance of the time.

A Los Angeles insurance salesman, Harry Baker, had originated the cake twenty years earlier and spent the intervening two decades preparing his custom masterpieces for famous Hollywood restaurants like The Brown Derby and for posh parties given by luminary hostesses of the period like Eleanor Roosevelt, Lily Pons, and Barbara Stanwyck. Although he received countless requests for the recipe, Harry Baker had always kept it a closely guarded secret.

Nearing retirement, he decided to give his creation to the homemakers of America. He had listened to the Betty Crocker radio program and helpful cooking hints for years and decided to present his great secret to Betty Crocker.

After purchasing the idea from Baker, Betty Crocker tested the baking techniques for a year to best adapt them for a typical household. The Mazola® and Wesson® oil sales-people were delighted when General Mills announced the "first really new cake in one hundred years." The mysteri-ous ingredient? Familiar salad or cooking oil.

Orange Chiffon Cake

General Mills, Inc.

Makes 1 cake

2¼ cups Softasilk® Cake Flour *or* 2 cups Gold Medal® All-Purpose Flour
1½ cups sugar
3 teaspoons baking powder
1 teaspoon salt
½ cup vegetable oil

5 egg yolks (with Softasilk®) *or* 7 egg yolks (with Gold Medal® Flour)
¾ cup cold water
2 tablespoons grated orange peel
1 cup egg whites (7 or 8)
½ teaspoon cream of tartar
Orange Butter Frosting (see page 399)

Preheat oven to 325°F. Mix flour, sugar, baking powder, and salt in bowl. Make a well and add in order: oil, egg yolks, water, and orange peel. Beat with spoon until smooth. Beat egg whites and cream of tartar in large bowl until very stiff peaks form. Gradually pour egg yolk mixture over beaten whites, gently folding with rubber spatula just until blended. Pour into ungreased tube pan, 10-by-4 inches. Bake about 1 hour 15 minutes or until top springs back when touched lightly. Hang upside down on heatproof funnel until cake is completely cold. Frost with Orange Butter Frosting.

Orange Butter Frosting

⅓ cup margarine *or* butter, softened

3 cups confectioners' sugar

1½ tablespoons grated orange *or* lemon peel

About 3 tablespoons orange *or* lemon juice

Mix all ingredients until smooth.

Variations

Lemon Chiffon Cake: Omit orange peel; add 2 teaspoons grated lemon peel and 2 teaspoons vanilla.

Spice Chiffon Cake: Omit orange peel; add with the flour 1 teaspoon ground cinnamon and ½ teaspoon each ground nutmeg, allspice, and cloves.

Chocolate Chip Chiffon Cake: Increase sugar to 1¾ cups. Omit orange peel; add 2 teaspoons vanilla. Gently fold 3 squares (1 ounce each) shaved sweet, semisweet, or unsweetened chocolate into batter.

Maple-Pecan Chiffon Cake: Substitute ¾ cup granulated sugar and ¾ cup packed brown sugar for the 1½ cups sugar. Omit orange peel; add 2 teaspoons maple flavoring. Gently fold 1 cup very finely chopped pecans into batter.

Easy Carrot Cake

Kraft General Foods, Inc.

Makes 10 to 12 servings

1 (2-layer) yellow cake mix	2 cups finely shredded
1¼ cups Miracle Whip®	carrots
Salad Dressing	½ cup chopped walnuts
4 eggs	Vanilla "Philly" Frosting
¼ cup cold water	(see below)
2 teaspoons ground cinnamon	

Preheat oven to 350°F. Beat cake mix, salad dressing, eggs, water, and cinnamon at medium speed with electric mixer until well blended. Stir in carrots and walnuts. Pour into greased 13-by-9-inch baking pan. Bake 30 to 35 minutes or until wooden toothpick inserted in center comes out clean. Cool. Frost.

Vanilla "Philly" Frosting

1 package (8 ounces)	1 tablespoon vanilla
Philadelphia® Brand	3 to 3½ cups sifted
Cream Cheese, softened	confectioners' sugar

Beat cream cheese and vanilla at medium speed with electric mixer until well blended. Gradually add sugar, beating well after each addition.

Preparation time: 25 minutes   *Cook time:* 35 minutes

Amazin' Raisin Cake

Best Foods, a division of CPC International Inc.

Makes 12 servings

3 cups unsifted flour	⅓ cup milk
2 cups sugar	2 eggs
2 teaspoons baking soda	3 cups coarsely chopped apples
1½ teaspoons cinnamon	
½ teaspoon nutmeg	1 cup raisins
½ teaspoon salt	1 cup coarsely chopped walnuts
¼ teaspoon cloves	
1 cup Hellmann's® or Best Foods® Mayonnaise	1 cup heavy or whipping cream, whipped

Preheat oven to 350°F. Grease and flour two 9-inch layer cake pans. In large bowl, combine flour, sugar, baking soda, cinnamon, nutmeg, salt, and cloves. Add mayonnaise, milk, and eggs. Beat at low speed 2 minutes, scraping bowl frequently. (Batter will be thick.) With spoon, stir in apples, raisins, and nuts. Spoon into pans. Bake 40 to 45 minutes or until cake tester inserted in center comes out clean. Cool in pans 10 minutes. Remove; cool on racks. Fill and frost with whipped cream.

Gelatin Poke Cake

Kraft General Foods, Inc.

Makes 1 cake

1 package (2-layer size) white cake mix or pudding-included cake mix	3½ cups (8 ounces) Cool Whip® Nondairy Whipped Topping, thawed, for garnish
1 package (4-serving size) Jell-O® Brand Gelatin, any flavor	Fruit for garnish (optional) Marzipan for garnish (optional)
1 cup boiling water	
½ cup cold water	

Preheat oven to 350°F. Prepare cake batter as directed on package and pour into well-greased and floured 13-by-9-inch pan. Bake 30 to 35 minutes, or until cake tester inserted in center comes out clean. Cool cake in pan 15 minutes; then pierce with utility fork at ½-inch intervals.

Meanwhile, dissolve gelatin in boiling water. Add cold water and carefully pour over cake. Chill 3 to 4 hours. Garnish with whipped topping and fruit or marzipan, if desired.

Alternate baking pans: Bake in one 10-inch tube pan for 45 to 50 minutes; remove from pan and place on waxed paper before adding gelatin. *Or* bake in two 8-inch or 9-inch layer pans for 30 to 35 minutes; remove from pans and place in clean pans or on waxed paper before adding gelatin. Fill and frost with 3½ cups (8 ounces) Cool Whip® Nondairy Whipped Topping, thawed.

Pineapple Upside Down Cake

Dole Food Company

Makes 8 servings

⅔ cup margarine	Zest and juice from 1 Dole®
⅔ cup brown sugar, packed	Lemon
1 can (20 ounces) Dole®	1 teaspoon vanilla extract
Pineapple Slices	1½ cups all-purpose flour
10 maraschino cherries	1¾ teaspoons baking powder
¾ cup granulated sugar	¼ teaspoon salt
2 eggs, separated	½ cup dairy sour cream

Preheat oven to 350°F. Melt *⅓ cup* margarine in 9- or 10-inch cast iron skillet. Remove from heat. Add brown sugar and stir until blended. Drain pineapple well, reserving *2 tablespoons* syrup. Arrange pineapple slices in brown sugar mixture. Place a cherry in the center of each pineapple slice. In large bowl, beat remaining ⅓ *cup* marga-rine with ½ *cup* granulated sugar until fluffy. Beat in egg yolks, *1 teaspoon* lemon zest, *1 tablespoon* lemon juice, and vanilla. Combine flour, baking powder, and salt. Blend into creamed mixture alternately with sour cream and reserved *2 tablespoons* pineapple syrup. Beat egg whites to soft peaks. Gradually beat in remaining ¼ *cup* granu-lated sugar to make stiff meringue. Fold into batter. Pour over pineapple in skillet. Bake 35 minutes or until cake springs back when touched. Let stand in pan on rack for 10 minutes, then invert onto serving plate.

Skippy's Honey Nut Peanut Butter Cupcakes

Best Foods, a division of CPC International Inc

Makes 24 cupcakes

1 package (18¼ or 18½ ounces) yellow cake mix (non-pudding type)
1 cup Roasted Honey Nut™ Skippy® Creamy Peanut Butter

½ cup grape jelly
Chocolate Honey Nut Frosting (see page 404)

Preheat oven to 350°F. Line twenty-four 2½-inch muffin cups with paper liners. In large bowl with mixer at me-dium speed, beat cake mix and peanut butter until coarse crumbs form. Continue, following package directions for yellow cake, omitting oil. Spoon some of the batter into cups, filling each about half full. Top each with *1 teaspoon* jelly. Carefully add enough batter to cover jelly and fill each cup three-fourths full. Bake 22 to 25 minutes or until toothpick inserted in center of 1 cupcake comes out clean. Cool in pan on wire rack 10 minutes; remove from pan and cool completely. Frost with Chocolate Peanut Butter Frosting.

Chocolate Honey Nut Frosting

⅓ cup unsweetened cocoa
¼ cup Mazola® Corn Oil Margarine
2 cups confectioners' sugar

3 to 4 tablespoons milk
½ teaspoon vanilla
⅓ cup Roasted Honey Nut™ Skippy® Creamy Peanut Butter

In large bowl, with mixer at medium speed, beat cocoa and margarine until smooth. Gradually beat in confectioners' sugar alternately with milk and vanilla. Beat in peanut butter until frosting is fluffy. Spread on cupcakes.

Coconut-Pecan Filling and Frosting

Kraft General Foods, Inc.

Makes about 2 cups, enough to cover tops of two 9-inch layers

⅔ cup (one 5.33 fluid-ounce can) evaporated milk
⅔ cup sugar
2 egg yolks, slightly beaten
⅓ cup butter *or* margarine

¾ teaspoon vanilla
1 cup Baker's® Angel Flake® Brand Coconut
⅔ cup chopped pecans

Combine milk, sugar, egg yolks, butter, and vanilla in saucepan. Cook and stir over medium heat until mixture thickens, about 10 minutes. Remove from heat; add coconut and pecans. Beat until cool and of spreading consistency.

SHOW-OFF CHEESECAKES

Northwest Cheesecake Supreme

Kraft General Foods, Inc.

Makes 10 to 12 servings

Crust

1 cup graham cracker
   crumbs
3 tablespoons sugar

3 tablespoons Parkay®
   Margarine, melted

Filling

4 packages (8 ounces each)
   Philadelphia® Brand Cream
   Cheese, softened
1 cup sugar
3 tablespoons flour

4 eggs
1 cup Breakstone's® Sour
   Cream
1 tablespoon vanilla
Sweet Cherry Sauce
   (see page 406)

Preheat oven to 350°F. Mix together crumbs, sugar, and margarine; press onto bottom of 9-inch springform pan. Bake 10 minutes.

In large mixing bowl, beat cream cheese, sugar, and flour, mixing at medium speed with electric mixer, until well blended. Add eggs; mix well. Blend in sour cream and vanilla; pour over crust. Bake 1 hour, 10 minutes. Loosen cake from rim of pan; cool before removing rim of pan. Chill. Top with sweet cherry sauce just before serving.

Sweet Cherry Sauce

Makes 2 cups

1 can (17 ounces) pitted dark sweet cherries	1 tablespoon cornstarch
1 tablespoon sugar	1 teaspoon lemon juice
	2 tablespoons kirsch

Drain cherries, reserving liquid. Add enough water to reserved liquid to measure *1¼ cups.* Combine sugar and cornstarch in saucepan; gradually add liquid and lemon juice. Cook, stirring constantly, until mixture is clear and thickened. Remove from heat; stir in cherries and kirsch. Cool.

Preparation time: 20 minutes   *Cooking time:* 1 hour, 20 minutes

Cookies and Cream Cheesecake

Kraft General Foods, Inc.

Makes 8 servings

2 cups (24) crushed creme-filled chocolate cookies	1 package (8 ounces) Philadelphia® Brand Cream Cheese, softened
6 tablespoons Parkay® Margarine, softened	½ cup sugar
1 envelope unflavored gelatin	¾ cup milk
¼ cup cold water	1 cup whipping cream, whipped
	1¼ cups (10) chopped creme-filled chocolate cookies

Combine cookie crumbs and margarine; press onto bottom and sides of 9-inch springform pan. (Use a food processor to crush the creme-filled chocolate cookies in an instant.)

Soften gelatin in water; stir over low heat until dissolved. Combine cream cheese and sugar, mixing at medium speed on electric mixer until well blended. Gradually add gelatin and milk, mixing until blended. Chill until mixture is thickened but not set. Fold in whipped cream. Reserve *1½ cups* cream-cheese mixture; pour remaining cream-cheese mixture over crust. Top with chopped cookies and reserved cream-cheese mixture. Chill until firm.

Preparation time: 25 minutes, plus chilling

Marble Cheesecake

Kraft General Foods, Inc.

Makes 10 to 12 servings

1 cup graham cracker crumbs	¾ cup sugar
3 tablespoons sugar	1 teaspoon vanilla
3 tablespoons Parkay® Margarine, melted	3 eggs
3 packages (8 ounces each) Philadelphia® Brand Cream Cheese, softened	1 square (1 ounce) Bakers® Unsweetened Chocolate, melted

Preheat oven to 350°F. Combine crumbs, sugar, and margarine; press onto bottom of 9-inch springform pan. Bake 10 minutes.

Turn oven up to 450°F. Combine cream cheese, sugar, and vanilla, mixing at medium speed on electric mixer until well blended. Add eggs, 1 at a time, mixing well after each addition. Blend chocolate into 1 cup batter. Spoon plain and chocolate batters alternately over crust; cut through batters with knife several times for marble effect. Bake 10 minutes. Reduce oven temperature to 250°F; continue baking 30 minutes. Loosen cake from rim of pan; cool before removing rim of pan. Chill.

Preparation time: 20 minutes, plus chilling

Cook time: 40 minutes

Beat-the-Heat Cheesecake

Nabisco Foods Group

Makes about 12 servings

2 envelopes KNOX Unflavored Gelatine	1 cup (½ pint) whipping *or* heavy cream
¾ cup sugar	1 tablespoon vanilla extract
1 cup boiling water	1 tablespoon fresh grated
2 packages (8 ounces each) cream cheese, softened	lemon peel (optional)
	Graham-Cracker Almond
1 cup (8 ounces) creamed cottage cheese	Crust (see below)
	Fruit for garnish (optional)

In large bowl, mix gelatine with *¼ cup* sugar; add boiling water and stir until gelatine is completely dissolved, about 5 minutes. With electric mixer, add remaining *½ cup* sugar, cream cheese, cottage cheese, cream, vanilla, and lemon peel, 1 at a time, beating well after each addition. Continue beating an additional 5 minutes or until mixture is smooth. Turn into Graham-Cracker Almond Crust; chill until firm, about 5 hours. Garnish, if desired, with fruit.

Graham-Cracker Almond Crust

1 cup graham-cracker crumbs	¼ cup melted butter *or* margarine
½ cup ground almonds	
2 tablespoons sugar	½ teaspoon almond extract

In small bowl, combine all ingredients. Press onto bottom and sides of 9-inch springform pan; chill.

Pineapple Cheesecake Squares

Dolc Food Company

Makes 12 servings

2¼ cups all-purpose flour, divided
½ cup Dole® Chopped Almonds
½ cup confectioners' sugar
⅔ cup margarine, softened
2 packages (8 ounces each) cream cheese, softened
¾ cup sugar, divided
2 eggs
⅔ cup Dole® Pineapple Juice
1 can (20 ounces) Dole® Crushed Pineapple, drained, with juice reserved
½ cup whipping cream, whipped

Preheat oven to 350°F. To make crust, combine *2 cups flour*, almonds, and confectioners' sugar in medium bowl. Cut in margarine until crumbly. Press firmly and evenly in bottom of ungreased 13-by-9-by-2-inch pan. Bake until very light golden brown, 15 to 20 minutes.

To make filling, beat cream cheese in medium bowl until smooth and fluffy. Beat in *½ cup sugar* and the eggs. Stir in *⅔ cup* pineapple juice. Pour over hot crust. Bake just until center is set, about 20 minutes. Cool completely.

To make topping, mix *¼ cup flour* and remaining *¼ cup sugar* in 2-quart saucepan. Stir in juice from drained pineapple. Heat to boiling over medium, stirring constantly. Boil and stir 1 minute. Remove from heat; fold in pineapple. Cool. Fold in whipped cream. Spread carefully over dessert. Cover loosely and refrigerate until firm, about 4 hours.

PRIZED PIES

Easy-as-Pie Crust

Best Foods, a division of CPC International Inc.

Makes 1 (9-inch) pie crust

1¼ cups flour	½ cup Mazola® margarine
⅛ teaspoon salt	2 tablespoons cold water

In medium bowl mix flour and salt. With pastry blender or 2 knives, cut in margarine until mixture resembles fine crumbs. Sprinkle water over flour mixture while tossing with fork to blend well. Press dough firmly into ball. On lightly floured surface roll out to 12-inch circle. Fit loosely into 9-inch pie plate. Trim and flute edge. Fill and bake according to recipe.

Light 'n Luscious Lemon Pie

Nestlé Food Company

Makes one 8-inch pie

2 cups water	1 envelope unflavored gelatin
1⅓ cups Carnation® Nonfat Dry Milk, divided	¼ cup lemon juice
1 package (3⅛ ounces) vanilla cook and serve pudding and pie filling mix	½ teaspoon grated lemon zest
	⅓ cup ice water
¼ cup granulated sugar	1 tablespoon lemon juice
	8-inch graham cracker crust

In large saucepan, combine water, *1 cup* nonfat dry milk, pudding and pie filling mix, sugar, and gelatin. Bring to a boil over medium heat, stirring constantly. Chill until mixture mounds from spoon. Beat in ¼ *cup* lemon juice and zest until smooth. In small mixer bowl, combine remaining nonfat dry milk and ice water. Beat at high speed about 3 to 4 minutes, until soft peaks form. Add *1 tablespoon* lemon juice; continue beating 1 to 2 minutes until stiff peaks form. Fold into pudding mixture. Spoon into crust; chill for 2 hours.

Ritz Mock Apple Pie

Nabisco Foods Group

Makes 10 servings
  Pastry for two-crust 9-inch pie
36 RITZ Crackers, coarsely broken (about 1¾ cups crumbs)
1¾ cups water
  2 cups sugar
  2 teaspoons cream of tartar
  2 tablespoons lemon juice

Grated rind of one lemon
  2 tablespoons FLEISCHMANN'S Margarine
  ½ teaspoon ground cinnamon

Preheat oven to 425°F. Roll out half the pastry and line a 9-inch pie plate. Place cracker crumbs in prepared crust. In saucepan, over high heat, heat water, sugar, and cream of tartar to a boil; simmer for 15 minutes. Add lemon juice and rind; cool. Pour syrup over cracker crumbs. Dot with margarine; sprinkle with cinnamon. Roll out remaining pastry; place over pie. Trim, seal, and flute edges. Slit top crust to allow steam to escape.

Bake for 30 to 35 minutes or until crust is crisp and golden. Serve warm.

ReaLemon® Meringue Pie

ReaLemon® Lemon Juice from Concentrate

Makes one 9-inch pie

1 (9-inch) baked pastry shell	4 eggs, separated
1⅔ cups sugar	1½ cups boiling water
6 tablespoons cornstarch	2 tablespoons margarine
½ cup ReaLemon® Lemon	*or* butter
Juice from Concentrate	¼ teaspoon cream of tartar

Preheat oven to 300°F. In heavy saucepan, combine *1⅓ cups* sugar and cornstarch; add ReaLemon®. In small bowl, beat egg *yolks;* add to lemon mixture. Gradually add water, stirring constantly. Over medium heat, cook and stir until mixture boils and thickens, about 8 to 10 minutes. Remove from heat. Add margarine; stir until melted. Pour into prepared pastry shell. In small mixer bowl, beat egg *whites* with cream of tartar until soft peaks form; gradually add remaining *⅓ cup* sugar, beating until stiff but not dry. Spread on top of pie, sealing carefully to edge of shell. Bake 20 to 30 minutes or until golden. Cool. Chill before serving. Refrigerate leftovers.

Variation: Substitute ReaLime® Lime Juice from Concentrate for ReaLemon.® Add green food coloring to filling if desired. Proceed as above.

Hershey's® Bavarian Chocolate Mint Pie

Hershey Foods Corporation

Makes 8 servings

1 envelope unflavored gelatin	½ cup chilled whipping cream
1½ cups milk	
1⅔ cups (10-oz. pkg.) Hershey's® Mint Chocolate Chips	8-inch packaged chocolate-flavored crumb crust (6 ounces)
1 teaspoon vanilla extract	Sweetened Whipped Cream (see below)

In medium saucepan, sprinkle gelatin over milk; let stand at least 5 minutes to soften. Stir in mint chocolate chips. Cook over low heat, stirring constantly with wire whisk, until chips are melted, chocolate flecks disappear, and mixture is smooth; do not boil. Remove from heat; add vanilla. Chill, stirring occasionally, until mixture begins to set. Beat *½ cup* whipping cream until stiff; carefully fold into chocolate mixture. Pour into crust; cover and chill until set. Garnish with Sweetened Whipped Cream.

Sweetened Whipped Cream

Makes about 1 cup
- ½ cup chilled whipping cream
- 1 tablespoon confectioners' sugar
- ¼ teaspoon vanilla extract

In small mixer bowl, beat ingredients until stiff.

Cherry Cheese Pie

Eagle® Brand Sweetened Condensed Milk
ReaLemon® Lemon Juice from Concentrate

Makes one 9-inch pie

1 (6-ounce) packaged graham cracker crumb pie crust

1 (8-ounce) package cream cheese, softened

1 (14-ounce) can Eagle® Brand Sweetened Condensed Milk (NOT evaporated milk)

⅓ cup ReaLemon® Lemon Juice from Concentrate

1 teaspoon vanilla extract

1 (21-ounce) can cherry pie filling, chilled

In large mixer bowl, beat cheese until fluffy. Gradually beat in Eagle® Brand until smooth. Stir in ReaLemon® and vanilla. Pour into prepared crust. Chill 3 hours or until set. Top with cherry pie filling before serving. Refrigerate leftovers.

Preparation time: 10 minutes

Banana Cream Cheese Pie

Kellogg Company

Makes 8 servings

4 cups *KELLOGG'S CORN FLAKES®* cereal, crushed to 1 cup

2 tablespoons sugar

2 tablespoons margarine, softened

2 tablespoons light corn syrup

3 medium bananas

1 package (8 ounces) light cream cheese, softened

1 can (14 ounces, 1⅓ cups) sweetened condensed milk

⅓ cup lemon juice

1 teaspoon vanilla

In medium-size mixing bowl, combine *KELLOGG'S CORN FLAKES*® cereal, sugar, margarine, and corn syrup. Press evenly and firmly in bottom and on side of 9-inch pie pan. Bake at 350°F about 5 minutes or until lightly browned. Cool completely. Slice *2 bananas* over bottom of pie shell. Beat cream cheese until smooth. Gradually beat in condensed milk. When mixture is smooth, stir in lemon juice and vanilla. Pour over sliced bananas and chill until firm, about 6 hours or overnight. Just before serving, slice *remaining* banana and use to garnish pie.

Fudge Pie

Nabisco Foods Group

Makes 8 servings

¾ cup BLUE BONNET 53% Vegetable Oil Spread	3 eggs, beaten
	1½ cups sugar
3 (1-ounce) squares unsweetened chocolate	⅓ cup all-purpose flour
	Vanilla ice cream, optional

Preheat oven to 325°F. In medium saucepan, over medium heat, heat spread and chocolate until melted and smooth; remove from heat. In small bowl, blend eggs, sugar, and flour; stir into chocolate mixture. Pour mixture into greased 9-inch pie plate. Bake about 45 to 50 minutes (center will be slightly soft). Cool completely on wire rack. To serve, cut into wedges and top with vanilla ice cream if desired.

Chocolate-Pecan and Caramel Pie

Nabisco Foods Group

Makes about 8 servings

1 envelope KNOX Unflavored Gelatine

¼ cup cold water

2 cups (1 pint) whipping *or* heavy cream

1 package (6 ounces) semi-sweet chocolate chips

2 eggs

1 teaspoon vanilla extract

1 cup (about 22) caramels

2 tablespoons butter

Chocolate-Pecan Crust (see page 417)

Pecans for garnish (optional)

In small saucepan, sprinkle unflavored gelatine over cold water; let stand 1 minute. Stir over low heat until gelatine is completely dissolved, about 3 minutes. Stir in *1 cup* cream. Bring just to the boiling point; then immediately add to blender with chocolate. Process until chocolate is completely melted, about 1 minute. While processing, through feed cap, add *½ cup* cream, eggs, and vanilla; process until blended. Pour into large bowl and chill until thickened, about 15 minutes.

Meanwhile, in small saucepan, combine caramels, *¼ cup* cream, and butter. Simmer over low heat, stirring occasionally, until caramels are completely melted and mixture is smooth. Pour onto Chocolate-Pecan Crust to cover bottom; let stand at room temperature to cool, about 10 minutes.

With wire whisk or spoon, beat gelatine mixture until smooth. Pour into prepared crust; chill until firm, about 3 hours. Garnish with remaining *¼ cup* cream, whipped, and, if desired, pecans.

Chocolate-Pecan Crust

1 box (8½ ounces) chocolate   ¾ cup finely chopped pecans
   wafer cookies   ½ cup melted butter *or*
                                     margarine

Preheat oven to 350°F. Crumble cookies to make about 2 cups crumbs. Combine with pecans and butter. Press into 9–inch pie pan and press up sides to form high rim. Bake 10 minutes. Cool.

No-Bake Old-Fashioned Coconut Cream Pie

Nabisco Foods Group

Makes about 12 servings

2 envelopes KNOX Unflavored Gelatine
¼ cup cold water
1 can (15 ounces) cream of coconut
1 cup (½ pint) light cream *or* half-and-half
3 eggs
1 (9-inch) baked pastry shell *or* graham cracker crust
4 cups whipped cream *or* whipped topping
2 tablespoons coconut, toasted

In small saucepan, sprinkle unflavored gelatine over cold water; let stand 1 minute. Stir over low heat until gelatine is completely dissolved, about 3 minutes.

   In blender or food processor, process cream of coconut, light cream, and eggs until blended. While processing, through feed cap, gradually add gelatine mixture and process until blended. Chill blender container until mixture is slightly thickened, about 15 minutes. Turn into pastry shell; chill until firm, about 3 hours. Top with whipped cream and coconut.

Variation: Instead of 3 eggs, use ¾ cup frozen cholesterol-free egg product, 1½ tablespoons butter or margarine, and ⅛ teaspoon salt.

Dream Pie

Kraft General Foods, Inc.

Makes one 8-inch pie

1   envelope Dream Whip® Whipped Topping Mix *or* 1¾ cups (4 ounces) Birds Eye® Cool Whip® Non-Dairy Whipped Topping, thawed

1   package (4-serving size) Jell-O® Instant Pudding and Pie Filling, any flavor

1⅓ cups cold milk

1   baked 8-inch pie shell *or* graham cracker crumb crust, cooled Sweetened sliced strawberries (optional)

Prepare whipped topping mix (if using Dream Whip®) as directed on package. Prepare pie filling mix with the milk as directed on package for pie. Blend in *1 cup* of whipped topping. Pour into pie shell. Chill at least 2 hours. Top each serving with strawberries and garnish with remaining whipped topping.

Black Bottom Banana Cream Pie

Nabisco Foods Group

Makes 8 servings

18 HONEY MAID Honey Grahams, finely crushed (about 1¼ cups crumbs)
¼ cup sugar
⅓ cup FLEISCHMANN'S Margarine, melted
¼ cup heavy cream
4 (1-ounce) squares semisweet chocolate
¼ cup PLANTERS Dry Roasted Peanuts, coarsely chopped

1 small banana, sliced
1 (4-serving size) package ROYAL Instant Vanilla Pudding & Pie Filling
2 cups cold milk
Whipped topping, for garnish
Additional coarsely chopped PLANTERS Dry Roasted Peanuts, for garnish

In small bowl, combine crumbs, sugar, and margarine; press on bottom and up side of 9-inch pie plate. Set aside.

In small saucepan, over low heat, heat heavy cream and chocolate until chocolate melts. Stir in peanuts. Spread evenly in prepared crust. Arrange banana slices over chocolate; set aside.

Prepare pudding according to package directions for pie using milk; carefully pour over bananas. Chill at least 2 hours. To serve, garnish with whipped topping and additional chopped peanuts.

Pineapple Pistachio Ice Cream Pie

Dole Food Company

Makes 8 servings

⅓ cup shelled Dole® Natural Pistachios

1 can (8 ounces) Dole® Crushed Pineapple, drained

2 tablespoons orange-flavored liqueur

Grated peel from 1 orange

1 quart vanilla ice cream, softened

1 (9-inch) prepared graham cracker crust

Toast pistachios. Fold pistachios, pineapple, liqueur, and orange peel into ice cream. Turn filling into graham cracker crust. Freeze 4 hours or until firm. Garnish with additional pistachios before serving.

To toast pistachio nutmeats (shelled pistachios): Preheat oven to 200°F. Toast nutmeats 10 to 15 minutes.

Famous Pumpkin Pie

Libby's, Nestlé Food Company

Makes one 9-inch pie

1 9-inch (4-cup volume) unbaked pie crust

2 eggs, lightly beaten

1¾ cups (16-ounce can) Libby's® Solid Pack Pumpkin

¾ cup granulated sugar

½ teaspoon salt

1 teaspoon ground cinnamon

½ teaspoon ground ginger

¼ teaspoon ground cloves

1½ cups (12-ounce can) *undiluted* Carnation® Evaporated Milk

Preheat oven to 425°F. In large mixing bowl, combine eggs, pumpkin, sugar, salt, cinnamon, ginger, cloves, and evaporated milk. Pour into unbaked pie crust. (*Note:* When using metal or foil pie pan, bake on preheated cookie sheet. When using glass or ceramic pie plate, *do not* use cookie sheet.) Bake 15 minutes. Reduce temperature to 350°F. Bake an additional 40 to 50 minutes, or until knife inserted near center comes out clean. Top cooled pie as desired.

THY OWN PUMPKIN PIE

The Story of Libby's Pumpkin

The versatile pumpkin became a highly regarded vegetable in America after some generous Indians introduced starving colonists to the large golden orb. For food in bitter winters, pumpkins could be stored in dugout root cellars along with winter squash, apples, and potatoes. In times of barley- and hop-crop failure, innovative colonists discovered that fermented pumpkins and persimmons, flavored with maple sugar, made an appealing-tasting substitute for beer. More importantly, the effect of the two drinks was the same.

Early pumpkin pies were simple dishes made by slicing off the tops of the fruit, scooping out the seed, adding milk, spices, and a sweetener like molasses, honey, or maple sugar, replacing the lid, and baking the whole pumpkin.

The familiar Halloween icon, the jack-o'-lantern, was introduced to America by Irish settlers. The Druid priests of their Celtic ancestors had believed the unearthly light emanating from carved faces warded off evil.

The type of pumpkin sold in markets for jack-o'-lanterns at Halloween is watery and not very sweet. The Dickinson variety, a meatier and sweeter version, is known as the eating pumpkin. By selectively breeding the sweet and rich Dickinson, Libby's was able to hybridize a variety, called the Libby's® Select, that has a richer, more golden color; a creamier texture; and a fresher flavor. Libby's introduction of solid-packed canned pumpkin in 1929 dramatically transformed America's humble pumpkin-pie-making efforts.

Besides being scrumptious, pumpkin is a rich, natural source of many important nutrients: vitamin A in the beta carotene form, vitamin C, potassium, iron, riboflavin, calcium, and protein. The calorie count, at 80 calories per cup, is low. One-third of the solids in a can of Libby's® pumpkin is natural dietary fiber.

Poet John Greenleaf Whittier has given us this beautiful thought for pumpkin pie makers: "And thy life be as sweet and its last sunset sky, golden-tinted and fair as thy own pumpkin pie!"

Harvest Cherry Pie

None Such® Ready-to-Use Mincemeat

Makes one 9-inch pie

1⅓ cups (½ jar) None-
       Such® Ready-to-Use
       Mincemeat (Regular *or*
       Brandy & Rum)
 ¾ cup chopped nuts

Pastry for 2-crust pie
1 can (21 ounces) cherry pie
    filling
1 egg yolk *plus* 2 table-
    spoons water (optional)

Place rack in lower half of oven; preheat oven to 425°F. Combine mincemeat and nuts; turn into pastry-lined 9-inch pie plate. Spoon cherry pie filling over mincemeat. Cover with top crust; cut slits near center. Seal and flute. For a more golden crust, mix egg yolk and water; brush over entire surface of pie. Bake 25 to 30 minutes or until golden brown. Serve warm or cool. Garnish as desired.

Sour Cream Peach Mince Pie

None Such® Condensed or Ready-to-Use Mincemeat

Makes one 9-inch pie

1 (9-inch) unbaked pastry
    shell
1 (15¼-ounce) can sliced
    peaches, well drained

1 (27-ounce) jar None Such®
    Ready-to-Use Mincemeat
    (Regular *or* Brandy & Rum)
1½ cups sour cream, at room
      temperature
 ¼ cup confectioners' sugar

Place rack in lowest position in oven. Preheat oven to 400°F. Reserve 3 peach slices; slice each in half to make

6 slices. Set aside. Chop remaining peach slices; place on bottom of pastry shell. Top with mincemeat. Bake 20 minutes. In small bowl, combine sour cream and sugar. Spread evenly over mincemeat. Return to oven; bake 10 minutes longer or until set. Cool. Chill thoroughly. Garnish with reserved peach slices. Refrigerate leftovers.

Tip: 1 (9-ounce) package condensed mincemeat, reconstituted as package directs, can be substituted for ready-to-use mincemeat.

Maple Pecan Pie

Cary's®, Maple Orchards®, and MacDonald's™ Pure Maple Syrup

Makes one 9-inch pie

1 (9-inch) unbaked pastry shell

3 eggs, beaten

1 cup Cary's®, Maple Orchards®, *or* MacDonald's™ Pure Maple Syrup

½ cup firmly packed light brown sugar

2 tablespoons butter *or* margarine, melted

1 teaspoon vanilla extract

1¼ cups pecan halves *or* pieces

Place rack in lowest position in oven; preheat oven to 350°F. In bowl, combine all ingredients except pastry shell. Pour into pastry shell. Bake 35 to 40 minutes or until golden. Cool. Serve at room temperature or chilled. Refrigerate leftovers.

Cinnamon Fruit Tart with Sour Cream Filling

Nabisco Foods Group

Makes 1 tart, 12 servings

1 envelope KNOX Unflavored Gelatine
¼ cup cold water
1 cup (8 ounces) creamed cottage cheese
¾ cup pineapple juice
½ cup sour cream
½ cup milk
¼ cup sugar
1 teaspoon lemon juice
Cinnamon Graham-Cracker Crust (see below)
2 cups any combination of fresh sliced strawberries, kiwi, or oranges; blueberries; and raspberries
2 tablespoons orange or apricot marmalade, melted

In small saucepan, sprinkle unflavored gelatine over cold water; let stand 1 minute. Stir over low heat until gelatine is completely dissolved, about 3 minutes.

In blender or food processor, process cottage cheese, pineapple juice, sour cream, milk, sugar, and lemon juice until blended. While processing, through feed cap, gradually add gelatine mixture and process until blended. Pour into Cinnamon Graham-Cracker Crust; chill until firm, about 3 hours. To serve, top with fresh fruit; then brush with marmalade.

Cinnamon Graham-Cracker Crust

¼ cup melted butter
1 tablespoon water
2 cups graham-cracker crumbs
1 tablespoon sugar
½ teaspoon ground cinnamon

Blend butter and water. In small bowl, combine all ingredients. Press into 10-inch tart pan. Refrigerate about 30 minutes before filling.

PUDDINGS, CUSTARDS, MOUSSES, AND SOUFFLÉS

Maple Bread Pudding

Cary's®, Maple Orchards®, and MacDonald's™ Pure Maple Syrup

Makes 6 to 8 servings

12 1-inch-thick slices French bread *or* 5 cups (about 6 ounces) French bread cubes

3 eggs

2½ cups milk

⅓ cup Cary's®, Maple Orchards®, *or* MacDonald's™ Pure Maple Syrup

¼ cup firmly packed light brown sugar

3 tablespoons margarine *or* butter, melted

½ teaspoon ground cinnamon

⅛ teaspoon ground nutmeg

Maple Almond Sauce (see page 427)

Preheat oven to 325°F. Arrange bread in 8-inch square baking dish or pan. In medium bowl, beat eggs. Add remaining ingredients except Maple Almond Sauce; mix well. Pour over bread, moistening completely. Bake 50 minutes or until knife inserted near center comes out clean. Serve warm or cold with warm Maple Almond Sauce. Refrigerate leftovers.

Maple Almond Sauce

Makes about ¾ cup

¼ cup water
2 teaspoons cornstarch
2 tablespoons margarine
   or butter

½ cup Cary's®, Maple
   Orchards®, *or*
   MacDonald's™ Pure Maple
   Syrup
2 tablespoons toasted sliced
   almonds

Combine water and cornstarch. In small saucepan, melt margarine. Add pure maple syrup and cornstarch mixture; cook and stir until slightly thickened. Remove from heat. Stir in almonds.

THE GAIL BORDEN STORY

The Story of Sweetened Condensed Milk

The name Borden has blazed brightly in American food-product history. The son of a frontiersman, Gail Borden was born in New York in 1801 and started his career as a school-teacher in Mississippi. He worked his way further across the country, landing in Texas in time to work in politics and help write that state's first constitution. Borden is credited with originating the battle cry "Remember the Alamo!" as a headline while writing newspaper reports of the heroic Texan struggle for independence from Mexico.

Borden became interested in scientific food preservation and developed his first product, a dehydrated meat biscuit, in Galveston, Texas. This nutritious hardtack sustained California gold seekers and the U.S. Army in 1849. For this invention, Borden was awarded a Gold Medal from Queen Victoria at the International Exposition in London in 1851. The meat biscuit wasn't a commercial success, however, because it didn't taste good.

His funds depleted, Borden was forced to return to America in steerage class with poor southern and eastern European immigrants. The cows that had been brought on board to provide milk were diseased. Borden witnessed many sick infants dying in their mothers' arms from the infected raw milk. Haunted by the sadness of those scenes, he vowed to do something about it.

In Lebanon, New York, he watched the Shakers, a religious sect, to learn their method of vacuum cooking to preserve fruit. Borden spent many months with the religious community developing and refining a similar procedure for removing water from milk to condense it.

In France at the time, Louis Pasteur was experimenting with ways to preserve milk, but he didn't yet understand the complete process of sterilization. Gail Borden learned that enough sugar in a product could retard bacterial growth. His genius was to add sugar to his condensed milk to prevent spoilage. In 1856, at age fifty-five, he received the first patent for the sweetened condensed milk that would be the beginning of one of America's greatest food corporations.

The Union Army ordered such large quantities of Borden's condensed milk to feed the troops during the Civil War that Borden was forced to license other manufacturers to help fill the quotas. He was incensed when he discovered that many licensees were selling an inferior product and chose the American Bald Eagle to represent the safe and wholesome qualities of his milk. Eagle Brand remains the name of his product today.

The Civil War propelled the Borden canned milk product into national consciousness. Returning to the North when the fighting had ended, Union soldiers remembered the sweet taste of the convenient food, and the ravaged South relied heavily on canned foods like Borden's milk to slave off starvation during the Reconstruction period.

Borden's milk also saved the lives of many infants in North America. Mothers followed feeding instructions on every Eagle Brand label until 1938, when doctors took over the business of prescribing infant formulas.

Refrigerators as standard household appliances capable of storing fresh whole milk changed the role of canned milk after World War 1. But during the forties, sugar became scarce, and Eagle Brand found a second role as a popular and convenient ingredient for homemade desserts.

Through the years, the Borden Company has been a milk-industry leader with a flow of innovations. Borden was the first company to sell fresh milk in bottles in 1885, the first to homogenize milk in 1927, and the first to fortify milk with vitamin D. Research at the company's Endicott, New York, plant led to the first federal pasteurization standards. And Borden continues to satisfy the needs of today's consumers with high-quality and wholesome product innovations in the Gail Borden tradition.

Creamy Banana Pudding

Eagle® Brand Sweetened Condensed Milk

Makes 8 to 10 servings

- 1 can (14 ounces) Eagle® Brand Sweetened Condensed Milk (*not* evaporated milk)
- 1½ cups cold water
- 1 package (4-serving size) *instant* vanilla-flavor pudding mix
- 2 cups (1 pint) whipping cream, whipped
- 36 vanilla wafers
- 3 medium bananas, sliced and dipped in ReaLemon® Lemon Juice from Concentrate

In large bowl, combine sweetened condensed milk and water. Add pudding mix; beat well. Chill 5 minutes. Fold in whipped cream. Spoon *1 cup* pudding mixture into 2½-quart glass serving bowl. Top with one-third *each* of the wafers, bananas, and pudding. Repeat layering twice, ending with pudding. Cover; chill. Garnish as desired. Refrigerate leftovers.

   Tip: Mixture can be layered in individual serving dishes.

All-Time Favorite Puff Pudding

Kraft General Foods, Inc.

Makes 8 servings

¼ cup (½ stick) Parkay Margarine
½ cup sugar *or* honey
1 teaspoon grated lemon rind
2 egg yolks
3 tablespoons lemon juice
2 tablespoons all-purpose flour
¼ cup Post® Grape-Nuts® *or* Raisin Grape-Nuts® Cereal *or* ½ C. W. Post® Hearty Granola Cereal
1 cup milk
2 egg whites, stiffly beaten
Cream *or* prepared whipped topping (optional)

Preheat oven to 325°F. Beat butter with sugar and lemon rind until light and fluffy. Beat in egg yolks. Stir in lemon juice, flour, cereal, and milk. (Mixture will look curdled, but this will not affect finished product.) Fold in beaten egg whites. Pour into greased 1-quart baking dish; place dish in pan of hot water. Bake 1 hour and 15 minutes or until top springs back when lightly touched. When done, pudding has a cakelike layer on top with custard below. Serve warm or cold with cream or prepared whipped topping, if desired.

   For individual puddings, pour mixture into five 5-ounce or four 6-ounce custard cups or soufflé cups. Bake about 40 minutes.

Indian Pudding

Nabisco Foods Group

Makes 8 servings

4 cups skim milk	1 egg, slightly beaten
¾ cup CREAM OF WHEAT Cereal (½-minute, 2½-minute, or 10-minute stovetop cooking)	¼ cup firmly packed light brown sugar
2 tablespoons FLEISCH-MANN'S Margarine	¾ teaspoon ground cinnamon
½ cup BRER RABBIT Light Molasses	½ teaspoon ground ginger Frozen Yogurt (optional)

In large saucepan, over medium heat, bring milk to a boil; gradually sprinkle in cereal, stirring constantly. Heat to a boil, stirring constantly; reduce heat. Cook 5 minutes for regular, 3 to 4 minutes for quick, and 2 to 3 minutes for instant, stirring occasionally until thickened. Remove from heat, stir in margarine, molasses, egg, brown sugar, cinnamon, and ginger.

Spoon mixture into 8 greased custard cups (6-ounce size) or 1½-quart greased casserole. Bake at 350°F for 20 minutes for custard cups or 35 minutes for casserole. Serve warm with frozen yogurt, if desired.

Variation: Substitute egg with ¼ cup EGG BEATERS Healthy Real Egg Product.

Cheesy Apple Yorkshire Pudding

Beatrice Cheese, Inc.

Makes 4 to 5 servings

2 eggs
½ cup all-purpose flour, sifted
¼ teaspoon salt
½ cup milk
2 medium apples, thinly sliced

⅓ cup County Line® Medium Sharp Cheddar Cheese, grated
¼ cup melted butter

Preheat oven to 425°F. In mixer bowl, beat eggs until light and fluffy. Sift together flour and salt; mix with ¼ *cup* milk. Add to eggs along with *remaining* milk; beat until smooth. Fold in apples, cheese, and melted butter; pour into a greased 8-inch baking pan. Bake 30 minutes.

Serve hot with butter and powdered sugar.

Original Banana Pudding

Nabisco Foods Group

Makes 8 servings

½ cup sugar
3 tablespoons all-purpose flour
Dash salt
4 eggs

2 cups milk
½ teaspoon vanilla extract
43 NILLA Wafers
5 to 6 medium-ripe bananas, sliced (about 4 cups)

Preheat oven to 425°F. Reserve *2 tablespoons* sugar. In top of double boiler, combine *remaining* sugar, flour, and salt. Beat in 1 whole egg and 3 egg yolks; reserve 3 egg whites. Stir in milk. Cook, uncovered, over boiling water, stirring constantly 10 minutes or until thickened. Remove from heat; stir in vanilla.

In bottom of 1½-quart round casserole, spoon ½ *cup* custard; cover with 8 wafers. Top with generous layer of sliced bananas, pour ⅔ *cup* custard over bananas. Arrange 10 wafers around outside edge of dish; cover custard with 11 wafers. Top with sliced bananas and ⅔ *cup* custard. Cover custard with 14 wafers; top with sliced bananas and remaining custard.

In small bowl, with electric mixer at high speed, beat reserved egg whites until soft peaks form. Gradually add reserved 2 *tablespoons* sugar, beating until mixture forms stiff peaks. Spoon on top of custard, spreading to cover entire surface.

Bake at 425°F for 5 minutes, or until surface is lightly browned. Garnish with additional banana slices if desired. Serve warm or cold.

Variations

Quick Banana Pudding: Prepare 1 package (6-serving size) ROYAL Instant Vanilla Pudding and Pie Filling according to package directions. Layer prepared pudding with wafers and bananas as above. Cover; chill at least 3 hours. Garnish with 2 cups prepared whipped topping and additional banana slices.

Fruit Variation: 4 cups sliced peaches, blueberries, or strawberries may be substituted for sliced banana.

Mexican Custard

Specialty Brands

Makes 10 to 12 servings

1 cup sugar	½ teaspoon Durkee® Ground Cinnamon
¼ cup water	
6 large eggs	¼ teaspoon Durkee® Ground Ginger
2 cups milk	
1 teaspoon Durkee® Vanilla	Assorted fruit (optional)

Preheat oven to 350°F. In heavy saucepan, combine ½ *cup* sugar and water. Bring to a boil, stirring until sugar dissolves. Continue boiling 6 minutes or until mixture becomes a light caramel color, stirring occasionally. Pour sugar syrup into greased 6-cup ring mold. Holding mold with pot holders, quickly rotate mold so syrup coats the bottom evenly. In a medium bowl, combine ½ *cup* sugar, eggs, milk, vanilla, and spices; mix well. Pour egg mixture into mold. Place mold in roasting pan filled with water 1 inch deep. Bake, uncovered, 55 minutes or until knife inserted in center comes out clean. Cool to room temperature. Loosen edge of custard with spatula and invert onto serving dish. Spoon any remaining caramel on top of custard; garnish with fruit, if desired.

St. Tropez Holiday Cranberry Mousse

Dole Food Company

Makes 8 to 10 servings

1 can (20 ounces) Dole® Crushed Pineapple

1 cup water

2 packages (3 ounces each) strawberry gelatin

1 can (16 ounces) whole-berry cranberry sauce

Zest and juice from 1 Dole® Lemon

¼ teaspoon ground nutmeg

2 cups dairy sour cream

½ cup Dole® Chopped Almonds, toasted

Drain pineapple well; reserve all juice. Heat juice and water to boiling. Stir into gelatin to dissolve. Blend in cranberry sauce. Add 1 teaspoon lemon zest, 3 tablespoons lemon juice, and nutmeg. Chill until mixture thickens slightly. Blend in sour cream. Fold in pineapple and almonds. Pour into 2-quart mold. Chill until firm. Unmold onto serving plate.

White Chocolate Mousse

McCormick & Company, Inc.

Makes 3 cups

16 ounces white chocolate
2 egg whites
¼ cup sugar
1 cup whipping cream
¼ cup confectioners' sugar

1 teaspoon pure McCormick/ Schilling® Vanilla Extract
½ teaspoon McCormick/ Schilling® imitation Rum Extract
Cherry Sauce (optional; see below)

Melt white chocolate in stainless steel bowl over hot water. Beat egg whites until foamy. Gradually add sugar, beating until stiff peaks form when beaters are lifted. Whip cream with confectioners' sugar and extracts. Fold together chocolate, egg whites, and cream. Spoon into dessert glasses. Chill. If desired, layer with Cherry Sauce or serve sauce separately.

Cherry Sauce

Makes 1 cup

1 cup cherry pie filling
¼ teaspoon McCormick/ Schilling® Cinnamon

⅛ teaspoon McCormick/ Schilling® Almond Extract

In food processor, mix ingredients. Run food processor 3 seconds. Scrape down sides of bowl and run 2 more seconds.

Piña Colada Soufflé

McCormick & Company, Inc.

Makes 16 servings, ½ cup each

- 2 envelopes unflavored gelatin
- 1½ cups canned pineapple juice, chilled
- 8 eggs, separated
- ½ teaspoon salt
- 1 cup sugar
- ⅛ teaspoon ground McCormick/Schilling® Mace
- ⅛ teaspoon ground McCormick/Schilling® Cardamom
- ½ teaspoon McCormick/Schilling® imitation Rum Extract
- 1 cup whipping cream
- 2 tablespoons confectioners' sugar
- ¼ cup dark rum
- 1 cup cream of coconut
- Sweetened whipped cream

Soften gelatin in ½ *cup* cold pineapple juice. In top of double boiler, combine egg yolks, salt, ¼ *cup* sugar, mace, cardamom, and remaining *1 cup* pineapple juice. Cook over boiling water, stirring constantly, until slightly thickened. Add gelatin mixture and rum extract. Stir until gelatin is dissolved. Pour into large bowl. Cool. To prepare 6-cup soufflé dish, fold a 30-inch strip of foil in half lengthwise. Tie foil with string around outside of dish to make a collar standing about 5 inches above rim. Beat egg whites until foamy. Gradually add remaining ¾ *cup* sugar. Beat until stiff peaks form when beaters are lifted. Whip cream with confectioners' sugar. Add rum and cream of coconut to gelatin mixture. Stir well. Gently fold in egg whites and whipped cream. Pour into prepared soufflé dish. Refrigerate at least 3 hours. Cut string and carefully remove foil collar. Garnish soufflé with sweetened whipped cream.

COOKIES AND BARS

FOOD OF THE GODS

The Story of Chocolate and Milton S. Hershey

More than two thousand years ago, the ancient Mayans worshiped the cacao bean as an idol. In fact, the scientific name for the cacao bean, *Theobraom cacao,* means "food of the gods."

The Spanish adventurers in Hernando Cortés' 1518 Mexican expedition watched with fascination as the last Aztec emperor, Montezuma II, drank from golden goblets filled with a bitter, spicy liquid prepared from roasted and ground cacao beans and chilled with snow carried down from the high sierra slopes. The drink was considered so prestigious that the golden goblets in which it was served were discarded after one use.

Cortés brought cacao beans back to Spain, where the nobility reserved for themselves exclusive rights to enjoy a heated chocolate drink prepared with cane sugar, another New World food discovery. The formula was too delicious to keep secret for long, however, and by the mid-1600s the chocolate drink was widely appreciated throughout France. The first chocolate shop was opened in England, and by the 1700s chocolate houses flourished and competed with coffeehouses throughout the country.

The New World's first chocolate-manufacturing facility was opened near Dorchester, Massachusetts, in 1765. Sixty years later a Dutch chemist, Conrad Van Houten, devised a chocolate press to mold cocoa butter and finely ground sugar into bar shapes.

Two Swiss contributions greatly enhanced the pleasures to be derived from the cacao bean. The Swiss learned to make smoother chocolate using a process called *conching*. The word *conch* comes from a Greek word meaning seashell and refers to the shape of the vat used to grind chocolate particles into a satiny texture. To cocoa liquor, a nonalcoholic end product of the bean, the Swiss added condensed milk to make the world's first milk chocolate. The later addition of fresh milk to produce superior candy would establish one of the United States' great fortunes.

Milton S. Hershey started life on a central Pennsylvania farm as a poor boy who dropped out of school before he was fourteen years old to apprentice with a printer. Soon he was fired after he dropped his straw hat into the printing press. His mother found him work as a candy maker's apprentice. Hershey spent his younger years learning to make good candy. He failed in several candy-making ventures before he began work with a Denver candy manufacturer who taught him to make incomparable caramels by adding milk to them.

Hershey raised capital to start the Lancaster Caramel Company in Lancaster, Pennsylvania. The German chocolate-manufacturing equipment displayed at the Chicago International Exposition in 1893 captured his interest. He purchased the equipment and was soon producing chocolate-covered caramels. Other chocolate experiments during this period led to some of today's major chocolate products: HERSHEY'S milk chocolate bar, HERSHEY'S milk chocolate bar with almonds, HERSHEY'S cocoa, and HERSHEY'S baking chocolate.

Hershey sold the Lancaster Caramel Company for $1 million in 1900 but retained the chocolate-manufacturing equipment and the rights to produce chocolate. His concept of a quality and affordable chocolate bar for the masses would make him the Henry Ford of the chocolate business.

In 1903 Hershey began building the world's largest chocolate-manufacturing facility to mass-produce milk chocolate. The chocolate business flourished. Hershey built a community for the workers, including churches, a school, a bank, a department store, golf courses, a zoo, and a trolley system to bring employees from nearby towns. The company is still headquartered in Hershey, Pennsylvania, where the aroma of chocolate wafts over the town.

Milton S. Hershey died at age eighty-eight, leaving the legacy that makes the company the leading chocolate and confectionery manufacturer in North America. He is remembered as the rarest of men, a dreamer as well as a builder, a philanthropic man who was acutely aware of the moral need to share the fruits of his success. The Milton Hershey School for orphaned boys, founded by Milton Hershey and his wife in 1909; became and continues to be the principal recipient of the Hershey fortune.

Reese's® Chewy Chocolate Cookies

Hershey Foods Corporation

Makes about 4½ dozen cookies

1¼ cups (2½ sticks) butter *or* margarine, softened	¾ cup Hershey's® Cocoa
2 cups sugar	1 teaspoon baking soda
2 eggs	½ teaspoon salt
2 teaspoons vanilla extract	1⅔ cups (10-oz. pkg.) Reese's® Peanut
2 cups all-purpose flour	Butter Chips

Heat oven to 350°F. In large mixer bowl, beat butter and sugar until light and fluffy. Add eggs and vanilla; beat well.

Stir together flour, cocoa, baking soda, and salt; gradually blend into butter mixture. Stir in chips. Drop by rounded teaspoonfuls onto ungreased cookie sheet. Bake 8 to 9 minutes. (Do not overbake; cookies will be soft. They will puff while baking and flatten while cooling.) Cool slightly; remove from cookie sheet to wire rack. Cool completely.

Variations

Pan Recipe: Spread batter in greased 15½-by-10½-by-1-inch jelly-roll pan. Bake at 350°F for 20 minutes or until set. Cool completely in pan on wire rack; cut into bars. Makes about 4 dozen bars.

Ice Cream Sandwiches: Prepare cookies as directed; cool. Press small scoop of vanilla ice cream between flat sides of cookies. Wrap and freeze.

Reese's® Cookies

Hershey Foods Corporation

Makes about 5 dozen cookies

1 cup shortening *or* ¾ cup (1½ sticks) butter *or* margarine, softened
1 cup granulated sugar
½ cup packed light brown sugar
1 teaspoon vanilla extract
2 eggs
2 cups all-purpose flour
1 teaspoon baking soda
1⅔ cups (10-oz. pkg.) Reese's® Peanut Butter Chips
⅔ cup Hershey's® Semisweet *or* Milk Chocolate Chips

Heat oven to 350°F. In large mixer bowl beat shortening, granulated sugar, brown sugar, and vanilla. Add eggs; beat well. Stir together flour and baking soda; blend into sugar mixture. Stir in chips. Drop by rounded teaspoonfuls onto ungreased cookie sheet. Bake 8 to 10 minutes or until lightly browned. Cool slightly; remove from cookie sheet onto wire rack. Cool completely.

Mini Chips Blondies

Hershey Foods Corporation

Makes about 3 dozen bars

¾ cup (1½ sticks) butter *or* margarine, softened
1½ cups packed light brown sugar
2 eggs
2 tablespoons milk
1 teaspoon vanilla extract
2 cups all-purpose flour
1 teaspoon baking powder
¼ teaspoon baking soda
¼ teaspoon salt
2 cups (12-oz. pkg.) Hershey's® Mini Chips® Semi-sweet chocolate

Heat oven to 350°F. Grease 13-by-9-by-2-inch pan and set aside. In large mixer bowl, cream butter and brown sugar until light and fluffy. Add eggs, milk, and vanilla; beat well. Combine flour, baking powder, baking soda, and salt; add to creamed mixture. Stir in chocolate. Spread into prepared pan. Bake 30 to 35 minutes or until lightly browned. Cool completely; cut into bars.

Chocolate-Caramel Bars

General Mills, Inc.

Makes 32 bars

- 1 package (14 ounces) vanilla caramels
- ⅔ cup evaporated milk
- 1 package Betty Crocker® SuperMoist® German Chocolate Cake Mix
- ½ cup margarine *or* butter, melted
- ¼ teaspoon vanilla
- 1 package (6 ounces) semi-sweet chocolate chips
- ¼ cup chopped nuts
- ¼ cup flaked coconut

Preheat oven to 350°F. Heat caramels and *⅓ cup* evaporated milk in 2-quart saucepan over low heat, stirring occasionally, until caramels are melted and mixture is smooth. Mix cake mix (dry), margarine, remaining *⅓ cup* evaporated milk, and vanilla in large bowl (mixture will be thick). With rubber spatula, pat half of mixture in bottom of ungreased 13-by-9-by-2-inch pan. Bake 6 minutes. Sprinkle with chocolate chips; pour caramel mixture over chocolate chips. Break remaining cake mixture into small pieces evenly over caramel mixture; sprinkle with nuts and coconut. Bake about 16 minutes or until coconut is light golden brown; cool. Cut into 2-by-½-inch bars.

The Ultimate Chocolate Chip Cookie

General Mills, Inc.

Makes 18 cookies

1 cup packed brown sugar
¾ cup granulated sugar
1 cup margarine *or* butter, softened
1 teaspoon vanilla
2 eggs
2½ cups Gold Medal® All-Purpose Flour (*not* self-rising flour)
¾ teaspoon baking soda
¾ teaspoon salt
12 ounces semi-sweet chocolate *or* milk chocolate, coarsely chopped, *or* semi-sweet chocolate chips (2 cups)
1 cup chopped walnuts

Preheat oven to 375°F. Beat sugars and margarine in large bowl on medium speed about 5 minutes or until fluffy. Beat in vanilla and eggs. Beat in flour, baking soda, and salt on low speed. Stir in chocolate and walnuts. Drop dough by ¼ cupfuls about 2 inches apart onto ungreased cookie sheet; flatten slightly with fork. Bake 11 to 14 minutes or until edges are light brown. Let stand 3 to 4 minutes before removing from cookie sheet. Cool on wire rack.

Hershey's® Premium Double Chocolate Drop Cookies

Hershey Foods Corporation

Makes about 3½ dozen cookies

1 cup (2 sticks) butter, softened
1½ cups sugar
2 eggs
2 teaspoons vanilla extract
2 cups all-purpose flour
⅔ cup Hershey's® Cocoa
¾ teaspoon baking soda
¼ teaspoon salt
½ cup toasted, slivered almonds
1¾ cups (10-oz. pkg.) Hershey's® Premium Milk Chocolate Chunks

Heat oven to 350°F. In large mixer bowl, beat butter, sugar, eggs, and vanilla until light and fluffy. Stir together flour, cocoa, baking soda, and salt; add to creamed mixture. Stir in almonds and milk chocolate chunks. Drop by tablespoonfuls onto ungreased cookie sheets. Bake 8 to 10 minutes or just until set. Cool slightly; remove from cookie sheet onto wire rack. Cool completely.

   To toast almonds: Preheat oven to 350°F. On shallow baking pan, place slivered almonds; toast until lightly browned, about 8 to 10 minutes.

Hershey's® Double Chocolate Mint Cookies

Hershey Foods Corporation

Makes about 2½ dozen cookies

⅔ cup butter *or* margarine, softened
1 cup sugar
1 egg
1 teaspoon vanilla extract
1 cup all-purpose flour
½ cup Hershey's Cocoa
½ teaspoon baking soda
¼ teaspoon salt
1⅔ cups (10-oz. pkg.) Hershey's® Mint Chocolate Chips

Heat oven to 350°F. In large mixer bowl, beat butter and sugar until light and fluffy. Add egg and vanilla; beat well. Combine flour, cocoa, baking soda, and salt; gradually blend into butter mixture. Stir in mint chocolate chips. Drop by rounded teaspoonfuls onto ungreased cookie sheet. Bake 8 to 9 minutes, or just until set; do not overbake. Cool slightly; remove from cookie sheet onto wire rack. Cool completely.

Hershey's® Vanilla Chip Chocolate Cookies

Hershey Foods Corporation

Makes about 4½ dozen cookies

1¼ cups (2½ sticks) butter *or* margarine, softened
2 cups sugar
2 eggs
2 teaspoons vanilla extract
2 cups all-purpose flour
¾ cup Hershey's® Cocoa
1 teaspoon baking soda
½ teaspoon salt
1⅔ cups (10-oz. pkg.) Hershey's® Vanilla Milk Chips

Heat oven to 350°F. In large mixer bowl, beat butter and sugar until creamy. Add eggs and vanilla extract; beat until light and fluffy. Stir together flour, cocoa, baking soda, and salt; gradually blend into butter mixture. Stir in vanilla milk chips. Drop by rounded teaspoonfuls onto ungreased cookie sheet. Bake 8 to 9 minutes. (Do not overbake; cookies will be soft. They will puff while baking; flatten upon cooling.) Cool slightly; remove from cookie sheet to wire rack. Cool completely.

Hershey's® Vanilla Milk Chip Cookies

Hershey Foods Corporation

Makes about 5 dozen cookies

- 1 cup (2 sticks) butter, softened
- ¾ cup granulated sugar
- ¾ cup packed light brown sugar
- 1 teaspoon vanilla extract
- 2 eggs
- 2¼ cups all-purpose flour
- 1 teaspoon baking soda
- ½ teaspoon salt
- 1⅔ cups (10-oz. pkg.) Hershey's® Vanilla Milk Chips
- 1 cup chopped nuts (optional)

Heat oven to 375°F. In large mixer bowl, beat butter, granulated sugar, brown sugar, and vanilla until light and fluffy. Add eggs; beat well. Stir together flour, baking soda, and salt; gradually add to butter mixture. Beat well. Stir in vanilla milk chips and nuts, if desired. Drop by rounded teaspoonfuls onto ungreased cookie sheet. Bake 8 to 10 minutes or until very lightly browned. Cool slightly; remove from cookie sheet to wire rack. Cool completely.

Magic Cookie Bars

Eagle® Brand Sweetened Condensed Milk

Makes 24 to 36 bars

- ½ cup margarine *or* butter
- 1½ cups graham cracker crumbs
- 1 can (14 ounces) Eagle® Brand Sweetened Condensed Milk (*not* evaporated milk)
- 1 cup (6 ounces) semi-sweet chocolate chips
- 1 can (3½ ounces; 1⅓ cups) flaked coconut
- 1 cup chopped nuts

Preheat oven to 350°F (325°F for glass dish). In 13-by-9-inch baking pan, melt margarine in oven. Sprinkle crumbs over margarine; pour Eagle® Brand evenly over crumbs. Top with remaining ingredients; press down firmly. Bake 25 to 30 minutes or until lightly browned. Cool. Chill, if desired. Cut into bars. Store, loosely covered, at room temperature.

Variation: Seven-Layer Magic Cookie Bars: Add 1 package (6 ounces) butterscotch-flavored chips after chocolate chips.

Chocolate Spice Cookies

None Such® Condensed Mincemeat

Makes about 6 dozen cookies

2 cups unsifted flour	2 teaspoons vanilla extract
½ cup unsweetened cocoa	1 package (9 ounces) None Such® Condensed Mincemeat, crumbled
1 teaspoon baking soda	
½ teaspoon salt	
1¼ cups sugar	1 cup chopped nuts (optional)
¾ cup shortening	
¼ cup margarine *or* butter, softened	Chocolate Glaze (optional)
2 eggs	Candied cherry halves (optional)

Preheat oven to 350°F. Stir together flour, cocoa, baking soda, and salt; set aside. In large mixer bowl, beat sugar, shortening, and margarine until fluffy. Beat in eggs and vanilla. Add flour mixture; mix well. Stir in mincemeat and, if desired, nuts. Roll into 1-inch balls; place 2 inches apart on ungreased baking sheets. Flatten slightly. Bake 8 to 10 minutes or until almost no imprint remains when lightly touched (*do not overbake*). Cool. Spread with Chocolate Glaze. Garnish with candied cherries, if desired.

Chocolate Glaze

Makes about ¾ cup

3 squares (1 ounce each)
semi-sweet chocolate

6 tablespoons water

2 tablespoons margarine
or butter

2 cups sifted confectioners'
sugar

1 teaspoon vanilla

⅛ teaspoon salt

In medium saucepan, combine chocolate, water, and margarine. Over medium heat, cook and stir until chocolate melts and mixture is smooth. Remove from heat; stir in sugar, vanilla, and salt.

Pecan Pie Bars

Best Foods, a division of CPC International Inc.

Makes 4 dozen bars

Bar Cookie Crust (see page 450)

4 eggs

1½ cups Karo® Light or
Dark Corn Syrup

1½ cups sugar

3 tablespoons Mazola®
Margarine, melted

1½ teaspoons vanilla

2½ cups chopped pecans

Preheat oven to 350°F. Prepare Bar Cookie Crust. In large bowl, beat eggs, corn syrup, sugar, margarine, and vanilla until well blended. Stir in pecans. Pour over hot crust; spread evenly. Bake 25 minutes *or* until filling is firm around edges and slightly firm in center. Cool completely on wire rack before cutting.

Bar Cookie Crust

2½ cups flour
1 cup cold Mazola®
Margarine, cut in ½-inch
pieces

½ cup confectioners' sugar
¼ teaspoon salt

Preheat oven to 350°F. Grease 15-by-10-by-1-inch baking pan. In large bowl with mixer at medium speed, beat flour, margarine, confectioners' sugar, and salt until mixture resembles coarse crumbs; press firmly and evenly into prepared pan. Bake 20 minutes or until golden brown.

Cake Mix Cookies

General Mills, Inc.

Makes about 4 dozen cookies

1 package Betty Crocker®
SuperMoist® Cake Mix
(any flavor except fudge
marble or carrot)
½ cup shortening

⅓ cup margarine *or* butter,
softened
½ teaspoon vanilla
1 egg

Preheat oven to 375°F. Mix about half of cake mix (dry), with shortening, margarine, vanilla, and egg in large bowl until well mixed. Stir in remaining cake mix.

Drop dough by rounded teaspoonfuls about 2 inches apart onto ungreased cookie sheet. Bake 9 to 11 minutes (centers will be soft). Cool 1 minute before removing from cookie sheet.

Variation: Mix ½ *cup* chopped nuts into dough. Shape dough by scant teaspoonfuls into balls. Place on ungreased cookie sheet. Bake 9 to 11 minutes (centers will be soft). Cool 1 minute before removing from cookie sheet.

Giant Skippy® Oat Cookies

Best Foods, a division of CPC International Inc.

Makes about 24 cookies

1¼ cups flour
1 teaspoon baking powder
1 teaspoon baking soda
¼ teaspoon salt
2½ cups quick oats
1 cup Mazola® Corn Oil Margarine

1 cup Skippy® Creamy *or* Super Chunk® Peanut Butter
1 cup sugar
1 cup firmly packed brown sugar
2 eggs
1 teaspoon vanilla

Preheat oven to 350°F. In medium bowl, stir flour, baking powder, baking soda, and salt. Mix in oats. Set aside. In large bowl with mixer at medium speed, beat margarine and peanut butter until smooth. Beat in sugars until blended. Beat in eggs and vanilla. Add flour/oat mixture; by hand, mix until well combined. Shape into 2–inch balls. Place 6 balls on ungreased cookie sheet; flatten each to 3-inch diameter. Bake 15 to 17 minutes or until golden. Remove from cookie sheet. Cool completely on wire rack. Store in tightly covered container.

Best Ever Peanut Butter Cookies

Best Foods, a division of CPC International Inc.

Makes 6 dozen cookies

2 cups quick oats
1¼ cups unsifted flour
1 teaspoon baking powder
1 teaspoon baking soda
¼ teaspoon salt
1 cup Mazola® Margarine

1 cup Skippy® Creamy *or* Super Chunk® Peanut Butter
1 cup sugar
1 cup firmly packed brown sugar
2 eggs
1 teaspoon vanilla

Preheat oven to 350°F. In small bowl, stir oats, flour, baking powder, baking soda, and salt. In large bowl with mixer at medium speed, beat margarine and peanut butter until smooth. Beat in sugars until blended. Beat in eggs and vanilla. Add flour mixture; beat until well blended. Drop by rounded teaspoonfuls 2 inches apart on ungreased cookie sheets. Bake 12 minutes or until lightly browned. Remove from cookie sheets. Cool completely on wire rack. Store in tightly covered container.

Whole-Wheat Orange Peanut Butter Cookies

Best Foods, a division of CPC International Inc.

Makes about 3 dozen cookies

1¼ cups unsifted whole-wheat flour
½ teaspoon baking powder
½ teaspoon baking soda
⅛ teaspoon salt
½ cup Mazola® Margarine
½ cup Skippy® Creamy *or* Super Chunk® Peanut Butter

⅔ cup firmly packed light brown sugar
⅓ cup sugar
1 egg
2 teaspoons grated orange peel
½ teaspoon vanilla
Sugar

Preheat oven to 350°F. In small bowl, stir together flour, baking powder, baking soda, and salt. In large bowl with mixer at medium speed, beat together margarine and peanut butter until well blended. Beat in sugars until well blended. Beat in egg, orange peel, and vanilla. Add flour mixture; beat well. Cover; refrigerate 1 hour. Shape dough into 1-inch balls. Roll in sugar. Place on ungreased cookie sheets 2 inches apart. Flatten with lightly sugared fork, making crisscross pattern. Bake about 12 minutes or until lightly browned. If desired, score with skewer after 5 minutes of baking. Cool on wire rack. Store in tightly covered container.

Variation: Reduced-Sugar Whole-Wheat Orange Peanut Butter Cookies: Omit ⅓ cup sugar. If desired, roll in additional sugar and flatten with lightly sugared fork.

Honey Nut Peanut Butter Oat Bars

Best Foods, a division of CPC International Inc.

Makes 39 bars

2 cups quick oats	2 tablespoons Mazola® Margarine
1½ cups unsifted flour	
1 teaspoon baking powder	1 cup sugar
¼ teaspoon salt	⅓ cup Karo® Dark Corn Syrup
⅔ cup Roasted Honey Nut™ Skippy® Super Chunk® Peanut Butter	2 eggs
	1 teaspoon vanilla
	2 cups raisins

Preheat oven to 400°F. Spread oats in 15½-by-10½-by-1-inch jelly-roll pan. Bake, stirring occasionally, 8 to 10 minutes or until lightly toasted. Cool. Turn down oven to 350°F. Grease 13-by-9-by-2-inch pan. In small bowl, stir together flour, baking powder, and salt. In large bowl with mixer at medium speed, beat peanut butter and margarine until well mixed. Beat in sugar, corn syrup, eggs, and vanilla until well blended. Beat in flour mixture until well mixed. With wooden spoon, stir in oats and raisins. Spread evenly in prepared pan. Bake about 25 minutes or until cake tester inserted in center comes out clean. Cool completely on wire rack. Cut into 3-by-1-inch bars. Store in tightly covered container or wrap individually in plastic wrap.

Variation: Reduced-Sugar Peanut Butter Oat Bars: Reduce sugar to ¾ cup.

Raisin Squares

Nabisco Foods Group

Makes 24 squares

⅔ cup all-purpose flour
½ cup CREAM OF WHEAT Cereal (½-minute, 2½-minute, or 10-minute stovetop cooking)
2 teaspoons DAVIS Baking Powder
1 teaspoon ground cinnamon
1 cup firmly packed light brown sugar
⅓ cup margarine, softened
½ cup EGG BEATERS Healthy Real Egg Product
1 cup seedless raisins
¼ cup walnuts, chopped
Powdered sugar glaze, optional

Preheat oven to 350°F. In small bowl, combine flour, cereal, baking powder, and cinnamon; set aside.

In medium bowl, with electric mixer at medium speed, beat brown sugar and margarine until creamy. Beat in egg product until smooth. Stir in flour mixture until blended. Add raisins and walnuts. Spread mixture in lightly greased 13-by-9-by-2-inch baking pan.

Bake for 20 to 25 minutes or until golden brown. Cool completely on wire rack. Drizzle with powdered sugar glaze if desired. Cut into squares to serve.

Peanut Butter Chips and Jelly Bars

Hershey Foods Corporation

Makes about 18 bars

1½ cups all-purpose flour
½ cup sugar
¾ teaspoon baking powder
½ cup (1 stick) cold butter
    or margarine

1 egg, beaten
¾ cup grape jelly
1⅔ cups (10-oz. pkg.) Reese's®
    Peanut Butter Chips,
    divided

Heat oven to 375°F. Grease 9-inch square baking pan. In large bowl, stir together flour, sugar, and baking powder; cut in butter with pastry blender or fork to resemble coarse crumbs. Add egg; blend well. Reserve half of mixture; press remaining mixture onto bottom of prepared pan. Spread jelly evenly over crust. Sprinkle with *1 cup* peanut butter chips. Stir together remaining crumb mixture with remaining *⅔ cup* chips; sprinkle over top. Bake 25 to 30 minutes or until lightly browned. Cool completely in pan on wire rack; cut into bars.

Date Almond Fingers

Dole Food Company

Makes 18 bars

1½ cups Dole® Chopped
    Dates
Zest and juice from 1 Dole®
    Orange
¾ cup brown sugar, packed
½ cup margarine
2 eggs

½ teaspoon almond extract
1 cup whole wheat flour
½ cup Dole® Whole Natural
    Almonds, toasted, and
    ground
2 teaspoons baking
    powder

Preheat oven to 350°F. Mix together dates in ½ *cup* hot orange juice in small bowl for 5 minutes. Purée in blender until smooth, 1 minute. Beat sugar and margarine until fluffy. Beat in eggs, *1 tablespoon* orange zest, and extract. Stir in date mixture. Combine flour, ground almonds, and baking powder. Add to date mixture. Stir until blended. Spread batter in greased 13-by-9-inch baking pan. Bake 20 to 25 minutes. Cool in pan 15 minutes. Turn onto wire rack to complete cooling. Cut into finger bars.

Fruit and Nut Cookies

Dole Food Company

Makes about 4 dozen cookies

1 cup margarine	1 teaspoon baking soda
1 cup granulated sugar	1 teaspoon ground cinnamon
½ cup brown sugar, packed	¼ teaspoon ground nutmeg
2 eggs	1 package (12 ounces)
1 tablespoon grated orange	Dole® Raisins
peel	1 package (8 ounces) Dole®
2 teaspoons grated lemon	Chopped Dates
peel	1 cup Dole® Chopped
2½ cups all-purpose flour	Almonds, toasted

Preheat oven to 375°F. Beat margarine and sugars until fluffy. Beat in eggs and orange and lemon peel. Combine flour, baking soda, cinnamon, and nutmeg. Beat into margarine mixture until blended. Stir in raisins, dates, and almonds. Drop by heaping tablespoon onto lightly greased cookie sheets. Spread slightly with back of spoon or fork. Bake 10 to 13 minutes. Cool on wire rack.

To toast almonds: Preheat oven to 350°F. Place in a shallow pan and bake for 10 minutes. Toasting time will vary depending upon the size of the almonds.

Jungle Bars

Dole Food Company

Makes 32 bars

2 ripe, medium Dole® Bananas, peeled	2 cups granola
½ pound dried figs	½ pound Dole® Chopped Natural Almonds, toasted (see below)
½ pound dried apricots	
½ pound Dole® Whole Pitted Dates	1 cup flaked coconut
½ pound Dole® Raisins	

Combine bananas, figs, apricots, dates, raisins, and granola in food processor, or run through food grinder. Stir in almonds. Press mixture into greased 13-by-9-inch baking dish. Sprinkle with coconut. Cover; refrigerate 24 hours to allow flavors to blend. Cut into bars.

To toast almonds: Preheat oven to 350°F. Place almonds in a shallow pan and bake for 10 minutes. Toasting time will vary depending upon the size of the almonds.

THE FIRST CEREAL FLAKES

The Story of W. K. Kellogg

Like so many great discoveries, the first breakfast cereal flakes were created accidentally. After long days as business manager at Michigan's Battle Creek Sanitarium, a Seventh Day Adventist institution with a regimen of vegetarianism, fresh air, sunshine, and water therapy, Will Keith Kellogg had been experimenting with ways to make grains more nutritious and digestible for the patients. He was running boiled wheat through rollers devised to create granola, one of the Sanitarium's previous breakfast discoveries. Distracted from his lab experiments one day in 1894, he left the cooked wheat exposed to air. The following day he decided to roll it through anyway. To his amazement, the rollers discharged a flake for each grain of wheat instead of a rolled sheet of wheat.

W. K. Kellogg and his brother, Dr. John Harvey Kellogg, the superintendent of the Sanitarium, believed that grains were very healthy foods. They served their creation to the patients, many of whom wrote after being discharged to ask for more of the breakfast treat they had eaten at "the San." This encouraged the Kellogg brothers to start a cereal company, The Sanitas Nut Food Company, to supply Sanitarium patients.

Here the corn flake was created in 1898. At first W. K. had trouble making corn flakes as appetizing as the wheat flakes, but he discovered that using malt flavoring and only the heart of the kernel created a much tastier flake.

While W. K. Kellogg was absorbed in his experiments, forty-two competitors also started cereal businesses in Battle Creek, many of them marketing Kellogg's own wheat-flake innovation. Only a handful of these companies would survive, and Kellogg had the business instincts to keep his company among the winners. He decided the way to fight these copycats was through consistent quality and effective marketing, advertising, and promotion.

Kellogg started his own Battle Creek Toasted Corn Flakes cereal company in 1906, soon to be known throughout the world as The Kellogg Company. The high demand for Kellogg products and W. K.'s desire to maintain quality prompted him to add this legend to each cereal box: "Beware of imitations. None genuine without this signature. W. K. Kellogg."

Kellogg's Corn Flakes® became an overnight triumph. W. K. Kellogg went on to earn his place among the movers and shakers and the great philanthropists of the early twentieth century—surprising achievements for a man who hadn't started his company until age forty-six, who once wrote in his diary, "Afraid I will always be a poor man."

Cherry Dot Cookies

Kellogg Company

Makes 5 dozen cookies

2¼ cups all-purpose flour
2 teaspoons baking powder
½ teaspoon salt
¾ cup margarine, softened
1 cup sugar
2 eggs
2 tablespoons skim milk
1 teaspoon vanilla
1 cup chopped nuts
1 cup finely chopped, pitted dates

⅓ cup finely chopped maraschino cherries
2⅔ cups *KELLOGG'S CORN FLAKES®* cereal, crushed to 1⅓ cups
15 maraschino cherries, cut into quarters
Vegetable Cooking Spray

Preheat oven to 350°F. Stir together flour, baking powder, and salt. Set aside. In large mixing bowl, beat margarine and sugar until light and fluffy. Add eggs. Beat well. Stir in milk and vanilla. Add flour mixture. Mix well. Stir in nuts, dates, and *⅓ cup* chopped cherries. Shape level measuring-tablespoon of dough into balls. Roll in *KELLOGG'S CORN FLAKES®* cereal. Place on baking sheets coated with cooking spray. Top each cookie with cherry quarter. Bake about 10 minutes or until lightly browned.

Easy S'more Treats

General Mills, Inc.

Makes 24 squares

¾ cup light corn syrup

3 tablespoons margarine *or* butter

1 package (11.5 ounces) milk chocolate chips

1 teaspoon vanilla

9 cups Golden Grahams® Cereal

3 cups miniature marshmallows

Grease rectangular pan, 13-by-9-by-2 inches. Heat corn syrup, margarine, and chocolate chips to boiling in 3-quart saucepan, stirring constantly; remove from heat. Stir in vanilla. Pour over cereal in large bowl; toss until completely coated with chocolate. Fold in marshmallows, 1 cup at a time. Press mixture evenly in pan with buttered back of spoon. Let stand at room temperature at least 1 hour or until firm. Cut into about 2–inch squares. Store, loosely covered, at room temperature, no more than 2 days.

To make 16 Treats: Grease square pan, 9-by-9-by-2 inches or 8-by-8-by-2 inches. Decrease corn syrup to ⅓ cup, margarine to 1 tablespoon, chocolate chips to 5.75-ounce package, vanilla to ½ teaspoon, cereal to 4 cups, and marshmallows to 1½ cups. Continue as directed above— except fold cereal gradually into chocolate mixture until completely coated. Fold in marshmallows. Press mixture evenly in pan with buttered back of spoon. Let stand at room temperature at least 1 hour. Cut 9-inch pan into 2¼- inch squares, 8-inch pan into 2-inch squares.

To microwave: Microwave corn syrup, margarine, and chocolate chips in 4-cup microwave-safe measure or medium, clear microwave-safe bowl, uncovered, on 1 minute, 30 seconds; stir until almost smooth. Microwave, uncovered, about 2 minutes, 30 seconds, or until large bubbles form on surface; stir in vanilla.

THE SWEET BEAN

The Story of Vanilla

Vanilla has long been regarded as the premier flavoring ingredient for pastries, cake mixes, soft drinks, candies, liqueurs, and other sweetened foods. What we think of as the taste of chocolate would not be possible without the addition of vanilla. The cacao bean itself has a bitter taste and needs to be married to the sweetness of vanilla to become the flavor that chocaholics crave.

Like so many of the world's important foods, vanilla was brought back from Latin America by New World explorers. In 1520, an officer of Cortés' expedition hesitantly accepted a taste of a frothy brew the Aztecs had prepared from ground cacao beans and corn, water, honey, and a flavoring agent they called *tlilxochitl*. Learning that the sweet new flavoring agent was from long, thin pods, the conquistadors called the additive *vainilla* from the Spanish word meaning "little bean."

The explorers liked the taste so much that they made room for vanilla on their voyage back to Spain. By the end of the sixteenth century, confectioners were blending chocolate treats flavored with vanilla. The apothecary of Queen Elizabeth I proclaimed vanilla to be a meritorious flavor with enough character to enhance foods on its own.

To keep up with increasing demand, the Spanish brought cuttings of the bean plant back to the homeland. The tropical plants flourished in greenhouses, but the fragrant orchid flowers never developed into bean pods. Finally, in 1836, a Belgian botanist, Charles Morren, discovered the reason for the problem. The bees and hummingbirds attracted to the orchids to pollinate the plants lived only in the New World. A method of hand pollinating the flowers with a bamboo stick was developed. This method is used for commercial cultivation to this day.

Most of our vanilla comes from the island of Madagascar, an island off the southeast coast of Africa that is three times larger than Great Britain. The vanilla beans are harvested by hand, then immersed in boiling water for two or three minutes. Daily the beans are spread to heat and dry in the sun, then wrapped in coverings to sweat until morning, for a period of ten to twenty days. A fermentation process occurs. The beans become dark brown, and the crystals that will frost the pods and impart the characteristic smell and flavor of vanilla begin to form. The beans are sun dried for up to six more months.

The Minister of Commerce of Madagascar meets annually with top worldwide purchasers of vanilla to discuss the annual crop and set prices. McCormick & Company is the largest purchaser involved in these negotiations. McCormick's agent personally selects the choicest vanilla beans. Crates packed with vanilla are loaded onto coastal steamers from small wooden boats floating just beyond the coral reefs. The coastal steamers enter the two main ports of Madagascar where the vanilla is transferred to ocean steamers for shipment to New York.

In the McCormick laboratory, each batch of vanilla is treated in a time-consuming process. Vanillin and water content is analyzed. The production facility is told how much alcohol and water to add to extract the flavor from each bean batch in order to comply with government regulations. Then the beans are ground, packed into baskets, and placed in large stainless-steel percolators where the flavor is extracted much the same as coffee is processed through percolation. An aging process and conscientious testing are the final steps to assure the correct degree of flavor and the mellow sweetness of excellent vanilla.

Ginger Bites

McCormick & Company, Inc.

Makes 12½ dozen 1-inch cookies

½ cup butter, softened	½ teaspoon McCormick/
½ cup sugar	Schilling® Cinnamon
½ cup molasses	3¼ cups flour
2 eggs	1 teaspoon McCormick/
1 teaspoon baking soda	Schilling® pure Vanilla
1 teaspoon McCormick/	Extract
Schilling® ground Ginger	

Preheat oven to 350°F. Cream butter with sugar. Beat in molasses and eggs. Combine next 4 ingredients and add gradually, mixing well. Stir in vanilla extract. On board dusted with confectioners' sugar, roll out small amount of dough at a time, to ⅛-inch thickness. Cut out cookies using very small, 1- to 1¼-inch cutters, or use a knife to cut 1-inch squares. Bake on ungreased cookie sheets 5 minutes. Cool on wire racks.

Merry Morsels (Holiday Cookies)

McCormick & Company, Inc.

Makes 14 dozen 1-inch cookies

1 cup butter
1 cup sugar
1 teaspoon McCormick/Schilling® pure Vanilla Extract
½ teaspoon McCormick/Schilling® Imitation Rum Extract
2½ cups sifted flour

¼ teaspoon McCormick/Schilling® Mace
¾ cup finely chopped green and red cherries (candied *or* maraschino that have been chopped and drained well on paper towels)
½ cup finely chopped pecans
¾ cup flaked coconut

Preheat oven to 375°F. Cream together butter and sugar. Stir in vanilla and rum extracts. Stir in flour, mace, cherries, and pecans. Chill dough. Shape into rolls 1 inch in diameter. Roll in coconut. Wrap in waxed paper and chill. Dough may be frozen at this stage and baked as needed. Slice ¼ inch thick. Place on ungreased cookie sheets. Bake 5 to 7 minutes or until edges are golden.

Holiday Wreaths

Kellogg Company

Makes 16 wreaths

⅓ cup margarine
1 package (10 ounces, about 40) regular marshmallows
1 teaspoon green food coloring

6 cups *KELLOGG'S CORN FLAKES*® cereal
Red cinnamon Imperial candies
Vegetable cooking spray

In large saucepan, melt margarine over low heat. Add marshmallows and stir until completely melted. Remove from heat. Stir in food coloring.

Add *KELLOGG'S CORN FLAKES®* cereal. Stir until well coated.

Using ¼ cup dry measure coated with cooking spray, evenly portion warm cereal mixture. Using buttered fingers, quickly shape into individual wreaths. Dot with cinnamon candies.

Variation: Press warm cereal mixture in 5½-cup ring mold coated with cooking spray or shape in ring on serving plate. Remove from mold and dot with red candies. Slice to serve.

To microwave: Microwave margarine and marshmallows at HIGH 2 minutes in microwave-safe mixing bowl. Stir to combine. Microwave at HIGH 1 minute longer. Stir until smooth. Follow steps 2 and 3 above.

Note: Do not use diet or reduced fat margarine.

Ginger-Orange Scones

Lipton

Makes 7 scones

- ½ cup milk
- 3 Lipton® Soothing Moments® Gentle Orange® Herbal Tea Bags
- 2¼ cups all-purpose flour
- 3 tablespoons PLUS ½ teaspoon sugar
- 1 tablespoon baking powder
- ½ teaspoon salt
- 5 tablespoons lightly salted butter, softened
- 3 tablespoons chopped crystallized ginger*
- 2 eggs

Preheat oven to 425°. In small saucepan, bring milk to the boiling point. Remove from heat and add Gentle Orange herbal tea bags; cover and steep 5 minutes. Remove tea bags and squeeze; cool. Reserve 1 tablespoon tea.

In large bowl, mix flour, *3 tablespoons* sugar, baking powder, and salt. With pastry blender or two knives, cut in butter until mixture is size of small peas. Stir in ginger; set aside.

Beat eggs and steeped tea. Make well in center of flour mixture; add tea mixture. With fork or spoon, stir just until flour is moistened. Turn dough onto lightly floured surface and press into 1-inch-thick circle. Cut into 2½-inch rounds. Press scraps of dough together; repeat. Brush tops with 1 tablespoon reserved tea, then sprinkle with remaining *½ teaspoon* sugar.

Arrange on ungreased cookie sheet and bake 15 minutes or until golden. On wire rack, cool 5 minutes.

Variation: Use 1¼ teaspoons ground ginger and 3 tablespoons raisins.

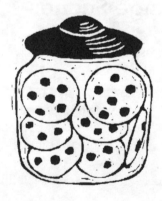

Strawberry Napoleons

Nabisco Foods Group

Makes 6 servings

1 (4-serving) package ROYAL Instant Vanilla Pudding & Pie Filling
1 cup cold milk
1 cup heavy cream, divided
1 cup diced strawberries

18 squares HONEY MAID Chocolate Grahams
Powdered sugar, strawberry slices, and chocolate fudge sauce, for garnish

Prepare pudding mix according to package directions using milk and *½ cup* heavy cream. Stir in chopped strawberries.

Place 1 graham square on each of 6 serving plates. Top each with 3 tablespoons pudding mixture and another graham square; repeat layers once. Chill until serving time.

Just before serving, beat *remaining* heavy cream until stiff. Sprinkle top of grahams with powdered sugar; garnish with whipped topping and a strawberry slice. Drizzle with chocolate fudge sauce.

Honey-Apricot Biscotti

Lipton

Makes 36 biscotti

¾ cup milk
4 Lipton® Soothing Moments® Honey & Lemon Flavored Tea Bags
2¾ cups all-purpose flour
1¼ cups sugar
¾ teaspoon baking soda

¾ teaspoon baking powder
½ teaspoon salt
2 egg yolks
⅓ cup whole almonds, lightly toasted
⅓ cup coarsely chopped dried apricots

Preheat oven to 350°. In small saucepan, bring milk to the boiling point. Remove from heat and add honey & lemon flavored tea bags; cover and steep 5 minutes. Remove tea bags and squeeze; cool.

In large bowl, mix flour, sugar, baking soda, baking powder, and salt. With electric mixer, beat in tea mixture and egg yolks to form a dough. Stir in almonds and apricots.

Turn dough onto lightly floured surface, then knead lightly. Divide in half. On greased and floured cookie sheet, with floured hands, shape each dough half into a 12-inch-long by 2-inch-wide, almost flat log.

Bake 35 minutes or until pale golden. Remove from oven and let cool on wire rack 10 minutes. Cut each log into ¾-inch-thick diagonal slices. Return slices to cookie sheet, cut side down, and bake, turning once, an additional 10 minutes or until golden.

CANDY

California White Chocolate Fudge

Kraft General Foods, Inc.

Makes about 2½ pounds

1½ cups sugar
 ¾ cup Breakstone's® Sour
   Cream
 ½ cup Parkay® Margarine
12 ounces white chocolate,
   coarsely chopped

1 jar (7 ounces) Kraft®
   Marshmallow Creme
 ¾ cup chopped walnuts
 ¾ cup chopped dried
   apricots

In heavy 2½- to 3-quart saucepan, bring sugar, sour cream, and margarine to full, rolling boil over medium heat, stirring constantly. Continue boiling 7 minutes or until candy thermometer reaches 234°F, stirring constantly. Remove from heat; stir in chocolate until melted. Stir in remaining ingredients until well blended. Pour into greased 8- or 9-inch square baking pan. Cool several hours or overnight; cut into squares.

(*Note:* To easily remove marshmallow creme from jar, remove lid and seal and microwave on HIGH 30 seconds.)

Preparation time: 30 minutes, plus chilling

Variation: Substitute macadamia nuts for walnuts.

Microwave Truffles

McCormick & Company, Inc.

Makes 50 truffles

24 ounces semi-sweet chocolate pieces
 2 tablespoons butter
 2 tablespoons dairy sour cream
 ½ teaspoon McCormick/ Schilling® imitation Brandy Extract
 ½ teaspoon McCormick/ Schilling® imitation Rum Extract
 ½ teaspoon McCormick/ Schilling® pure Vanilla Extract
Cocoa
Flaked Coconut
Finely chopped pecans

To microwave: Put chocolate, butter, and sour cream in 3-quart covered heatproof glass casserole. Heat in microwave oven on HIGH 2 minutes. Stir thoroughly. Heat 1 minute longer. Stir. Divide mixture into three portions. Add one extract to each portion and mix well. Shape into 1-inch balls and roll in cocoa, coconut, or chopped pecans. Store in airtight container.

Foolproof Dark Chocolate Fudge

Eagle® Brand Sweetened Condensed Milk

Makes about 2 pounds

3 cups (18 ounces) semi-sweet chocolate chips
1 can (14 ounces) Eagle® Brand Original, Low-Fat, *or* Fat-Free Sweetened Condensed Milk (*not* evaporated milk)
Dash salt
 ½ to 1 cup chopped nuts
1½ teaspoons vanilla extract

In heavy saucepan, over low heat, melt chips with Eagle® Brand and salt. Remove from heat; stir in nuts and vanilla. Spread evenly into aluminum foil-lined 8- or 9-inch square pan. Chill 2 hours or until firm. Turn fudge onto cutting board; peel off foil and cut into squares. Store, loosely covered, at room temperature.

To microwave: In 1-quart glass measure with handle, combine chips with Eagle® Brand and salt. Cook on HIGH 3 minutes or until chips melt, stirring after each 1½ minutes. Stir in remaining ingredients. Proceed as above.

Preparation time: 10 minutes

Fantasy Fudge

Kraft General Foods, Inc.

Makes 3 pounds

¾ cup Parkay® Margarine
3 cups sugar
⅔ cup evaporated milk (*not* sweetened condensed milk)
1 package (12 ounces) Baker's® Real Semi-sweet Chocolate Chips
1 jar (7 ounces) Kraft® Marshmallow Creme
1 cup chopped nuts
1 teaspoon vanilla

Preparation time: 10 minutes   *Cooking time:* 15 minutes

To microwave: Microwave margarine in 4-quart bowl or casserole on HIGH 1 minute or until melted. Add sugar and milk; mix well. Microwave on HIGH 5 minutes or until mixture begins to boil; stir after 3 minutes. Mix well, scraping bowl. Microwave 5½ minutes; stir after 3 minutes. Gradually stir in chocolate until melted. Add remaining ingredients; mix well. Pour into greased 9-by-9-inch or 13-by-9-inch pan. Cool at room temperature; cut into squares.

Stir together margarine, sugar, and evaporated milk in heavy 2½- to 3-quart saucepan; bring to full boil, stirring constantly. Boil 5 minutes over medium heat, or until candy thermometer reaches 234°F, stirring constantly to prevent scorching. Remove from heat. Gradually stir in chocolate until melted. Add remaining ingredients; mix until well blended. Pour into greased 9-by-9-inch or 13-by-9-inch pan. Cool at room temperature; cut into squares.

Variations

Omit nuts. Substitute 1 cup peanut butter for chocolate pieces.

Substitute 4 cups Kraft® Miniature Marshmallows for Kraft® Marshmallow Creme.

Substitute 40 Kraft Marshmallows for Kraft® Marshmallow Creme.

Double recipe. Use 13-ounce jar Kraft® Marshmallow Creme and 5-quart Dutch oven.

Substitute 1 cup Kraft® Party Mints *or* Butter Mints for nuts.

Substitute 1 cup Kraft® Peanut Brittle, crushed, for nuts.

Omit nuts. Add ½ cup crushed peppermint candy.

Substitute 8 squares (8 ounces total) Baker's® Semisweet chocolate, broken in half, for chips.

Five-Minute Fudge

Carnation, Nestlé Food Company

Makes 2 pounds

2 tablespoons butter *or* margarine

⅔ cup *undiluted* Carnation® Evaporated Milk

1⅔ cups sugar

½ teaspoon salt

2 cups (4 ounces) miniature marshmallows

1½ cups (9 ounces) Nestlé® Toll House® Semi-Sweet Chocolate Morsels

1 teaspoon vanilla

½ cup chopped nuts

In medium saucepan combine butter, evaporated milk, sugar, and salt. Bring to a boil over medium heat, stirring constantly. Boil 4 to 5 minutes, stirring constantly. Remove from heat. Stir in marshmallows, chocolate, vanilla, and nuts. Stir vigorously for 1 minute until marshmallows melt and blend. Pour into buttered 8-inch square pan. Cool. Cut into squares.

Variations

Fancy Fudge: Omit chopped nuts. Substitute ¼ cup toasted chopped almonds and ½ cup finely chopped candied mixed fruit.

Five-Minute Fudge Rolls: Make Five-Minute Fudge as directed above. Spread about 1 cup chopped nuts on waxed paper. Pour fudge mixture over nuts. As fudge cools, form into roll. Slice.

Peppermint Fudge: Sprinkle ¼ cup coarsely broken peppermint candy over top of fudge in pan.

Upside-Down Coconut Fudge: Spread 1 cup flaked, toasted coconut on bottom of buttered 8-inch square pan. Top with fudge.

Peanut Fudge: Substitute ½ cup chopped peanuts for nuts.

Hershey's® Vanilla Milk Chips Almond Fudge

Hershey Foods Corporation

Makes about 4 dozen candies

1⅔ cups (10-oz. pkg.) Hershey's® Vanilla Milk Chips

⅔ cup sweetened condensed milk

1½ cups coarsely chopped slivered almonds, toasted

½ teaspoon vanilla extract

Butter 8-inch square pan. In medium saucepan over very low heat, melt vanilla milk chips and sweetened condensed milk, stirring constantly, until mixture is smooth. Remove from heat. Stir in almonds and vanilla. Spread in prepared pan. Cover; refrigerate until firm, about 2 hours. Cut into 1-inch squares.

To toast almonds: Preheat oven to 350°F. Spread almonds on cookie sheet. Bake, stirring occasionally, until lightly browned, 8 to 10 minutes; cool.

Chocolate Pizza

Kraft General Foods, Inc.

Makes one 12-inch pizza

1 package (12 ounces) Baker's® Real Semi-sweet Chocolate Chips

1 pound white almond bark, divided

2 cups Kraft® Miniature Marshmallows

1 cup crisp rice cereal

1 cup peanuts

1 jar (6 ounces) red maraschino cherries, drained, cut in half

3 tablespoons green maraschino cherries, drained, quartered

⅓ cup Baker's® Angel Flake® Brand Coconut

1 teaspoon oil

Melt chocolate chips with *14 ounces* almond bark in large saucepan over low heat, stirring until smooth; remove from heat. Stir in marshmallows, cereal, and peanuts. Pour onto greased 12-inch pizza pan. Top with cherries; sprinkle with coconut. Melt remaining *2 ounces* almond bark with oil over low heat, stirring until smooth; drizzle over coconut. Chill until firm; store at room temperature.

To microwave: Microwave chocolate pieces with *14 ounces* almond bark in 2-quart bowl on HIGH 2 minutes; stir. Continue microwaving 1 to 2 minutes or until smooth when stirred, stirring every 30 seconds. Stir in marshmallows, cereal, and peanuts. Pour onto greased 12-inch pizza pan. Top with cherries; sprinkle with coconut. Melt remaining *2 ounces* almond bark with oil in 1-cup measure on HIGH 1 minute; stir. Continue microwaving 30 seconds to 1 minute or until smooth when stirred, stirring every 15 seconds. Drizzle over coconut. Chill until firm; store at room temperature.

Variations

Substitute 1 cup chopped or halved pecans or walnuts for peanuts.

For smaller pizzas, shape mixture into four 6-inch rounds or twelve 4-inch rounds on waxed paper–lined cookie sheets.

Preparation time: 15 minutes, plus chilling

Caramel Nut Bites

Kellogg Company

Makes about 2 dozen

¼ cup margarine
½ pound caramels (about 28)
2 tablespoons skim milk
3½ cups *KELLOGG'S CORN FLAKES®* cereal

½ cup chopped nuts
½ cup shredded coconut
Vegetable cooking spray

In large saucepan, combine margarine, caramels, and milk. Cook and stir over low heat until melted and smooth, stirring instantly. Remove from heat. Add remaining ingredients, mixing until evenly combined.

Drop by rounded measuring-tablespoon onto baking sheet coated with cooking spray. Cool. Store tightly covered at room temperature.

EASY, YET IMPRESSIVE

Easy Cherries Jubilee

Pepperidge Farm, Inc

Makes 6 servings

1 package (10 ounces) Pepperidge Farm® Frozen Puff Pastry Shells

1 can (17 ounces) cherry pie filling

2 tablespoons water

3 tablespoons brandy

Vanilla ice cream

Prepare pastry shells according to package directions. In mixing bowl, combine pie filling and water. In small saucepan, heat brandy until hot. Ignite and pour over filling. Stir until flame goes out. Spoon ice cream into pastry shells and top with warm sauce.

Napoleons

Pepperidge Farm, Inc.

Makes 12 napoleons

1 sheet Pepperidge Farm® Frozen Puff Pastry, thawed 20 minutes

1 package (4½ ounces) instant chocolate pudding

1 cup sour cream

1 cup confectioners' sugar

1 cup milk

1 tablespoon milk

2 ounces semisweet chocolate, melted

Preheat oven to 400°F. Cut pastry into 4 strips, 2½ inches wide. Cut each strip crosswise into thirds. Bake strips on an ungreased baking sheet for 12 to 15 minutes. Prepare pudding according to package directions, substituting sour cream for 1 cup milk. Cut pastry rectangles in half, making a top and a bottom. Generously spoon pudding on bottom half and top with other half. Blend sugar and milk. Spread on top and drizzle with chocolate.

Elephant Ears

Pepperidge Farm, Inc.

Makes about 32 pastries
- 1 sheet Pepperidge Farm Frozen Puff Pastry, thawed 20 minutes
- Granulated sugar
- Cinnamon
- 1 egg beaten with 1 tablespoon water

Preheat oven to 425°F. Unfold and cut pastry sheet in half. Roll out 1 piece to an 8-by-14-inch rectangle. Sprinkle generously with sugar and cinnamon. Fold the short edges of the pastry one-quarter the distance toward the center. Sprinkle again with sugar and cinnamon and fold short edges again toward the center, leaving a ¼-inch space between edges. Fold 1 side over onto the other, making an 8-layer rectangle. Chill 10 minutes. Repeat with another piece. Slice chilled rolls crosswise into ½-by-¾-inch pieces. Brush with egg mixture. Place on ungreased baking sheets and bake 10 minutes, or until golden brown. Remove immediately from baking sheets and let cool.

Variation

For appetizers, substitute grated Parmesan cheese for sugar/cinnamon mixture.

Fruit 'n Cheese Dessert Salad

Sargento Cheese Company, Inc.

Makes 6 servings, 1 cup each

1 package (0.8 ounces) sugar-free cook-and-serve vanilla pudding

1 can (15 ounces) pineapple chunks packed in juice, drained, with juice reserved

¼ cup orange juice

6 cups assorted fresh fruits, cut into 1-inch chunks

¾ cup (3 ounces) Sargento® Preferred Light® Fancy Shredded Mozzarella Cheese

In a saucepan, combine dry pudding, reserved liquid from pineapple, and orange juice to make fruit glaze. Heat over medium, stirring constantly until thickened, about 1 minute. Cool. Gently toss fruit glaze with pineapple chunks and fresh fruit chunks. Cover and chill until ready to serve. Top each 1-cup serving with 2 tablespoons cheese.

TOPPINGS

Whipped Topping

Nestlé Food Company

Makes 3 cups

½ cup ice water

½ cup Carnation® Nonfat Dry Milk

1½ teaspoons unflavored gelatin

2 tablespoons cold water

2 tablespoons boiling water

¼ cup confectioners' sugar

1 teaspoon vanilla

In mixing bowl, combine ½ *cup* ice water and nonfat dry milk. Chill bowl, beaters, and nonfat dry milk mixture. In small bowl, combine gelatin and *2 tablespoons* cold water. Let stand 3 minutes. Add *2 tablespoons* boiling water. Let cool to room temperature. Whip chilled nonfat dry milk mixture until stiff peaks form. Add gelatin, confectioners' sugar, and vanilla. Whip until well blended. (*Note:* If whipped topping develops an airy appearance, simply stir vigorously to restore smooth appearance. For best results, prepare same day as serving.)

Nutmeg Brandy Sauce

Nestlé Food Company

Makes 1½ cups

½ cup sugar
1 tablespoon cornstarch
½ teaspoon nutmeg
⅝ cup (5-ounce can) *undiluted* Carnation® Evaporated Milk

½ cup apricot nectar
2 tablespoons butter
4 teaspoons brandy
½ teaspoon vanilla

In small saucepan combine sugar, cornstarch, and nutmeg. Gradually stir in evaporated milk, apricot nectar, and butter. Cook over medium heat, stirring constantly, until mixture comes to a boil; boil 1 minute. Remove from heat. Stir in brandy and vanilla.

Serve warm or chilled over fruit, ice cream, or cake.

Index